THE
SENIOR
TOUR

THE SENIOR TOUR

STEVE HERSHEY

DOUBLEDAY

NEW YORK   LONDON   TORONTO   SYDNEY   AUCKLAND

PUBLISHED BY DOUBLEDAY
a division of Bantam Doubleday Dell Publishing Group, Inc.
666 Fifth Ave., New York, New York 10103

DOUBLEDAY and the portrayal of an anchor with a dolphin are
trademarks of Doubleday, a division of Bantam Doubleday Dell
Publishing Group, Inc.

BOOK DESIGN BY CLAIRE NAYLON VACCARO

Library of Congress Cataloging-in-Publication Data
Hershey, Steve.
    The Senior Tour / Steve Hershey.
        p.   cm.
    1. Senior PGA Tour (Association)   2. Golfers—United States.
    3. Golf—Tournaments—United States.   I. Title.
GV969.S46H47   1992
796.352′66—dc20   91-28709
                                                              CIP

ISBN 0-385-41705-5
Copyright © 1992 by Steve Hershey
Appendix copyright © 1992 by the PGA Tour Inc.

1   3   5   7   9   10   8   6   4   2

FIRST EDITION

To Linda, my computer expert, confidant, counselor and best friend. It couldn't have happened without you, babe.

FOREWORD

I am as astonished as anybody about the phenomenon that is the Senior PGA Tour. As my 50th birthday approached in the late 1970s, I really wasn't thinking about a serious extension of my playing career—nor, I suspect, were any of my contemporaries who are among the subjects in this book.

The first inkling of what might be out there for us players whose careers peaked in the 1950s and 1960s cames with the instant popularity among television's golfing public of the "made for TV" Legends of Golf. That's the two-man, better-ball tournament that Fred Raphael and Jimmy Demaret created for the over-50s and settled in Austin, Texas, in 1978. I figured I might play there in 1980 after I had turned 50, as well as in the PGA Seniors, which was being upgraded from its longtime position as a part of the PGA's annual winter series for vacationing club professionals. Beyond that, it seemed to be just a question of whether I could be competitive and continue to play on the regular tour in events besides the majors and several annual PGA tournaments that were favorites of mine.

But the success of the first two Legends—particularly the exciting playoff in 1979 involving Roberto De Vicenzo, Julius Boros, Tommy Bolt and Art Wall—got a lot of people thinking, including me. The USGA got into the act by creating a Senior Open for 1980, but it didn't mean much to me then because the USGA put a 55-year-old age minimum on the field. The PGA Tour decided to test the waters in 1980 and arranged tournaments in Atlantic City and Melbourne, Florida. *Golf Digest* liked the idea and set up an event at historic Newport Golf Club in Rhode Island. My entry into the picture came in Charlotte, North Carolina, which had just lost the Kemper Open to Washington, D.C. I had automobile and real estate interests in Charlotte; a number of longtime friends there were receptive to my suggestions of a World Seniors Invitational and supported its establishment.

With this nucleus, and the logical decision of the USGA to lower the age minimum to 50 for the 1981 Senior Open, we began to see that senior tournament golf might be more than just a passing fancy. But 42 tournaments of various types, and overall prize money of some $24 million, just a decade later? No way!

The tournament stars of the past who were already seniors comprised the bulk of the fields the first couple of years. But with the obvious success of the new tour clearly in view, the players from then on came from several directions. The players on the PGA Tour in their forties were ready, willing and anxious to change ships as soon as they passed the 50 mark. By and large, they have been the stars since those first seasons. Others who enjoyed success on the PGA Tour in their younger days but dropped off the circuit long before their 50th birthdays recycled their games and returned to action; several had greater success than they ever enjoyed on the regular tour. Even a few men who never made much of a mark on the PGA Tour—Don Bies, Larry Mowry and Rives McBee, for instance— have done very well on the Senior PGA Tour. The lure of the Senior

PGA Tour also has prompted several scratch amateurs to turn pro and take a crack at its money and prestige.

I never was able to play the Senior PGA Tour on a full-time basis because of the demands of my business and other activities, but I did manage to win now and then through the 1980s. I have enjoyed the competition and the camaraderie with the players whom I have tried to beat for so many years. I've also enjoyed the fans who have supported us so well. Who could have thought back then that Arnold Palmer would still be playing a schedule of more than 20 tournaments a year when he was in his sixties? Not me.

I have enjoyed reliving these early years of senior tournament golf through this first book on the subject and through the eyes and words of Steve Hershey, whose duties as golf writer for *USA Today* have kept him in close touch with the Senior PGA Tour and its players over the years. *The Senior Tour* gives golf's historians another worthwhile book for their libraries, and it gives the game's fans an entertaining and informative look at some of the new kids on the golfing block.

—Arnold Palmer

CONTENTS

CONTENTS

INTRODUCTION

The pioneers of the Senior PGA Tour—the players who started what flourished into the business phenomenon of the 1980s—experienced a riches-to-rags-to-riches saga unique in all of sports. There is no other sport where players have ended their careers, then recaptured them to the fullest 10 years later. Nowhere else have athletes been given the opportunity after age 50 to compete just as intensely, face all the same hazards, endure the same pressure and make more money in three or four years than they made in a lifetime.

This collection of reminiscences is not meant to be a history of the Senior Tour, which, remarkably, still is in its adolescence. Nor does it propose to select the best players, or even the nicest guys. The people were chosen for this book because they had a story to tell and, perhaps, even a lesson to convey.

To all those who appear in this book, I wish to express my sincerest gratitude. They all were particularly gracious and generous with their time. I also would like to thank members of the Senior PGA Tour staff, particularly Phil Stambaugh and media director Tim Crosby. Oh, yes, and a special toast of thanks for the encouragement to two very special and successful sons, enterprising Steve Jr., and budding Dr. Jimmy.

Steve Hershey
Seabrook, Maryland

THE
SENIOR
TOUR

IN THE
BEGINNING

It was as if a genie popped out of a bottle and, with the touch of a magic wand, granted many of the former great stars of professional golf one more wish.

Some, such as Arnold Palmer and Gary Player, were doing quite well financially, while others, such as Orville Moody, Al Geiberger, Dave Hill and Jim Dent, were hard pressed to pay their bills. But they all had one thing in common: They hungered for that lingering taste of competition. They longed for the thrills of the past, when the juices flowed and the crowds roared. They were like aging actors starving for one more part, a last significant role, a final chance to perform in front of an audience and once again experience the cheers, the adoration, the affection of their fans.

All the money in the world can't bring back those moments in baseball, football, basketball or any other sport—except golf. With the birth of the Senior Tour, the stars of the fifties, the sixties and now the early seventies have been given a second chance—or, as the golfers say, a mulligan in life.

It began one cold afternoon in January of 1980 in a conference room at the PGA Tour headquarters in Ponte Vedra, Florida. Six aging professional golfers sat down to explore how to retrieve the echoes, revive glories past and, yes, find a way to put a few bucks in their pockets. This was no social affair, no cocktails and shrimp, no replaying great shots.

Sam Snead, Julius Boros, Don January, Bob Goalby, Dan Sikes and Gardner Dickinson—all leaders on the career money list—met with PGA Tour Commissioner Deane Beman and talked about starting a Senior Tour, just a couple of events a year for the 50-and-over set. They had been encouraged by the public's enthusiastic response to the Liberty Mutual Legends of Golf two-man team tournament, and they wondered if there would be any support for regular tournaments featuring the top names of the past. Snead, then 67, the PGA Tour's all-time winner with 81 victories, knew he couldn't compete with most of the seniors, but he was willing to give his time, money and effort to help this project get off the ground. Boros was 59 and knew his days of winning were numbered, but he had an ulterior motive, which he would laugh about with the boys over some beers at the airport.

Goalby, January and Sikes were all 50 and itching to get this 50-and-over tour started, and, at 52, Dickinson was just as eager to start playing competitively again. Sikes was named chairman of what would be known as the Senior Advisory Council.

"We really didn't know what the hell we were doing," Goalby says. "When we first started talking, we didn't know whether we should run it ourselves or go under the PGA Tour umbrella. We didn't have one rule, or really much of a plan. We just wanted to explore the possibilities of playing tournaments again. I guess it was a dream, but it made sense to some of us.

"We decided pretty quickly that we would be better off working with the Tour. Deane put the whole thing together. He knew what he was doing; he had done a great job with the regular tour, so when we left, we put it in his hands."

The meeting broke up about four o'clock that afternoon. The players were on their own and headed back to Jacksonville International Airport. There, after a few beers while waiting for various flights, Boros—a father of six, with two grandchildren having recently moved into his home in Fort Lauderdale, Florida—was talking to the others about the chances of the Senior Tour's success and his ability to compete.

"It sure would be great if we could get this thing off the ground, guys," he said with a grin. "I don't care if I win or not; I just want to be competitive enough to warrant leaving home once in a while."

For his part, Beman left the meeting impressed with the players' desire to begin another venture at their age, but he knew it wouldn't be easy to implement their plan.

"That was a pretty tough group of people," Beman recalls with a laugh. "They had been tough competitors all their lives; no Caspar Milquetoasts there. They weren't a real trusting group, and the first meeting could be called tumultuous. They wanted to play, but they weren't sure how they wanted to do it. Also, they didn't know how much they wanted to play. Their kids were grown and, frankly, they didn't have a hell of a lot to do.

"After that first meeting, I went to our Tournament Policy Board and asked the authority to get the plan under way. I told them it would cost $350,000 to staff the operation. I was met with overwhelming support, but nobody knew how much it would cost to get the Senior Tour where it is today. We invested $7.7 million to get the Senior Tour rolling during its first 10 years."

Thus, the sports phenomenon of the 1980s was born. An idea initiated by six former players and put in place with the organizational

T I P

"I played with Ben Hogan in the 1956 Texas International Open. I was new on the Tour and looking for any help I could find. After the round, I asked him if he saw anything that could help me with my swing. He said to me, 'Is there anything wrong with your elbow?' I thought he was talking about my left elbow, but it was five years later before I discovered he meant the right one. I always had my right elbow away from my body, and this produced a long and loose swing. I would shoot 63 or 83! Once I tucked my right elbow in close to my body, I tripled what I was making per week. This just allowed me to put the club in the same plane every time on every swing. Most amateur players are not in their proper position at the golf ball. It all depends on a person's height, length of arm, length of leg, length of torso, distance from the ball, and so forth. Most pros don't teach position; they're too worried about where the hands are going."

Don January

skills of the existing PGA Tour would mushroom from two events worth $125,000 each in 1980 to 42 tournaments with total official purses of $17,950,000 in 1990.

When it comes to golf, it takes a lot to surprise Arnold Palmer, but there he was one day, flashing one of the world's most familiar grins and admitting he was wrong.

"I never thought it could grow so fast," he said. "It's taken off in popularity beyond anyone's belief. Our only problem now is not being able to provide enough dates for everyone."

The Senior Tour really got its start with Fred Raphael, who in the early 1960s produced Shell's "Wonderful World of Golf" and filmed matches of the world's top players. Jimmy Demaret was one of the television commentators for CBS, and he and Raphael started talking about starting a tournament of their own, a team event to bring back some of the old favorites. Demaret had helped design a course at Onion Creek Club in Austin, Texas, and he suggested they take the tournament there.

The first best-ball event was held in 1978, and with NBC television focusing in, it couldn't have had a more dramatic, more appealing finish. Snead and Dickinson were trailing the Australian duo of Peter Thomson and Kel Nagle, 1-down, going into the 16th hole. Thomson, the five-time British Open champion, rolled in a 20-foot birdie putt, and if Snead didn't make his from 12 feet, his team would be 2-down with two holes to play. Ol' Sam knocked it in, then made another birdie from 8 feet on the next hole to even the match. On the 590-yard 18th, Snead pitched his third shot from down in a swale to within 3 feet and made the putt to win. Three birdies in the last three holes from golf's all-time winner. Cecil B. De Mille couldn't have directed a better finish.

The television ratings were surprisingly high, and they skyrocketed the following year, when the Legends had the most dramatic finish in its 14-year history. Boros and Roberto De Vicenzo strung together a mind-boggling six consecutive birdies in a playoff—and they needed every one to edge Tommy Bolt and Art Wall, who made five. Six birdies in a row! These old guys could still play, and for many middle-aged golfers sitting around the 19th hole at their local country club, it was exciting to see their old favorites stalking the fairways in search of glory again.

"I think that a big part of the appeal of those Legends of Golf shows is that they show so much more golf," Snead says. "It's not all that boring junk you're usually forced to watch: you know, the blimp flying overhead, pretty scenery, somebody hitching up his pants. In the Legends they show golf shots—isn't that what people want to see?"

As the Legends awoke the world to the fact that these old-timers could still make birdies and compete, it became easier to sell a couple of Senior events in 1980. There already were the PGA Seniors Championship at the PGA National Course in Palm Beach Gardens, Florida, and the U.S. Senior Open. But now Snead and his pals came up with two Senior Tour events of their own.

"Leo Fraser was a good friend of ours, and he owned a course in Atlantic City," Goalby says. "He offered us the course, so our first event was the Atlantic City International, which Don January won. Our other event was in Melbourne, Florida, where Harold Staub was the tournament director. That was the Suntree Classic, and Charlie Sifford won. We still play in Melbourne.

"That was a start; that got us off the ground. But we still didn't know what we were doing. At first, our qualifications were the top 20 on the all-time money list, the top 20 on the all-time victory list, six qualifying spots and four sponsor exemptions for our 50-man field. We found out in a hurry that didn't work."

It didn't work because guys came out of the woodwork. It was only two tournaments in warm-weather sites, and wouldn't it be nice to see all your old buddies again? This was just like an outing, right?

So here they came. One of the first to arrive was Britain's "Light-Horse" Harry Cooper, a wonderful golfer in his day, but this wasn't his day. He won 30 times over a 27-year career, but his last victory came in the 1939 Goodall Palm Beach Round Robin. Then there was Jim Ferrier, an Australian with 18 career victories, but none since the 1961 Almaden Open Invitational. Cooper was 76 and Ferrier 65. They couldn't beat their amateur partners, so the eligibility rule had to be changed.

"We had some battles, but we eliminated the all-time wins category in a hurry," says Goalby. "We went to the top 36 available players on the all-time money list and that's basically where it stayed."

The schedule increased to five events in 1981. Rookie Miller Barber, who has been on the road all his life and won as recently as 1978 (the Phoenix Open) on the regular tour, came along and won three times. Between both tours, this happy wanderer never missed a week, winning $49,325 on the regular tour in 1981 and finishing first on the Senior Tour money list with $83,136. The next year, he again led the Senior Tour money race with $106,890. The old Arkansas Razorback was in hog heaven.

"I know what makes Miller happy," his wife, Karen, once said. "Having a hotel key in his pocket."

Despite one of the worst-looking swings in captivity, Barber has been a consistent winner in the first decade of the Senior Tour. He leads in victories with 24 and was the No. 1 money winner in the eighties with $2,214,603—the only player with more than $2 million in earnings in that decade. He still tells the story of Snead trying to convince him to get rid of that jerky three-part loop in his backswing, but it didn't work.

"Sam kept after me and after me to smooth out my backswing," Barber says. "I tried. But the more normal I got it, the worse I hit the ball. So, I figured I'd better stick with what got me this far."

Meanwhile, the Legends still was the Senior Tour's major showcase, and its only television showing. And the old-timers still were putting on a show. Snead had his sidesaddle-style putting stroke on laser beam in 1982; he and partner January had a 10-shot lead on the final day when Snead rolled in a long birdie putt at No. 15 and another at the 16th. On the next tee, January turned to his partner and said, "Damn, Sam, how much do you want to win by?" Snead replied, "You never know, son, those folks up ahead of us might be cheating."

The following year, the schedule jumped from 11 to 18 events, and a fellow named Brian Henning, a South African who joined the Senior Tour staff in 1981, was kept hopping. It was Henning's job as tournament director to find sponsors willing to support a tournament, then go to the site and run the event. It wasn't easy.

"Most of the good cities were taken [by the PGA Tour and LPGA], so we went to places where they never had tournaments before," Henning says. "We didn't have a policy regarding the type of courses we needed. I'd go in, sell the pro-am and barely look at the course. In those days we couldn't be choosy.

"We played in Nashville once and the course didn't even have a driving range, but they were putting up $150,000, so we showed up. Once, I was dealing with a guy from Daytona Beach, and I called to ask him when I could come to his office and sign a contract. 'Office?' he said. 'What office? My truck is my office.'

"I went up to Marlboro, Massachusetts, one time on the Saturday before the tournament and asked for some ropes and stakes to rope off the gallery area. The guy said he didn't have any. We finally called Hartford and asked if we could borrow some. The next day a truck arrived and the rope wasn't even rolled up. It was just all tangled in the back. The course was in terrible shape. But we still teed it up.

"Many places we went, the people had no idea how to put a tournament on. We had to teach them everything. And the crowds. When we started, we were lucky to get 1,000 people. But as long as they knew the top players were coming, we could sell two Pro-Am days and that's what kept us going." (The two days of Pro-Ams with local businessmen paying at least $1,000 to play with the pros, was a lifeblood of the Senior Tour in the early days.)

T I P

"Anytime I've been in contention to win a tournament, I always concentrate on tempo in my golf swing down the stretch. It's easy to get very fast when you're anxious, so I try to keep the tempo of the swing slow and in keeping with the tempo that got me in the position to win. We see it every week during pro-ams. Everyone's very anxious to hit the ball long and show the pro that he's a good player. He would do well just to keep within himself, to keep his swings at a good pace and a good tempo. The key is to take it back slowly about a foot to two feet away from the ball. If you take it slow there, your tempo should be pretty good. You cannot take it slow for the first foot or two and then jerk the club back all of a sudden. It can't be done. Most of the time when people get out of tempo, it's right as they draw the club head away from the ball."

Gene Littler

That year, January, then 53, won six times and led the money list with $237,571. Now the old boys were getting into serious money, but where would it all end? How many tournaments would there be next year? January, for one, thought they had reached a comfortable limit.

"When we first talked about a Senior Tour, I think a lot of us envisioned playing 8, 10, 12 tournaments a year," January says. "It was sort of a club, a group of guys who wanted to get together, show up once a month and have a good time. I don't think any of us thought it would ever become this big."

January and Barber should have worn a mask and a gun the way they took all the money in the early years. January ranked 2-2-1-1 on the money list the first four years and Barber 1-1-2-2. They were in their prime at the perfect time, and rarely did anybody beat them until Peter Thomson's magical year of 1985.

At 56, suddenly everything Thomson did was right. Every time he putted, the hole got in the way of the ball. Although January won 6 times and Barber 4, they were far outdistanced by Thomson, who won 9 times and set a record not even Lee Trevino could match in his sensational rookie season in 1990. Not since Snead won 10 in 1950 had any golfer been so successful. And the irony of it all was that Thomson never won again. Within two years he had become a part-time player while devoting most of his energy to designing and developing 25 golf courses in Japan and the Pacific Basin.

"Ah, that was a wonderful year," Thomson recalled with a twinkle in his eye at the 1990 British Open at St. Andrews, Scotland. "I didn't live anywhere, just bounced from town to town with my wife and daughter. The Senior Tour took over my life. I won the first tournament of the year [MONY Tournament of Champions] at La Costa, and my confidence was so high, I thought I'd make every putt all year. Damn near did, too. But once the year was over, it was a letdown. I didn't have anything more to prove and, at my age, it was difficult to get motivated again."

With the schedule expanding to 27 tournaments and the purses growing to more than $6 million, there was a need for more players. Suddenly it was difficult for the regulars to play every event. After all, guys like January and Gene Littler said they only wanted to play 10 or 12, although as the purses increased, so, not surprisingly, did their schedules.

"When we had 18 to 20 tournaments, everybody played in all of them. It made it easy to sell the pro-ams," Henning says. "I could guarantee that Snead, Palmer, Boros would be there. The players would show up and go to all the parties. It was great. Snead and Lionel Hebert would play the trumpet and it was a lot of fun. But as the schedule increased, the players simply couldn't go to all the tournaments and all the parties."

Goalby was one of the players trying to do it all, and it caught up with him, too.

"We created our own monster," he says. "All of a sudden, with all the money out there, you couldn't play once a month because none of us practice when we're at home. So we had to start playing more to stay competitive. It started out real friendly, but as the money got bigger, it turned a little cutthroat."

By then, the Senior Tour was large enough to merit its own division within the PGA Tour. Beman recommended to the Advisory Board that a separate board be set up, and it was easily approved.

"The Senior players wanted to be in control of their own destiny," Beman says. "Ironically, it was the same group of players who had fought for their own independence from the PGA of America in 1968 and '69. They wanted to form their own organization then, and now they wanted to again. I immediately moved to get it approved, and it went through without a hitch, no acrimony at all.

"None of the regular tour players asked about the money. I had told them it would cost $350,000 a year, but it was probably double, with all the administrative costs. But if I would have told them $700,000 in 1980, it might have scared some off. The Senior Tour is in the players' long-term interest, but sometimes it's tough to get players to invest in the future. If they're really doing well, they won't need it, and if they're doing lousy, they won't benefit. To their credit, they all agreed."

One of the first things the seniors did was form a Senior Player Retirement Plan. Starting in 1985, any player who finished 40th or better in a tournament received one unit, worth $512. Therefore, if a player finished in the top 40 in 30 events, he would receive $15,360 in an annuity that he paid no taxes on until he withdrew it.

That's a comforting cushion for a bunch of guys who hadn't expected a dime a decade before, and they unhesitatingly credit some of those players who met back on that cold January day in 1980.

"Snead and Boros were our catalyst," says Goalby. "I don't think there would be a Senior Tour today without them. Back in the beginning, we had to sell our product, and nobody did it better than Sam. In the first four years, Sam played in every tournament, went to every banquet, every clinic. He was going to four parties a week sometimes, and that's not easy when you have to play the next day. But he did whatever it took, whatever was needed to get the job done."

Snead insists to this day that he had more fun playing the Senior Tour than the regular tour. His only regret was that he wasn't able to be more competitive.

"I'll tell you a great story," he said one day during a promotional tour at Tantallon Country Club in Fort Washington, Maryland. Of course, that's the way he starts most conversations these days.

"I was playing down at the Senior Roundup in Sun City [Arizona] and shot 69. This old guy—he looked to be 80 if he was a day— came up to me and said I changed his life. He said he used to be a 5, 6 handicapper, then his game started deteriorating, and he ended up a 19. He said he got so disgusted he quit the game. Then he saw me play the year before at Sun City and said to himself, 'If ol' Sam can still break 70, I ought to be able to play a little.' So he went back, starting practicing again and got his handicap down to 13. He said it made a tremendous difference in his life, and his wife says he's a hell of a lot easier to live with now that he's playing golf again."

The best example of those players' dedication may have been their pitch for a cable television package for the 1985 season. Snead, Goalby, Dickinson, January, Sikes and Doug Ford all played at an outing in South Bend, Indiana, one Monday in the summer of 1984. Bright and early the next morning, they took a puddle jumper to Chicago, then flew to New York for a meeting with Don Ohlmeyer and Ray Volpe.

"We had a heck of a time getting ol' Sam up at five in the morning," Goalby laughs. "He's not much for flying, and that little prop job to the Windy City had him worried. But he went. He knew it was important. And—you're not going to believe this—he paid his own way. We all did."

The players had become impatient over lack of television coverage, and they agreed to pay Ohlmeyer and Volpe $100,000 to try to get them a contract on ESPN. The players were able to set up a deal for Beman to negotiate with Mazda to carry six events in 1985.

"We negotiated a five-year deal with Mazda, and Don [Ohlmeyer], to his credit, returned the $100,000 to the players," Beman says. "That was the first major breakthrough with television."

Terry Hanson, former vice president of communications for the PGA Tour, said the biggest hurdle in television negotiations was that the regular tour had all the 4–6 P.M. slots, leaving ESPN an early 2–4 P.M. show. The early finish upset sponsors, who didn't want fans leaving that early. The other alternative was tape delay (6–7:30 P.M.), which ESPN didn't like.

At the time, the only network television coverage involved two events, both sponsored by Chrysler. The Vintage Invitational was played at the posh Vintage Club in Indian Wells, California, and the Chrysler Cup was a team competition between American and international players. Joe Campana, a hulking man of six feet four inches and more than 300 pounds, put the Chrysler Cup together, and the day he made the announcement, Arnold Palmer and Gary Player, the respective captains, were at the TPC at Avenel in Potomac, Maryland.

Player, the physical fitness fanatic, kept eyeing Campana's massive girth. When it was time to thank Chrysler, he just couldn't resist.

"You know the Senior Tour is just starting out, and for a corporation to take this kind of risk is a very bold move. It takes a lot of guts," then, pausing, he patted Campana's stomach and added, "and this man has a lot of guts."

In 1987, the Vantage brand of R. J. Reynolds Tobacco Co. made a major commitment to the Senior Tour. The elements of the brand's initial involvement grew into an electronic scoreboard system (Vantage Scoreboards); an individual player bonus pool and a tournament charity bonus pool based on season-long performance of players (Vantage Cup); and a separate yet coinciding competition at 25 tournaments for players age 60 and over (Vantage Classics). In addition, the company sponsors the richest event on the circuit, the $1.5 million Vantage Championship.

But the big breakthrough, the financial move that finally put the Senior Tour in the black, was the Cadillac Series, which carried 14 events in 1990, 15 in 1991 and 16 this year.

"Mazda for its early commitment, R. J. Reynolds for putting together the Vantage Cup program, and most recently Cadillac were the forces that really put the Senior Tour over the top," Beman says. "They were very vital to our growth and came along when we really needed support."

Another way the Senior Tour gained exposure was by being included in the Infiniti Tournament of Champions each January at the La Costa resort near San Diego. The only way to qualify for this high-profile event was to win a PGA Tour event the previous year, and it was a wonderful reward for some 30 winners, who played for purses that reached $800,000 in 1991.

In 1983, Goalby was having breakfast with Allard Roen, the longtime chairman of the Infiniti tournament who brought the tournament from the Stardust in Las Vegas in 1969.

"Wouldn't it be nice if you could have Snead, Boros, Palmer and those guys in this tournament?" Goalby asked Roen.

"I'd love it," Roen replied.

"Well," Goalby said, "you could have them if you invited the Senior Tour winners, too."

"Hell, I barely have enough money to sponsor the regular tour," Roen said. "Where am I going to get more money for the seniors?"

That afternoon, Roen came up to Goalby and said, "I just took a nap, and when I woke up, I thought what a dumb ass I am. If I had 10 seniors, I could sell 10 more pro-am spots at $8,000 each. That's $80,000, and that's all I need. This is a retirement area, and their presence will boost the gate, so it won't cost me anything to have the seniors."

The seniors started playing at La Costa in 1984, and by 1991 their purse had grown to $350,000. Miller Barber walked off with the $50,000 first prize in 1989, a pretty good way to start the season. It certainly took care of that year's room service bills. Bruce Crampton won the 1991 Tournament of Champions and collected his largest single payday ever—$80,000.

As the Senior Tour grew, so did the size of the fields. In 1987 they were expanded to 72 players: 28 from the all-time money list, 28 from the current Senior Tour money list, 8 from the National Qualifying Tournament, 4 from local qualifying and 4 sponsor exemptions. Also, for the first time, the pro-am portions and the tournament were separated, with pro-ams being held on Wednesday and Thursday and the 54-hole tournament starting Friday. It wasn't always like that. At the beginning they played pro-ams on Thursday and Friday, and the Friday scores counted in the tournament.

"The players couldn't handle that," Goalby says. "They were too nervous in the pro-ams, with the score counting. They were jumpy and not real friendly. It wasn't like the regular tour where you could go out, have fun, shoot anything in the pro-ams. Finally, we suggested the present format of two days of pro-ams, then a three-day tournament starting Friday."

One who resisted the most was Palmer, who had trouble adjusting to the fact that he was a senior, playing in Senior tournaments. He wanted every tournament to be 72 holes, but after a few distractions from his amateur partners, he came back and told the seniors, "You guys are right. I can't handle it, either."

When there were only 50 players in a tournament, everybody had to play in both pro-ams, but as the fields grew to 72, then to the current 78, the top money winners had the option to play in just one. Playing two makes for a long week: it means the player has to get to the tournament by Tuesday afternoon, and in many cases, he doesn't have time to go home between tournaments.

But most players travel with their wives now, and they say that makes such a big difference. With their kids grown, they can travel much easier than during the old days, and since the players aren't closing down the bars anymore, it's nice to have a dinner companion. There are a few exceptions, of course. Jim Ferree, who turned 60 last June, travels with his 3-year-old son, Randall, and Al Geiberger often has 2-year-old Al, Jr., in tow. Geiberger's wife, Carolyn, has had three children since he joined the Senior Tour in 1987.

"We're all one big happy family out here," Geiberger says with a smile. "It's a terrific atmosphere. It's like a class reunion every week, and so much more fun than the regular tour because the pressure is off. We're all winners on the Senior Tour."

In the 1990s, the cast of characters will change. The current players are the first to admit that their careers are limited—and that each year, more of those "young 50-year-olds from the junior tour" are arriving to challenge them, not only for the money, but for the glory, the adoration, the thrill of being champions again.

"It's been a great ride. It's been fantastic," Goalby sums up. "For a lot of these guys, it's been a reason to live."

LEE TREVINO

N o one has done more for the popularity of golf among the pull-cart brigade than Lee Trevino, and no one did more in his first year on the Senior PGA Tour to heighten interest, attract fans and stimulate the foggy memories of the fiftysomething set.

Anyone who has ever guzzled a beer at a 19th hole has a Trevino story, a Trevino saying or at least a well-remembered quote. Some of the ivy-covered ones will live as long as golf is played and be repeated whenever the situation arises during a round:

- "You can talk to a slice, but a hook won't listen."
- "Two things that won't last long: a dog chasing cars and a pro putting for pars."
- "You don't know what pressure is until you've played for $10 with $5 in your pocket."
- "Rules? They ought to write 'em on the back of a book of matches. You hit it there; hit it again."

As Fuzzy Zoeller, a scratch player in any lounge, once said, "Lee has more lines than the Illinois railroad."

Lee Buck Trevino, the Merry Mex, came out of Texas with his mouth running. He chattered between shots, tossed one-liners at the gallery and played a type of game that anyone who ever has hit balls off a rubber mat at a driving range can fantasize about. "No one who ever had lessons would have a swing like mine," he says.

An eighth-grade dropout who never knew his father, Trevino learned the game at Glen Lakes public course near Dallas, where he caddied, then at Hardy's Driving Range. At Hardy's, he worked seven days a week, helped build a pitch-and-putt course and hustled bets on the side, including his now famous gimmick of playing with a Dr Pepper bottle. He would wrap tape around the neck of the bottle so it wouldn't slip out of his hand. Then he'd challenge somebody— tossing the ball up, hitting it with a baseball swing, then putting it croquet-style. What made it work, he admits now, was that he was always taken lightly, underestimated. The other guy would give him half a stroke a hole and not really concentrate. That's where he first learned about pressure and the advantages of being the underdog. He still relishes the role, although it's become almost impossible on the Senior Tour.

As his reputation grew, the pigeons stopped flocking to Hardy's, and Trevino needed new hunting grounds. He found one in 1965 when Martin Lettunich, an El Paso cotton farmer, thought enough of his game to offer him a job as an assistant pro. Trevino took his wife, Claudia, and two kids and packed all their belongings in a small U-Haul, which he pulled with his 1958 Oldsmobile to El Paso. He had $50 in his pocket when he went to work with Don Whittenton and his cousin Jesse at Horizon Hills Country Club, a windblown course in the wastelands outside of El Paso. For $30 a week, Trevino shined shoes, tended bar, picked up driving range balls and, in his spare time, beat balls until his hands bled. By this time he was 26, had served as a Marine Corps gunnery sergeant in the Pacific, had a little boy and a little girl and wondered if they could live on $30 a week. He didn't know where his next dollar was coming from, but he knew how to get it, when the opportunity presented itself.

It did one day at Horizon Hills, when who should turn up but Raymond Floyd, who had been on the PGA Tour for three years and, as a good-looking freewheeling playboy, was always looking to hustle a buck. A couple of pals suggested he come to Horizon Hills for a little high-stakes game, so he showed up one morning. After a young Mexican carried his clubs to the clubhouse, Floyd yawned and asked who he was playing. "Me," said Trevino. "You mean they bet on you?" a startled Floyd replied. When someone asked Floyd if he wanted to look at the course first, he said, "Nah, let's play cards until we're ready to tee off."

The first day, Floyd shot 66 and lost by a stroke. The next day, he shot another 66 and lost by two. The third day, Floyd eagled the last hole to beat Trevino by a shot. "I sent him home COD," Trevino says. "Don't ever play a good player on his home course."

After that, Trevino was anxious to join the PGA Tour, but he had trouble getting anyone to endorse his application before Bill Eschenbrenner, the pro at El Paso Country Club, finally agreed to do so in 1967. That year Trevino qualified for the U.S. Open at Baltusrol Golf Club in Springfield, New Jersey, and made his first splash in the national press. He arrived with a battered set of clubs and a couple of shirts, but he surprised everyone who saw his short, flat swing (which someone called a calculated lurch) by shooting consistent rounds of 72-70-71-70 for 283 to finish fifth—eight shots behind Jack Nicklaus. His consistent play won him $6,000, plus an exemption for next year's Open. When asked if he had ever won that much before, Trevino answered, "Did I ever win that much? I never saw that much before."

With his newfound riches, Trevino stayed on the Tour the rest of the year, earning $45,472 to finish 45th on the money list and qualify for the following year. Still, he was relatively unknown, a fast talker with a jalapeño personality, when he headed for Rochester, New York, for the 1968 U.S. Open.

"I wasn't very happy when I started off for Rochester," he recalls, warming up to one of his favorite stories. "A couple of weeks earlier at Houston, I had a one-shot lead over Roberto De Vicenzo with two holes to play, and I bogeyed both of them to lose by a shot. Two weeks later, I finished second again in Atlanta to Bob Lunn. I was really down. I didn't want to go home. I hadn't won and it bothered me, bothered me bad. So I drove to Stamford [Connecticut], stayed with friends, drank some beer and tried to forget.

"After a few days I headed for Rochester. I wasn't sure where I was—somewhere near Utica [New York]—and all of a sudden, I saw these lights. It was a kids' tee-ball game, so I got a six-pack and a bucket of chicken and watched them play. I was sort of crying in my beer, but watching those kids having so much fun picked me up. I started thinking how lucky I was just to be playing in the U.S. Open."

Rochester was different in one way for Trevino, who usually would find the cheapest motel that had room service and spend his evening there alone. The Paul Kircher family wanted to play host to a young player that week, and Trevino decided he could use a break from motel monotony, so he took them up on their offer.

"I'll never forget the first day I got home from the course. Paul's wife, Barbara, was unpacking all this canned Mexican food she'd bought," he says. "She thought I'd like that, but I told her I was raised on that stuff and hated it."

Trevino received a boost from an unexpected source before the tournament began on Thursday. He played all three practice rounds with Doug Sanders; Sanders kept telling him how well he was playing, then told the press that Trevino could win the tournament.

"I played the first two rounds with Deane Beman and Gay Brewer and just concentrated on making the cut," Trevino says. "Even though I shot 68-69, just two shots off Bert Yancey's lead, I never thought about winning. It didn't dawn on me that I was doing something big."

Trevino carved out another 69 on Saturday to slice Yancey's lead to a single shot, yet much of the attention was on defending champion Jack Nicklaus, even though he was seven shots back. Nobody expected much from the final twosome of Yancey and Trevino. Yancey, a tall, erect, dignified former West Point cadet, was a fanatic about the golf swing and had won four times in three years. Trevino, who hadn't won anything, was a wisecracking, squat, swarthy Mexican with a tattoo on his arm and a homemade, flat left-to-right swing.

"I skulled my first tee shot, didn't get it to the fairway," Trevino says now that he can laugh about it. "But I swear I wasn't nervous. I figured all the pressure was on Yancey and that he was more worried about Nicklaus than me. The Bear was smoking; he was hitting it stiff. He just couldn't make a putt."

Yancey and Trevino both bogeyed the first hole, and the cheers could be heard ahead as Nicklaus was making birdies at the third and fourth holes. Trevino one-putted for a par on the second hole, then tied Yancey, who bogeyed the third. Now Nicklaus was just three shots back, but he missed birdie putts on the seventh and eighth holes when seemingly he could have put his inexperienced challengers away.

Trevino took the lead for the first time in the tournament on the fifth hole when Yancey caught a bunker, blasted within 3 feet and missed the putt. After a birdie at No. 6, Yancey visited two more bunkers at the eighth and ninth holes and made the turn one shot behind after a 38. His wheels were coming off, and all Trevino had to do was keep making pars. Yancey drove into the woods at No. 10 for another bogey, then as Trevino was about to stroke a 35-foot birdie putt at No. 11, there was a thunderous roar as Nicklaus made another birdie ahead of him. He backed away, then stepped up and sank the putt.

"That was the turning point," Trevino says. "I also birdied the

12th hole, and Yancey bogeyed 10 and 13. At the 13th green, I told Joe Dey [executive director of the USGA], 'I'm just trying to build up as big a lead as I can, so I won't choke.' " Yancey, who later dropped off the Tour with depression induced by chemical imbalance, had blown a five-shot lead after 45 holes and would shoot 76 to finish third. Nicklaus had closed with a 67 for 279 and Trevino knew he had it. Surprisingly, there was little emotion, no flair for dramatics, waving or smiling as Trevino walked down the 18th fairway. With a four-shot lead and no water or out-of-bounds, he could have played the last hole with a Dr Pepper bottle and won. "I don't remember much," says the player who usually seems to have an ironclad memory. "I guess I was in shock. I know I wasn't saying much."

That's the shocker. The only time Trevino is quiet now is when he's sleeping, and he says he has trouble doing that because "I can't wait to wake up and hear what I'm going to say." With his final-round 69, Trevino had matched Nicklaus' record of 275 and became the first player in U.S. Open history to play all four rounds (69-68-69-69) in the sixties. Players might occasionally still make fun of his flat swing, but he would never be an unknown at a golf tournament again. Lee Buck had arrived.

It was a long haul from where he grew up, in that four-room, dirt-floor shack with no electricity and no running water, next to a cemetery in rural Dallas where his mother's father, Joe, dug graves. And still to come were many more duels with Nicklaus, five more major championships, fortunes made and fortunes lost, lightning, two back operations, two divorces. The only thing that remained constant was Trevino's personality.

FIRST VICTORY: *A relatively subdued Lee Trevino waves to the crowd after holing his final putt and winning the 1968 U.S. Open at Oak Hill Country Club in Rochester, New York, his first victory as a touring professional.*

HAPPY WINNER: *Trevino tries to get a smile out of runner-up Jack Nicklaus after winning the 1968 U.S. Open at Oak Hill Country Club in Rochester, New York.*

Bill Eschenbrenner, the pro at El Paso Country Club who endorsed Trevino's application for the PGA Tour, says, "I've never known a guy who's so great who's changed so little. Lee's exactly the same person he was back in 1965."

"I come from a different era," Trevino says. "I'm from the club era. I started out shining shoes, giving lessons, selling 10E shoes to some guy who wears a 12C and making him like it."

Naturally, life changed for Trevino after he won the U.S. Open. Now he was accepted, part of the crowd, a member of the establishment—except he didn't want to be. He remembered where he came from, where he had been, how hard he had worked, and he wasn't ready to slip into a dinner jacket and backslap with the country club set. During his first trip to The Masters, he was asked why he didn't go into the palatial clubhouse. He looked up quizzically and said, "Why do I want to go in there? There's *golfers* in there. And they'll come over with a thousand questions and you have to be *nice*."

Later, of course, it came out that Trevino resented the entire atmosphere at Augusta National. Although he qualified, he refused to play three times in the early 1970s. When he did return, he insisted on changing his shoes in the parking lot.

The Masters always has been a problem for Trevino. It's the only major championship he hasn't won twice, hasn't won at all, hasn't even come close. In addition to his disdain for the Old South aura, the course itself has been his waterloo, and he has convinced himself he can't play it well. His best finishes were ties for 10th in 1975 and 1985. But after missing the cut in 1987 and 1988, he came back the following year at age 49 and shot an opening-round 67.

"If somebody would have wanted to bet me $1,000 I would break 76, I wouldn't have taken a quarter of it, and I'm a betting man," Trevino said afterward. "But this means a lot to me. I might come back and shoot three 80s, but this 67 is a real confidence booster. It proves that there still is a spark in the fireplace. I just have to throw the right wood on it.

"At my age, it's tough to concentrate for four days. Hell, I can't remember where I live sometimes, I can never find my car keys and I got one of them ropes around my glasses so I know where they are. Boys, I'm ready for that Senior Tour right now."

Nicklaus got a chuckle out of Trevino's latest lament about the perils of Augusta National. "Lee says he can't draw the ball, that this is a hooker's course," he said. "Well, we all know Lee can do anything he wants to with a golf ball. I've played a lot of golf with him and, believe me, he can hit it any way he wants. He's got it in his mind he can't play here, but that 67 shows that he can."

Trevino's retort to his good friend was simple. "Tell Jack we'll play $1,000 Nassau, but he has to play my drive and I'll play his and see how he likes it. If he had to play my drives on this course, he couldn't break 80."

Just as Trevino was always filled with trepidation about The Masters, he usually approached the U.S. Open brimming with a quiet confidence—although his first defense was a disaster. After finishing fifth in 1967 and winning the following year at Rochester, he was one of the favorites when the championship returned to Texas in 1969 at Champions Golf Club in Houston. But he shot 74-75—149 and missed the cut by a shot, one of the biggest disappointments of his career. The only thing that softened his feeling was that his longtime Texas pal, Orville Moody, shocked the golf world by turning back Deane Beman, Al Geiberger and Bob Rosburg to win by a stroke.

But surprisingly, in 1990, after so many major championships, Ryder Cup matches, victories and near victories, when asked about his biggest disappointment, Trevino chose a tournament in Portland, Oregon, in 1969, when he felt he still had to prove himself. He was leading Billy Casper by four shots with four holes to play. He bogeyed the 16th hole, then on the par-3 17th, he hit his tee shot under a lip of a bunker and made six. Meanwhile, Casper birdied the last four holes to win. "Instead of drinking a six-pack of beer that night, I drank a case," he says. "That's still my most disappointing loss."

In 1971, Trevino came to the U.S. Open at Merion Golf Club, near Philadelphia, at the top of his game. He had won the Tallahassee Open and the Danny Thomas Memphis Classic. He had finished second twice and third in three other events. Since late April, he had played seven tournaments, and in six of them he finished in the top five. Once again, Nicklaus was the favorite after having won the PGA

FRIENDLY ALLY: *Trevino poses with the rubber snake he used to fool spectators during a practice round before the 1971 U.S. Open at Merion Golf Club in Ardmore, Pennsylvania. Later, before a Monday playoff with Jack Nicklaus, he would pull the snake out of his golf bag and playfully toss it at the Golden Bear.*

Championship at the PGA National Golf Club in Palm Beach, Florida, in February and finishing second to Charlie Coody at The Masters. After rounds of 70-72-69 for 211, Trevino was four shots behind young Jim Simons and two behind Nicklaus going into the final round. With birdies at Nos. 13 and 14, he took a one-shot lead, but he missed the 18th green to the right and made bogey to fall into a tie with Nicklaus, setting up a moment that would brand him forever.

As he and Nicklaus were waiting to tee off the next day for their 18-hole playoff, Trevino suddenly pulled a rubber snake out of his golf bag and playfully tossed it at his revered rival. This was the U.S. Open, the most dignified event of the year, and with all the blue-blazered officials standing sanctimoniously around the first tee, here was this irreverent Mexican acting like a child.

Trevino's attitude toward the dignity of the U.S. Golf Association is well documented. "When I retire," he says, "I'm going to get a pair of gray slacks, a white shirt, a striped tie, a blue blazer and a case of dandruff and go stand on the first tee so I can be a USGA official."

Nicklaus fell two shots back after three holes and never caught up as Trevino won his second U.S. Open title in four years. In his next start, Trevino won the Canadian Open in another playoff, this one with Art Wall. Then it was off to the British Open at Royal Birkdale, where he battled stroke-for-stroke with Britain's popular Tony Jacklin and Taiwan's Liang Huan Lu and held a one-shot lead going into the final round. Trevino birdied the last hole to win by a shot and became only the fourth player to win the U.S. Open and the British Open the same year. (Bobby Jones in 1930, Gene Sarazen in 1932 and Ben Hogan in 1953 were the others.)

It was almost more than the golf historians could handle the following year when Trevino, now a crowd favorite in Scotland as well as the United States, arrived at Muirfield to defend his title. Looming in his path once again was Nicklaus, who brought quite a story with him. The Golden Bear had won his fourth Masters that April and added his third U.S. Open championship in June. Now he was closing in on Ben Hogan's great accomplishment, in 1953, of winning the first three major championships. Within his reach was the elusive Grand Slam, a collection of victories in all four major championships in the same year, a feat that has never been achieved.

There was a logjam atop the leader board after two rounds, but Trevino's torrid stretch run the next day broke it wide open. He sank birdie putts of 20 feet on the 14th and 15th holes, holed out a bunker shot at the 16th, two-putted for a birdie at the par-5 17th and sank a 30-yard chip shot from behind the 18th green for a closing birdie to finish with a 66 for a three-round total of 207. Jacklin, his dogged pursuer the previous year, was only a shot behind, but the next challenger was Doug Sanders at 211, and Nicklaus was a distant 213. In the final round, Nicklaus made an early charge and took the lead after successive birdies at 9, 10 and 11, but his four-iron shot to the 16th hole bounced off the green into the rough and he made bogey. Trevino and Jacklin were tied going to the par-5 17th hole. Trevino hooked his drive into the rough, punched out, pulled his third shot into rough short of the green, chipped strong, then with bogey or double bogey staring him in the face, chipped in for a par. A stunned Jacklin three-putted from 20 feet for a bogey, and Trevino's par on the last hole made him the first player, since Arnold Palmer in 1962, to successfully defend the Open championship.

At the 1973 Danny Thomas Memphis Classic, Trevino achieved another milestone. With his second-place finish, he reached the $1 million mark in official earnings, and no one at that time had ever done it quicker: 6 years 11 months. Trevino was a certified millionaire, but before long he would lose it faster than he earned it.

After Trevino won the 1974 PGA Championship, shooting a final-round 69 to hold off Nicklaus by a shot, things started to turn the other way for him. It may be difficult to imagine now that he's back on top again, the toast of the Senior Tour, after becoming the first to win $1 million in a single year, but his career was in peril several times.

During a thunderstorm in the second round of the 1975 Western Open at Butler National Golf Club just outside of Chicago, Trevino, Bobby Nichols and Jerry Heard took refuge under a tree. Lightning struck a nearby lake and traveled through the ground to where Trevino was leaning against his golf bag. The bolt went up the metal shafts and pierced his left side.

"The pain in my left arm and shoulder was killing me, but I kept fighting it," he recalls. All three players were rushed to a nearby hospital. Doctors found small spidery marks on Trevino's left shoulder, the lightning's exit wounds. They said later that they usually see those marks in a morgue. That round was rained out and so was Saturday's. After being hospitalized for 36 hours, Heard, who was burned on the upper right leg, returned and tied for fourth. Nichols, burned on the head, took the next three weeks off, and although he

LIGHTNING STRIKES: *Trevino is comforted by spectators after being struck by lightning during the second round of the 1975 Western Open at Butler National Golf Club in Oak Brook, Illinois.*

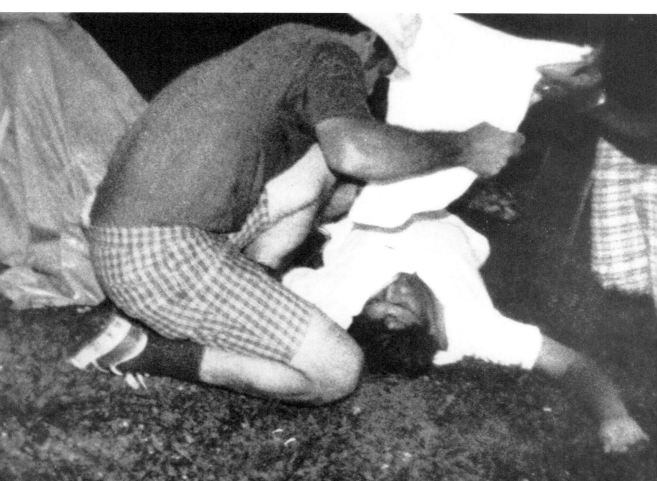

had won 12 times in the previous 13 years, he never won another PGA Tour event.

There were lingering effects for Trevino, too. His theory is that the electricity dried out the lubrication around his disks. True or not, 17 months later he was being wheeled into an operating room at a Houston hospital to have a herniated disk repaired. The story goes that he looked up at the surgeon, Dr. Antonio Moure, and said, "Doc, your reputation is on the line. Blow this one and you can use those scalpels to eat your dinner." Not surprisingly, Trevino was overanxious to start playing, and he came back too soon the next year. He tied for 39th at the Jackie Gleason Inverrary Classic, came in 75th at the Florida Citrus Open, missed the cut at Doral and withdrew from the Tournament Players Championship. When the warm weather arrived, he heated up, finishing 11th at the Colonial, 7th at the Memorial and tied for 9th at Memphis when Al Geiberger shot his 59.

That was it until the Canadian Open, where he started 67-68-71 and had a six-shot lead over Nicklaus, Tom Kite and Raymond Floyd. Everybody's score went up in the gusty winds Sunday, but Trevino easily won by four shots. Was he back? Were his troubles behind him? Hardly.

Late that year—his worst on the Tour since his rookie year, with earnings of just $85,198—Trevino learned that although he had earned more than $1.5 million lifetime, he was broke. He had let his two pals, Don and Jess Whittenton—the guys who had given him the job in El Paso and backed him when he started on the Tour—invest his money in a development called the Santa Teresa Country Club in New Mexico, not far from El Paso. The government had filed an $82,000 tax lien against him, and he found out he didn't have enough cash to pay it off. Lee Trevino Enterprises was bankrupt.

Trevino figures he lost $1.5 million. He had to liquidate all his assets. He sold his house overlooking the golf course, the clubhouse, the course he owned, the condos, everything. Although he never has

blamed them publicly, he severed all relationships with the Whit-
tentons and now has this advice for all investors: "Whenever a guy
comes up to me and says he's got a great deal, I tell him, 'If it's such
a good deal, go tell your family.' Why should a complete stranger
want to make money for me?"

Trevino was back where he started when he had joined the Tour
in 1967. His financial setback seemed to ignite his desire again,
revitalize his determination and give him more incentive than ever.
He started the 1978 season with a flourish, tying for fourth at the Joe
Garagiola Tucson Open, second at the Phoenix Open and ninth at
the Bob Hope Desert Classic. After finishing second at the Byron
Nelson Classic, he won the Colonial National Invitation, closing with
a four-under-par 66 to finish four shots ahead of Jerry Heard and Jerry
Pate.

Two starts later, Trevino had another fine finish, shooting 65 to
force a playoff with Andy Bean at Memphis, but he lost when Bean
sank a long birdie putt on the first hole. Trevino also lost another
playoff in Milwaukee, a marathon duel with Lee Elder, when he
bogeyed the eighth playoff hole. He wound up sixth on the money
list with $228,723. He moved up to fourth the following year, when
he won the Canadian Open for the third time, and second in 1980,
when he was a three-time winner.

The following year promised to be more of the same after Trevino
won the Tournament of Champions by two strokes with a final-round
69, but two weeks later he was stacking boxes in his garage when his
career took another sudden turn.

"I reached up and pinched a nerve," he says. "I didn't know
what it was at the time, but I knew it wasn't another disk problem.
It was different—the pain was worse. There were times I couldn't
even put my socks on. The pain was killing me. It was so bad, I really
thought about giving up golf. Everything fell apart: my course management, my strategy, concentration. I was listless and uninspired."

He tried everything, he said, even acupuncture. He wasn't play-

FRUSTRATING TIMES: *Trevino bends and bites his putter in frustration after missing a birdie attempt that would have tied him for the lead going into the final round of the 1980 Kemper Open.*

ing well because he was unable to get his right side down and through the swing. He lost his leg action, his power and his confidence. Finally, he tried another doctor in Dallas, who discovered the problem. A nerve in his back had swollen to three times its normal size. It was repaired by a microsurgical procedure, a laser used to burn and deaden the nerve. The excruciating pain was gone, but the effects lingered.

Now Trevino was like a lot of players his age. He was in his midforties and he was struggling. In 1982, he entered 20 tournaments: he missed seven cuts and withdrew four times. His only top-10 finish was a tie for ninth at the Colonial. There were a lot of doubts—so many, in fact, that he planned a second career as a television commentator. He landed a job with NBC.

"I took the job with NBC because I didn't know if I could win anymore," he says. "I was struggling and had to look for another way to make money. I was fortunate to work with guys like Vin Scully and Charley Jones. Scully is a pro's pro. He and Charley worked hard and knew what was going on all the time. They did the work. I had the easiest job. I just sat there until somebody asked me a question. I didn't mind the booth. It was pretty good money, like tying for third every week.

"In the beginning, even though they hired me because I was me, I tried to think of what to say, how it was going to come out and what it was going to sound like. That's not me. The NBC people encouraged me just to be myself, so I loosened up. It gave me a perfect balance. If I didn't have that job, I don't know if I would have been happy playing because I probably would have played too much, and I was too damn old for that."

There was one glorious interruption in Trevino's struggling years in the 1980s, one last curtain call, a major championship. Ironically, it was much the same as Jack Nicklaus experienced in the 1986 Masters, his only victory between the 1984 Memorial and the Senior Tour.

Trevino's one-week visit to glories past came at the 1984 PGA Championship at Shoal Creek Country Club near Birmingham, Alabama. At age 44, he outbattled two other former PGA Champions—Gary Player, 48, and Lanny Wadkins, 35—on the last day, turning them away with a hot-putting 69 to win by four shots with four sub-70 rounds.

During the third round, someone in the gallery started heckling Herman Mitchell, Trevino's 300-pound-plus caddie. Then he yelled at Trevino, "Hey, Lee, what do you feed that guy?" Without breaking stride, Trevino turned and said, "Rednecks, and he's hungry."

Trevino started the final round leading Wadkins by a shot and Player by two. Many were wondering if a player his age could maintain his concentration level enough to continue putting the way he had. Trevino showed the skeptics on the 1st hole when he rolled in a 60-footer for birdie. Wadkins pulled ahead by a shot but lost the lead

LONGTIME TEAMMATES: *Trevino checks his yardage with longtime caddie Herman Mitchell at the Senior Tournament Players Championship in Dearborn, Michigan.*

KISS OF VICTORY: *Trevino couldn't toss his hat because he borrowed it, and he said he was too old to jump, so he kissed his putter after winning the 1984 PGA Championship at Shoal Creek, Alabama.*

when he three-putted the 12th hole. Trevino increased his lead to two strokes with an 8-foot birdie at 14. Wadkins birdied 15, then gave it back with a bogey at 17. He bogeyed again at 18, and Trevino ran in a 15-footer for birdie to win by four.

"I was too old to jump," he says of that humid, rain-dampened day. "I can jump as high as I ever could, but I can't stay up as long. I didn't want to throw my hat because it wasn't mine. I forgot my hat and an elderly gentleman in the clubhouse loaned me his. So I did what made sense. I kissed the putter that won it for me. The PGA absolutely gave me new life. I never really got depressed about my game, but I was sure worried. It had been so long since I won. No matter what happened from then on, this one will stick out in my mind more than any of them. This one just meant so much in so many ways."

In addition to his sixth major championship trophy, Trevino was greatly rewarded in other ways. He signed a long-term contract to be the major spokesman for Toyota cars and trucks. He re-signed with Vlasic Foods and received many offers to play overseas, with appearance money guaranteed up to $50,000.

"That win really stretched out my career as far as both playing and contracts," Trevino says. "It meant a tremendous amount of money, probably in the millions." He would need it because he wouldn't win again until he reached the Senior Tour five years later. During that span, his official earnings dropped to $423,324, an average of slightly less than $85,000 a year. In 1988, he played only 10 tournaments, and his best finish was a tie for 19th at the Canon Greater Hartford Open. But already he was talking about the Senior Tour, about playing with the round bellies instead of the flat bellies.

"I'd go right now if they'd let me," he said at the 1989 Masters. "Hell, if I could find my birth certificate, I might be eligible. I knew I was on the wrong tour when I tried to bum a cigarette in the locker room. There must have been 25 guys in there and none of them smoked. All those guys do at night is putt on the rug and eat bananas."

Trevino took his preparation for the Senior Tour extremely seriously. As he hit balls on the practice range at the MCI Heritage Classic at Hilton Head, he talked about starting over.

"I've let all my contracts run out," he said between seven-iron shots. "I told NBC I didn't want to work; I cut my ties with Toyota and all my other businesses. I want to go into the Senior Tour exactly the way I went into the regular tour, with no strings, no obligations. I'll play for myself the first year and then negotiate on the strength of what I've done. I'm starting all over and that's the way I want it."

He increased his PGA Tour schedule to 14, mostly in the second half of the year, and boosted his confidence with ties for fourth at Hartford and fifth at the Western Open. If he could play well on 7,000-yard courses, he told himself, he would be primed for the 6,600-yard courses on the Senior Tour. He sequestered himself in a house in Palm Springs in October before the Skins Game and went into a grueling physical conditioning program. He would play 36 holes a day, then hit 200 practice balls, or play 18 holes and hit 500 balls. His birthday was December 1, and he was gearing up for his debut at the GTE Kaanapali Classic in Maui, Hawaii.

Then he almost didn't go. Claudia, whom he married in 1984 after meeting her when she was a 17-year-old volunteer at the Greater Hartford Open, wasn't going. Her mother had abdominal surgery in Connecticut, and Claudia went to be with her. Lee wanted to accompany her, but Claudia insisted he go to Hawaii.

It was hardly an auspicious debut. He bogeyed the first two holes, then got himself together and posted a three-under-par 69, but that was five shots behind Joe Jimenez. Trevino was three-under-par at the turn Friday, but a pair of three-putts on the back nine left him with another 69, six strokes behind Don Bies. Back in his suite at the Kapalua Bay Hotel, he received a birthday card signed by most of the players—a picture of Charles Schulz's Snoopy fainting at the mention of his age. There was also a hint of the respect he had earned throughout his career when Butch Baird wrote, "We took up a collection, $150,000 not to play. Will you accept?"

The third and final round was rained out, so Trevino finished in a three-way tie for seventh and missed out on his first goal: to qualify for the Tournament of Champions at La Costa in January.

His first victory on the Senior Tour came in the opening event of 1990, the Royal Caribbean Classic at Key Biscayne, Florida. It

PRESIDENTIAL ADVICE: *Trevino offers advice to President George Bush during the pro-am at the 1990 Doug Sanders Kingwood Celebrity Classic in Houston.*

was an outright gift from Jim Dent, who blew a seven-shot lead with nine holes to play and a five-shot edge with three left, finishing bogey, bogey, double bogey to lose by a shot.

"I never should have won," Trevino says. "Never in my wildest dreams did I think I could catch Jim. I was just hoping to finish second."

He finished second the next week to Mike Hill at the GTE Suncoast Classic. The following week, Trevino came back and won the Aetna Challenge at Naples, Florida, with a sand save on the last hole to edge Bruce Crampton (who shot 65-66 the last two rounds) by a shot with a 16-under-par 200. In 9 of his first 11 rounds on the Senior Tour, Trevino shot in the sixties, and the other two were 71s. He won again the next week at the $400,000 Vintage Chrysler Invitational at Indian Wells, California, again by one shot.

"Trevino is in a league by himself," Chi Chi Rodriguez says. "We don't even count him. We figure when you come in second, you're a winner."

After taking a little time off, Trevino didn't win again until the Doug Sanders Kingwood Celebrity Classic outside of Houston, an event highlighted by the appearance of President Bush. The President played with his son George, Sanders and PGA Tour Commissioner Deane Beman in Saturday's round. Bush drew a huge gallery and distinguished himself in the scramble format. Two weeks later, Trevino added his 5th victory in 10 starts. He outlasted 67-year-old Mike Fetchick with a 10-foot birdie putt on the fifth playoff hole at the NYNEX Golf Digest Commemorative at Sleepy Hollow Country Club in Scarborough, New York.

OLD-TIMERS HUG: *Trevino gives Mike Fetchick, 67, a hug after sinking a birdie putt to beat him on the fifth playoff hole at the NYNEX Commemorative at Sleepy Hollow Country Club in Scarborough, New York.*

Fetchick won three times on the PGA Tour, including the 1956 Western Open, which was considered a major championship at the time. In 1985, he became the oldest winner in Senior Tour history when he birdied the final hole to win the Hilton Head Senior Invitational at age 63. He had dropped each year on the money list since and was 64th in 1989.

Still, there he was, battling Trevino head-to-head in the playoff after firing a final-round 64 to tie Trevino, Rodriguez and Jimmy Powell at 11-under-par 199. Having recently switched to a long-shafted putter, Fetchick looked like a winner on the first extra hole when he ran in a 20-footer for birdie. Powell was bunkered and out of it, and Rodriguez missed from 18 feet, leaving it up to Trevino, who says he told Fetchick, "I bet I'm the last man you want to see over this putt, right?" Then he calmly knocked in the 15-footer. After sinking a couple of 3- and 4-footers for pars, Fetchick finally succumbed on the fifth extra hole when his 25-footer for birdie slid by on the right and Trevino sank a 10-footer.

Trevino was back in the same white-hot groove where he started the season. He finished second the next two weeks—once to Nicklaus' record-breaking 27-under-par at the Mazda Senior Tournament Players Championship—and then he had the highlight of his year, a dramatic come-from-behind victory over Nicklaus in the U.S. Senior Open at storied Ridgewood Country Club at Paramus, New Jersey.

After skipping practice rounds Tuesday and Wednesday to spend more time working on an unfamiliar right-to-left draw off the tee, Trevino charged out of the box with a 67 and a 68 to take a one-shot lead over Jim Dent and five over the guys he was most concerned about, Nicklaus and Gary Player. After he slipped to a 73 Saturday when his putter suddenly went cold, Trevino found himself tied with Dent and Player, a shot behind Nicklaus. He passed Nicklaus with birdies on the 2d and 3d holes, slipped back into a tie with a bogey at the par-5 13th, then sank birdie putts of 20 and 15 feet on the 15th and 16th holes to go 13-under-par. Nicklaus also birdied those holes,

"In my first year on the Senior Tour, I had trouble in the early rounds of the Transamerica Senior Golf Championship in Napa, California. I caught myself forward-pressing the putter in the last round on the fourth hole. I was starting the putter back on line, but with the forward press, it opened the blade. This caused all my putts to miss on the right side of the hole. On the back nine, I concentrated on taking the hands back with the putter head, without any forward press. I birdied five of the last seven holes and ended up winning the tournament. Most everyone will start a putter on their intended line, and it's usually the line they read correctly. When they start regripping and forward-pressing, that takes the putter off line, which means they have to compensate in some way to get it back on line during the stroke. The easiest way for me is just to move the hands and the putter head back at the same time."

Lee Trevino

but he had bogeyed 14 and was 12-under coming to the par-5 17th hole. After his one-iron second shot left him 128 yards from the hole, he chunked an eight-iron 10 yards short, chipped within 4 feet and missed the putt for a bogey.

"Never in my wildest dreams did I expect Jack to bogey the 17th hole," Trevino said. "It's great to beat him again. It's always a feather in your cap to beat Jack Nicklaus because he's the best. I was on a mission today."

It was quite a trip and now Trevino had come full circle. In 1967, he had come to New Jersey a virtual unknown. The following year he won the U.S. Open at Baltusrol, outlasting runner-up Jack Nicklaus. Now, 23 years later, he had come to the Garden State for his first U.S. Senior Open and again outdueled Nicklaus down the stretch.

"A U.S. Open is a U.S. Open as far as I'm concerned," Trevino said. "This year has far exceeded my expectations. I never dreamed it would be like this. I'm astounded at what's happened to the Senior Tour."

There was an obvious letdown after that. Some of the desire and intensity drained out of Trevino that day, and it took a while to regain it. He tied for 16th the following week—only his second finish of the year out of the top 10—and didn't challenge again until a last-day 68 brought him within a shot of Rives McBee at the Showdown Classic at Jeremy Ranch in Park City, Utah. He had a chance to win at the Crestar Classic near Richmond, but he could only par the last two holes, and his final-round 67 wasn't strong enough to hold off Jim Dent's sizzling 65.

"I'm a little worn out," Trevino said two weeks later, before the $1.5 million Vantage Championship. "It's been a long year, but I've still got one goal left. I want to win $1 million."

It was the first time he had revealed that goal. With earnings of $740,101 and only six tournaments left on his schedule, it added another heavy load to his broad shoulders. A victory at the Vantage,

A TROPHY IS A TROPHY: *Trevino says, "A U.S. Open is a U.S. Open," while squeezing the trophy after winning the 1990 U.S. Senior Open at Ridgewood Country Club in Paramus, New Jersey.*

the Senior Tour's richest tournament, was worth $202,500 and certainly would have given him a boost. But the best he could do was tie for fourth when he started four shots behind second-round leader Charlie Coody and merely matched his two-under-par 70. Bob Charles finished with a brilliant eight-under-par 64 to tie 1987 champion Al Geiberger for second.

The next week, Trevino finished second, needing a final-round 67 to come within four shots of wire-to-wire winner Bruce Crampton at the Gatlin Brothers Southwest Classic. But it served notice that he was ready to win again, and he did the following week at the Transamerica Championship at Silverado Country Club in Napa, California. After an opening 73, he came back with a 67 to tie for the lead, then won going away with a 65 for his seventh victory of the year.

His seemingly unrealistic goal of winning $1 million was assured when he reached the season's grand finale at the New York Life Championship, a new $1 million tournament for the top 30 money winners. But now Trevino had deftly placed still another carrot in front of his own nose, still one more seemingly impossible dream—he wanted to be the No. 1 money winner in the United States, not just the Senior Tour. He wanted to overtake Greg Norman, who had won the Arnold Palmer Trophy as the PGA Tour's top money winner with $1,165,477.

After starting with a pair of 68s, Trevino was three back of Mike Hill and Dale Douglass, but he caught them with a blazing 65 on Sunday. Now it was playoff time, but Trevino had already reached his ultimate goal. Even when Hill rolled in a 40-foot birdie to win on the first extra hole, Trevino earned $95,000 for tying for second, boosting his official winnings to $1,190,518—$25,041 more than Norman.

So the Merry Mex had done it all, climbed every plateau, achieved every goal in his first, and so far most memorable, season on the Senior PGA Tour. He won seven times, finished second on eight occasions and set a scoring record with a 68.69 average. He led in putting, greens hit in regulation and, of course, the all-important money list.

"It's leading the league in batting average, runs batted in and home runs. This makes it a '71 year," Trevino said, referring to the year he won the U.S., Canadian and British Opens. "I achieved all my goals."

So what's left for golf's all-time goodwill ambassador? What can he possibly do for an encore? Well, how about more of the same?

There was no letup in Trevino's 30-tournament schedule in 1991, but the intensity, at times, was missing. After winning the Aetna Challenge by a shot over Dale Douglass in February and the rain-shortened Vantage at the Dominion in March, he didn't win again until Sunwest Bank/Charley Pride Classic in late August.

After letting all his commercial contracts expire and playing relatively sponsor-free (except for Toyota) in 1990, Trevino signed with business advisor Chuck Rubin, brother-in-law of his good friend Tom Watson, and literally held an auction for his services.

"Being the leading money winner last year has become very profitable," Trevino said before the 1991 PGA Seniors Championship at Palm Beach Gardens, Florida, the week after The Masters. "I signed with Cadillac; I signed with Motorola and Spalding. And I went to Japan to do some commercials [cigarettes for RJR Tobacco]. I've played nine tournaments already and have done a lot outside of golf. I love it. I'll do as much as I can for my sponsors. I like to work.

"There have been times this year when I've gone out and played a little tired, but I love it. Golf is all I know, all I want to do. I can't wait to wake up in the morning because I know I'm going to play golf. I love to play, I want to play every day and hopefully I'll be able to play for many years to come."

ORVILLE MOODY

They were standing behind the scorer's tent: Al Geiberger, Bob Rosburg and Deane Beman, all eagerly awaiting what they felt surely would be the first four-way playoff in U.S. Open history.

The two former PGA champions and Beman had tied at two-over-par 282 on that hot, windy June afternoon in 1969 at Champions Golf Club in Houston. They were waiting for a paunchy, moon-faced, sad-eyed former army sergeant to three-putt from 12 feet and join them.

There was no reason for them to expect him to get down in two because he was, unquestionably, the worst putter on the PGA Tour— and this was for the U.S. Open championship.

Moody had joined the Tour the previous year after spending 14½ years in the Army. Although he was a very accurate driver and an excellent long-iron player, he hadn't come close to winning because he played like an amateur on the greens, stabbing and jabbing.

Lee Trevino had been the center of attention before the tournament started. The Merry Mex had come out of Texas to win the U.S. Open the previous year at Oak Hill in Rochester, and he was a sentimental favorite to repeat in his native state. Amid all his quips and laughter, Trevino tossed out one line in the direction of his longtime Texas pal that would live forever: "If I don't win this week, I think you will, Sarge."

It was easier to find someone in a three-piece suit with a Boston accent at Champions than anyone else who thought Moody had a chance that week. Not even after he followed an opening 71 with a 70 to pull within four shots of the front-running Beman did anyone seriously think Moody could hold up in such a pressure situation. In one of the greatest exhibitions in Open history, the short-hitting Beman used fairway woods on seven par-4 holes and one par-3 and shot 68 in the opening round, a stroke behind Bob Murphy. The next day, the future commissioner of the PGA Tour tamed the 7,187-yard Cypress Creek course again with a 69 and gained a one-shot edge over Murphy and Miller Barber.

Not all the attention was focused on the leaders. The biggest gallery was following Trevino, but his fans went away disappointed when he followed an opening 74 with a 75 and missed the cut by a stroke. Some folks surely asked some tough questions while swigging their long-neck Lone Star beers: Was he a flash in the pan? Hell, could that flat, left-to-right swing really hold up? Was Lee going to turn out to be another Jack Fleck, the 1955 U.S. Open champion, who rarely competed again and wound up a long career with total earnings of $129,898?

Anyway, it was Moody this time, not Trevino, who had come out of nowhere to challenge for the U.S. Open title. Ol' Sarge didn't

ON TARGET: *A slender Orville Moody waves his fist after sinking a birdie putt during a third-round 68 in the 1969 U.S. Open at Houston.*

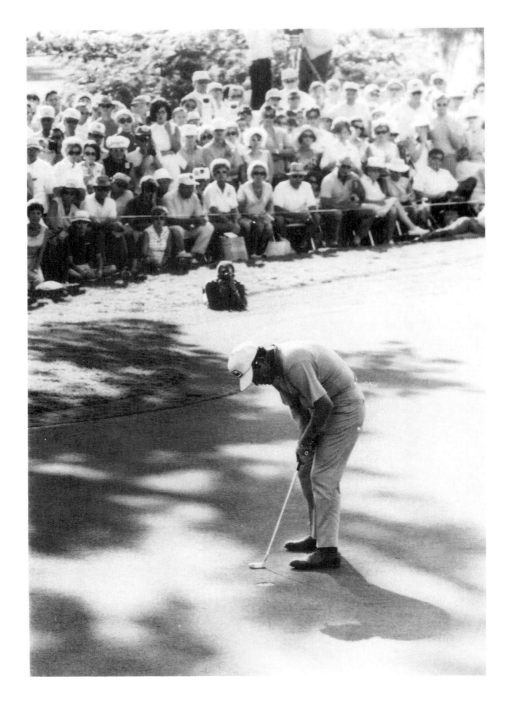

MOODY WINS OPEN: *Moody taps in his winning par putt on the last hole to win the 1969 U.S. Open at Houston, his only victory on the PGA Tour.*

crack the third day when his awkward-looking, cross-handed putting stroke produced a 68. However, Barber also shot 68 and bolted into the lead when Beman faded to a 73 and Murphy to 74.

Now it came down to the last day, and everyone wondered how the portly part Choctaw Indian from Oklahoma, who looked more like the local plumber than a pro golfer, would hold up. It was a hectic day on the leader board, with eight players within two shots of the lead on the back nine. But nobody made a charge, least of all Barber, who blew to a 78.

Arnold Palmer was in the group at two-over-par playing the 416-yard 15th hole. After hooking his drive into the rough, he made one of his miraculous recovery shots, a low hook around some trees onto the green. Then he three-putted and lost yet another chance to win a second U.S. Open title.

Moody, meanwhile, was plugging along with Barber in the last group. They were tied going into the 213-yard, par-3 12th hole. They both pushed their tee shots into the right woods, overcompensating for the lake on the left. Moody chipped close enough to slap in his par putt, while Barber dumped his pitch into a bunker, made five and didn't threaten again.

Geiberger, the 1966 PGA champion, made a move with a birdie at No. 15, but he three-putted 16 and needed a birdie on the last hole to catch Moody. His 20-footer curled away in the last few inches, and he went to sit and wait for Moody to falter.

Beman had been scrambling all day. He missed birdie putts on the 15th and 16th holes and appeared out of it; but then he hit a six-iron within 15 feet and sank the birdie putt on the last hole to tie Geiberger. Rosburg was next. All he needed was a par to tie Moody at one-under-par, but he hooked his drive and put his second shot in a bunker to the right of the green. He blasted a magnificent sand shot within 2 feet of the hole, then stepped up quickly and jabbed his putt.

"That bunker shot was probably the greatest shot I ever played," says Rosburg, now a television commentator for ABC. "And the putt had to be one of the worst. Still, I thought there was a good chance for a playoff because nobody knew how Sarge would hold up."

Now Moody needed only pars on the last two holes to gain golfing immortality. He was pumped up at 17, hitting his approach shot over the long, narrow green, but from 30 feet he chipped close enough to shake in another tester. But how long could this one-putting go on?

"I knew I had to par the last hole," Moody recalls with a smile. "I hit a big, big tee shot right down the middle, then an eight-iron to 12 feet from the hole. I eased the first putt down, then turned my hat sideways and said to myself, 'You stupid idiot!' for leaving it 2 feet short."

Beman recalls standing there with Geiberger and Rosburg watching Moody. "There wasn't anybody who thought Moody would make that putt, including Sarge," he says, laughing. "We were all thinking about a playoff." As Beman, Geiberger and Rosburg stood gaping, Moody managed to rattle in one more knee-knocker and he was the U.S. Open champion.

Jim Murray, the incomparable columnist for the *Los Angeles Times*, described this once-in-a-lifetime achievement best when he wrote, "It was like unhitching a horse from a plow and having it win the Kentucky Derby or a guy stepping out of the audience, removing his coat and knocking out the heavyweight champion of the world."

Had Moody realized just how much that putt meant, how far it would have to carry him financially, how long it would be before he could raise his hand in victory on the 18th green again, it's doubtful that he could have drawn the putter back, let alone guided the ball into the cup.

Moody's official earnings in the next 10 years bottomed out at $290,470, an average of $29,470 a year before taxes and travel ex-

CROSS-HANDED: *Moody displays his unorthodox, cross-handed putting style, one of many methods he tried while struggling on the PGA Tour.*

penses, hardly adequate for a wife and four kids. He came close to winning a couple of times, but it always came down to putting and, well, he just never quite figured out that part of the game.

The best example was a stinging defeat in the 1973 Bing Crosby National Pro-Am at Pebble Beach. Moody had a four-shot lead going into the final round, but he started pushing and pulling. He finally fell into a playoff with Jack Nicklaus and Raymond Floyd when he three-putted the 18th green—missing his victory attempt from no more than 14 inches. He lost the playoff to Nicklaus.

"I used to go home so disgusted after a round of golf that I wanted to quit," Moody recalls. "I would just be so torn up. It was like an electrical shock would hit me."

His fellow seniors now will talk about that ugly stroke on the greens, how they had to turn their backs because they couldn't bear to watch, how some of them even felt embarrassed for him.

After winning only $13,283 in 1974, Moody decided to leave the Tour and try to make it in the golf course business. That decision resulted in some of the funniest, most bizarre experiences of his life.

First, he got a job as head pro at Lake Arbor in Arvada, Colorado, a suburb of Denver.

"We had this young teenage girl, maybe 14, working with us on weekends, a real nice kid that everybody liked. But it turned out that she was stealing us blind," Moody recalled one day before a U.S. Senior Open. "At first, there would be $10, $20 missing when I checked in on Saturdays. Then, it got to be more and more. It had to be an inside job, and after a while we figured she was doing it, but she always denied it and we couldn't prove anything. Finally, I just let her go; but I worked a lot of weeks for nothing."

Moody stayed at Lake Arbor for two years, but it was driving him crazy: he kept thinking he could make more money back on Tour. He returned in 1977 and at times was teased into thinking his game was back. He shot 66 the final day to finish 2nd to Mike McCullough at the Magnolia Classic in Hattiesburg, Mississippi, a tournament opposite The Masters. But a tie for 16th at the Danny Thomas Memphis Classic was his only other good showing, and he wound up making only $15,521 that year.

The next year he was worse, missing the cut in his first seven starts. His stroke average was a dismal 74.76. Then, suddenly, at the Heritage Classic in Hilton Head, South Carolina, his putter behaved on the tiny greens at Harbour Town, and he tied for 3rd with Larry Nelson with a 67-71 finish, collecting $13,275—his biggest check since the 1973 San Antonio Open. The next week he was 14th at the Greater Greensboro Open in North Carolina, and later that month he was 16th at Houston after opening 67-68.

A second-round 64 that paved the way for a tie for 3rd at Houston was the highlight of 1979; the year ended with a tie for 5th behind Curtis Strange's first victory in the season-ending Pensacola Open. There were only lowlights the following year, and a disgusted Moody tossed in his towel once more. He was discouraged and flat broke.

"I was 47 and couldn't make a living out there anymore," he says. "The only checks I was getting were for working my butt off at Monday outings. And if it wasn't for winning the U.S. Open, I wouldn't have had those.

"So, I got a job at a club in a little town near where I lived in Plano, Texas—Sulphur Springs. Plano was a small town, about 15,000. We had about 175 members. I got $24,000 a year and made another $30,000 with carts and giving lessons. It was just enough to make a living."

Moody got quite an orientation to small-town living. One of the first days he was there, he got a call in the pro shop informing him that there was a football game going on in the 14th fairway.

"I jumped in a cart and headed out, expecting to find a few kids playing touch football," Moody says. "Well, you can imagine my surprise when I got there and there was an entire high school football team in full equipment tearing up my grass. When I started screaming and yelling, this guy—I guess he was the coach—came up to me

calmly and informed me that the junior varsity always practices here when the varsity is using the main field."

There were a lot of other hazards in Moody's path during his years in Sulphur Springs while he waited for his 50th birthday and a chance to cash in on the riches of the Senior Tour.

"This guy came in one afternoon and, after having a drink, complained that the Weller was weak, that it tasted watered down," Moody says. "Naturally, I told him he was crazy, but the second time somebody complained, I decided to try it. Damn if it wasn't weak as hell. That night I hung around, pretending to be busy in the shop, but watching to see who drank Weller. Sure enough, the bartender's best buddy came in and had a bunch of Weller without leaving much money as far as I could see. The bottle was at least half empty when I left, but the next morning it was damn near full.

"It was the same thing with cigarettes. There would be a bunch missing—a certain brand, usually—so you just looked around, found out who smoked that brand and let 'em know you were watching 'em.

"Hell, I knew all the tricks. I was in the Army for 14 years, and those soldiers will steal you blind. I ran enough golf shops to learn the deals. I had a hell of a time with my inventory at Fort Hood [Killeen, Texas]. Everybody had to pay for greens fees—not much, but it was cash. It seemed like we got a fair amount of play in the mornings, but when I came in, there was hardly anything in the register. So one day, I decided to come early. I took a cart and counted 19 guys on the front nine. When I got to the pro shop, the guy had only seven receipts. I don't know if he was letting them play for free or pocketing the money; all I know is that he was reassigned the next day.

CHORUS LINE: *Moody kicks up his foot after a 15-foot putt for his par drops on the par-4 17th hole during the third round of the 69th U.S. Open.*

"I had this guy who worked for me in the pro shop who never wore socks. He used to come in every morning wearing tennis shoes and no socks, but that wasn't really unusual with young guys. I didn't think anything of it until I started taking inventory and came up missing a bunch of socks. At first, I recounted, asked around, then I remembered this kid. So I watched him, and sure enough, every day for a week when he left, he was wearing socks.

"I didn't report him because he could have gotten court-martialed. In the Army, they send you to jail for that sort of stuff, so I figured I kept him out of jail by just reaming his ass and letting him know he better not pull that shit again."

Moody was raised on a golf course in Chickasha, Oklahoma, where his father was a greens superintendent. "I started playing when I was about 3," Moody says. "But I never played on anything but sand greens until I was 13 or 14."

Moody won the Oklahoma state high school championship and was offered a scholarship to the University of Oklahoma, but it didn't take him long to realize that academics were tougher than downhill putts on sand greens, so he left shortly to join the Army. After he served for a while as a rifle instructor, his golf talents were discovered, and he was placed in charge of instruction, and maintenance and supervision of golf courses. Of course, there was plenty of hustling on the side. An enlisted man has got to have beer money.

"I played guys on one leg, sitting down, on my knees, cross-handed and left-handed," Moody says. "I beat a guy sitting in a chair. I could break 90 doing that. Once, after I sprained my ankle and had a cast on my leg, I shot 65. Hit it just as damn far as I ever did."

He served in Japan, Korea and Germany, and he found time to

ARMY SPECIAL: *During his 14 years in the Army, Moody found plenty of time to tune his game.*

win the 1958 All-Army Championship, the 1962 All-Service title and three Korean Opens.

"I was stationed in Japan for four years, so I ought to know a little Japanese," Moody says. "I also know some German, Korean and even a little English."

Although he had risen to the rank of staff sergeant, the army life was wearing on Moody when he was running the pro shop at Fort Hood in 1967, and he kept listening to his buddies who told him he could make it on the PGA Tour. It was a gamble, giving up his pension after 14½ years, but he decided to take it. He'd go to the Qualifying School and give the Tour a try for 2 years; if he couldn't cut it, he could come back to the security of the Army and finish out his 20 years.

He almost went back to the Army a couple of times in the early going, but he managed to hang on. That victory at the U.S. Open kept a lot of doors ajar and gave him enough opportunities to stay afloat financially, although it was never easy. Especially tough were his last two years at Sulphur Springs, where all he could do was practice his putting and count down to the day when he would turn 50 and become eligible for the Senior Tour.

His birthday is December 7, so Moody couldn't start playing on the Senior Tour until 1984, which by then had grown to 24 events and a total purse of $5,156,000. His arrival was hardly greeted with any fanfare by the media or concern by the other players. Based on his past performances, he certainly wasn't considered a threat to start taking anybody's money. Ol' Sarge was just another nice guy who needed a job.

Well, if there is a Fountain of Youth, it certainly showered on Moody right away. Early in the year, he chipped in to beat Palmer and Dan Sikes at Daytona Beach, Florida—his first victory since the 1969 U.S. Open. Now, qualified for the Tournament of Champions at La Costa in Carlsbad, California, he won the elite event in a runaway by seven strokes.

At last, Moody was a winner. He finished fifth on the money list that year, winning $183,920, and seemed to have solved his putting problems. Alas, it was only temporary. The more he played, the more he started to shake—just a little at first, then more and more.

He started 1985 on a strong note, losing to Miller Barber by a shot at the opening Sunrise Classic in Fort Pierce, Florida, but it went steadily downhill from there. He looked like the ol' Sarge again, stabbing and jabbing.

"Holding that putter was like trying to hold a rattlesnake," he says. "I didn't have any confidence at all. I'd get over a three-footer and just hope I didn't fan it."

Finally, he made a decision that would change his life. It turned him from a guy who lived week to week into one with financial security for the first time.

The long putter. Many have tried it, but no one has reaped more rewards.

"I was struggling. I had the yips so bad on all short putts, I didn't know what to do," Moody says. "You know, when you have the yips, it doesn't help to practice. Hell, you can stand on the putting green all day and roll them smooth. But as soon as you get on the course, get in competition with a little money riding, those old hands start shaking. You can see them moving, you can step away, but by then you've lost your concentration."

Moody probably spent more time on the practice green than any of the seniors, trolling for tips, trying new stances and new grips, asking questions, seeking any sort of advice that might help. Finally one day, late in that frustrating summer of 1985, he saw Charles Owens using a putter with a 50-inch shaft.

Owens is another classic success story on the Senior Tour. He started playing cross-handed as a kid growing up in Winter Haven, Florida, and never changed. He played football briefly at Florida A&M. While in the Army in 1952, he injured his left knee during a parachute exercise at Fort Bragg, North Carolina. After several

GIVE IT A RIP: *Moody was an immediate success on the Senior Tour, winning the Daytona Beach Classic in his rookie year.*

operations failed to completely repair the injury, the knee was finally fused in 1965. Owens started to play golf again after a 13-year layoff, and in 1967 he turned pro. Three years later he qualified for the PGA Tour and won the Kemper-Ashville Open, a satellite event, in 1971.

Then his other knee started bothering him, and after several operations, he dropped off the Tour. He continued to support his wife and five kids by playing on the Florida mini-tour, winning the West Palm Beach Open in 1971 and 1972 and the Florida Open in 1974. When the Senior Tour started he was ready, although it took him several years to crack the top 50 on the money list.

Switching to a 50-inch putter that weighed almost three pounds, Owens earned $78,158 in 1985. The following year he won the season-opening Treasure Coast Classic at Fort Pierce, Florida, shooting 65-69-68 to finish 14-under-par. A month later, he won the Senior PGA Tour Roundup after a second-round 64 moved him within a shot of front-running Dale Douglass; a final-round 67 caught Douglass, and a par on the second playoff hole beat him.

Owens won $207,813 that year and $103,030 the next year, when he had a third and three fifths. But physical problems—including bottled iritis, which occasionally blinds him in his right eye—continued to plague him, and he drastically curtailed his schedule in 1989, 1990 and 1991. Fortunately for Moody, Owens was quite active and successful in that fall of 1985 when Sarge's game was floundering.

"I had always fooled around with different putters, ever since I was in the Army," Moody says. "One day I was on the putting green when I noticed Charlie Owens using that awkward-looking long putter he called Slim Jim. At that stage, I was willing to try anything. I tried it and liked it right away. It took a little getting used to, but it was a godsend. Thank God for Charlie Owens."

At the Citizens Union Classic in Lexington, Kentucky, Moody fired a final-round six-under-par 65 to get in a playoff with Lee Elder, Walt Zembriski and Dan Sikes before losing to Elder's birdie on the third extra hole. Three weeks later, Sarge was at it again, tying for second behind Mike Fetchick at the Hilton Head International.

"Almost overnight, I went from a mediocre scorer to a really good scorer," Moody says. "My game probably improved two shots all the way around. I felt like I had a chance to win again."

Finally shedding his Army Surplus specials, Moody went spiffy in 1986, donning the Hogan-style caps, bright-colored striped shirts and, of all things, plus fours. It didn't help him win, although his new long putter carried him to 12 top-10 finishes. There still was one ingredient missing, and Sarge acquired that the following year when he convinced his attractive daughter, Michelle, to caddie for him.

"Michelle was 17, had good eyes and could see the greens," Moody explains. "I was 54 and couldn't see too good. It made sense."

Michelle caddied until the 1990 season, when she married Senior Tour staff member Brett Shelton and enrolled at Southern Methodist University. But ol' Sarge knew a good thing. He hired a friend of Michelle's, Stacey Trimble, to replace her.

With Michelle reading his putts, encouraging him along the way and, just as important, keeping him company, Moody enjoyed one of his best years as a professional golfer in 1987. He won three times, including the Liberty Mutual Legends of Golf with Bruce Crampton, where they combined for a tournament-record 11-under-par 59 in the third round and made a string of 11 consecutive birdies over two days. With Crampton rubbing Moody's big belly for luck, they closed with a 64 to win by four shots.

His confidence boosted, Moody went on to win the Rancho Murieta Gold Rush at Rancho Murieta, California, gaining a two-shot lead with a second-round 67 and holding off Butch Baird to win by two. He was second at the Greenbrier (West Virginia) American Express Championship to Crampton, second again to Chi Chi Rodriguez at the Digital Seniors Classic in Concord, Massachusetts, and again at the Gus Machado Classic in Key Biscayne, Florida, before winning the final event of the year, the rain-shortened GTE Kaanapali Classic on Maui, Hawaii, by three shots.

A milestone he never dreamed was attainable came true at the $1 million Vantage Championship. There he finished fourth (four shots behind Al Geiberger), collected $56,050 and went over the $1 million mark in combined PGA Tour earnings. At long last, the part Choctaw Indian from Chickasha, Oklahoma, who learned to putt on sand greens and spent 14½ years in the Army, was officially a millionaire. And the best was yet to come.

At 55, ol' Sarge really hit it rich. He won four more tournaments, finished second four times, third twice and won $411,859—more than he had won in 14 years on the regular tour.

His best performance came early in a record-smashing effort at the Vintage Chrysler Invitational in Indian Wells, California, the first week of March. He opened by tying the tournament record of 64 and closed by beating it with a 63. His 72-hole total of 25-under-par 263 was another Senior Tour record (until Nicklaus broke it by two shots at the 1990 Tournament Players Championship), and so was his winning margin of 11 strokes. Next month, Moody teamed with Crampton again to successfully defend their title at the Legends of Golf, and it was Moody's putting that made the difference. He sank a 14-foot downhiller for birdie on the sixth playoff hole to beat Lou Graham and Tommy Aaron.

The week after finishing second to Bob Charles at the Sunwest Bank/Charley Pride Classic in Albuquerque, New Mexico, Moody shot a final-round 66 at the Senior Players Reunion in Dallas, then won a four-way playoff against Charles, Bobby Nichols and Don Massengale with a birdie on the first extra hole. His fourth victory came at the Greater Grand Rapids Open, where he shot a second-round 65, then held off a charging Gary Player (66) to win by one.

"Sarge is a real threat every week now," Player said afterwards. "He's always been a great player from tee to green, and now that he's putting well, he's going to win a lot of tournaments." More remarkable than his 15 top-five finishes, his $411,859 in prize money or his 4 victories, was one telling statistic that told everything about the long-shafted putter, Michelle reading his putts and the contentment of a man who finally had cured the lifelong yips. Moody finished No. 1 in putting statistics. Yes, he had come from the worst to the best.

"A lot of guys started asking me about my putter," Moody says. "They used to make fun of ol' Sarge, but not so much after that. Jim Ferree started using one, and so did Gay Brewer and Harold Henning."

John Paul Cain, the successful stockbroker from Houston who burst on the Senior Tour in 1989 by qualifying for the Greater Grand Rapids Open on Monday and winning the tournament that weekend, first encountered Moody back in 1967. Fresh out of the Army, Moody was in his hustling days and was taken down to Houston by some potential Tour sponsors to play with Cain, one of the state's top amateurs.

"I beat his brains out for three days," Moody says. "But he told the sponsors I couldn't putt well enough to make it on Tour. So when I won the U.S. Open, one of the sponsors was kicking himself. He told me, 'That's OK, John Paul never made me any money in the stock market, either.' "

Cain still insists he was right. "Sure, that's a true story. Sarge is the best ball-striker I've ever known, but I've seen beginners putt better than he could."

With his newfound confidence, his new equipment, and Michelle still at his side, Moody went on to have his best year in 1989,

RECORD BREAKER: *Mastering his strange-looking putter, Moody set a Senior Tour record at the Vintage Chrysler Invitational with a 25-under-par 263 total.*

at an age (56) when most Senior players start their decline. By this time, he had seven victories plus two more at the Legends, but none of them were what Gary Player calls "majors." Player gets a lot of kidding about his emphasis on the so-called major championships, but only because he's not reluctant to discuss it with the media.

Anyway, one of the prized possessions on the Senior Tour is the Mazda Senior Tournament Players Championship, modeled after the rich Tournament Players Championship (now The Players Championship) on the regular tour. It carried a purse of $700,000, with a first prize of $105,000, and was played at the Tournament Players Club Valley Course at Ponte Vedra, Florida, home of PGA Tour headquarters.

Moody showed up in early June without a victory, but he got off to a good start with a 67, which tied him with five others for the lead. Gary Player took a one-shot lead after 36 holes with a 66, then Moody mounted his charge with a tournament-record eight-under-par 64 to build a comfortable six-shot cushion.

"I felt like I was in a trance out there," he said afterward. "I just kept hitting one good shot after another."

It was a walk in the park on Sunday and Moody knew it, playing for pars, shooting 71 and cruising to a two-shot victory over charging Charlie Coody, who had 67. It was just four days shy of the 20th anniversary of his unforgettable triumph at Champions in Houston, and Moody said he was going to put the trophy right next to a brand-new U.S. Open trophy (his original one was destroyed by fire in 1977 and just recently replaced).

A better trophy was only three weeks away at Laurel Valley Golf Club, in Ligonier, Pennsylvania, about 10 miles from the birthplace of Arnold Palmer.

Moody had finished fourth in the two previous U.S. Senior Opens, which were growing in prestige and media coverage every year. The atmosphere was undeniably USGA, with its red, white and

T I P

"I went to the long putter because of the simple fact that I was a guy that had the yips real bad. The first day that I used the long putter, I putted much better and got over the yips. The more I used it, the smoother I eventually got with the stroke. This, combined with a few other small changes that I made, gave me more confidence as I went along. I think the straighter you can stand, the less chance you have of your nerves taking control of you. You're more relaxed. Standing higher also makes it easier to swing the putter, and it works more like a pendulum on a clock. If you bend over too much, you want to hit at the ball."

Orville Moody

ANOTHER RECORD: *Saying he felt as though he was "in a trance," Moody cruised to victory in the 1989 Mazda Senior Tournament Players Championship on the Tournament Players Club Valley Course in Ponte Vedra, Florida.*

blue bunting and blue-blazered officials everywhere. It's a special event and the players all felt it.

Al Geiberger opened with a four-under-par 68 to take a one-shot lead over Harold Henning and amateur Frank Boydston, who owned what he called "the slowest-growing restaurant chain in America, a hamburger joint in Arizona where they drink beer out of mason jars and use tuna fish cans for ashtrays."

"What will my buddies say when they see my name on the leader board?" Boydston said, answering a reporter's question. "Oh, they'll just say, 'He'll choke tomorrow like all amateurs do.' "

Using clubs so worn the caddie said he couldn't read the numbers, Boydston skied to a 76 the second day, but Moody wasn't much better, with a 73 after an opening 72. He appeared totally out of contention when rookie Frank Beard shot 69 for a five-under-par 139. But it all changed the next day, when Moody went into one of his "trances" and shot a U.S. Senior Open record 64 to tie Beard at 207. He finished with a flourish, making birdies at Nos. 14, 15 and 16, then an eagle on the 472-yard finishing hole, when he hit a five-wood 12 feet past the hole and sank the putt.

"It was one of those days when everything was in the groove," Moody says. "The first four holes I didn't make a putt, but then I got started. I drove the ball so well and hit my irons almost perfect. But I really wasn't thinking about a good score until I birdied 14.

"Under the conditions, this is probably the best round I've played," Moody said at the time. "Oh, I've had a couple of 62s down in Texas, but those courses are nothing like this."

When pressed, Moody, in his best "aw, shucks" delivery, added, "Well, I did shoot 57 once in a gambling match in 1979 at a little old club in Texas—Bowie Country Club, down near the Alamo. It was only about 6,200 or 6,300 yards, and I made three eagles. But hey, you gotta hit some good shots to score 57 on a par-72 course. I don't care how short it is. After I did it, some guys down there said

ANOTHER U.S. OPEN: *Moody doesn't let his ample girth interfere as he shoots a U.S. Senior Open record 64 on his way to victory in 1989 at Laurel Valley Golf Club in Ligonier, Pennsylvania.*

I couldn't do it again, so I went out and played nine more holes and shot 30."

But this wasn't a little town in Texas, playing with guys wearing jeans and chewing Red Man. This was the U.S. by-God Senior Open, and now Moody had a chance to do what only three other players (Palmer, Player and Billy Casper) had ever done—win both the U.S. Open and the U.S. Senior Open. (Nicklaus matched them by winning the 1991 U.S. Senior Open.)

On a bright, clear Sunday, Moody and Beard, winner of 11 titles on the PGA Tour and its leading money winner in 1969, battled head-to-head. Moody cracked first, bogeying the first hole, but he came back with an eagle at the 509-yard sixth, sinking a 30-footer.

"It's tough to beat a competitor like Frank," Moody says. "It could have gone either way. At the start, Frank had a couple of birdie putts. If he had made them, it might have been different. I was just hanging in there, and then all of a sudden I make a 30-footer for eagle and the blood started flowing."

Moody birdied the 8th and 11th holes, and by that time Beard, in his first pressure situation in years, had faded. After a three-putt from 40 feet at No. 14, Moody parred in for a 70 and a two-shot victory.

"The long putter and Michelle reading the putts made the difference," Moody says. "I've always been able to play from tee to green, but I had this terrible jerk with the other putters. The long putter allows me to stroke the ball a lot smoother, and now I've developed a lot of confidence, which is so important."

In his down-home, country-spun drawl, Sarge unwittingly summed up his career in what would be his last victory until the 1991 PaineWebber Invitational. "Winning the Senior Open is a tremendous honor, but I have to admit, winning the U.S. Open in 1969 meant more to me," Moody said, remembering all the tough times in between. "That meant a lot more money to me over a long, lean period of 15 years. I could never have made it without that."

AL GEIBERGER

If Al Geiberger had known just how much of a financial lifeboat that round of golf would be, he might never have finished his miraculous 59 one hot steamy Friday in June of 1977.

"That day the pressure built and built," he recalls, as if it was yesterday. "Everybody on the course was flocking to our group. You could hear the buzzing, feel the excitement.

"I thought, 'Holy criminy, what have I gotten myself into?' But walking to the 15th tee, I said to myself, 'I'm hitting it so well and putting so well, why not pull out all the stops?' If you see me going for the pins, you know I'm really playing well. I really started thinking birdie."

Geiberger started on the 10th tee that second round of the Danny Thomas Memphis Classic, at the 7,249-yard Colonial Country Club in Cordova, Tennessee, just outside of Memphis. He was playing the front nine as he came down the stretch.

At the 388-yard sixth hole, he feathered a three-wood off the tee, then hit a crisp pitching wedge 13 feet past the hole and sank the putt for birdie. That put him 11-under-par with three holes to play.

"I really didn't know that 59 would be the record," he says, his eyes sparkling as he warms to recalling his favorite story for perhaps the 10,000th time. Then he laughs. "Stupidity comes in handy at moments of crisis."

A birdie hole was next—a 564-yard par-5 that Geiberger could come close to reaching with two good wood shots. He made them, then hit a pitching wedge that sucked up 9 feet from the cup. Once again, displaying nerves of steel—or, as he says, no nerves at all— he rolled in the birdie attempt. Now he was 12-under-par; he could par in for 60. He knew few players had ever achieved that magical number, not Nicklaus, not Hogan, not Palmer, not any of the legends of the game save ol' Sam Snead, in the second round of the 1957 Dallas Open at Glen Lakes Country Club in Dallas—and that was 20 years ago.

The pressing thought on the tee at the difficult 439-yard eighth hole was not how he was going to make a birdie, but how he was going to be able to salvage a par. He did it with a booming drive, a five-iron to 20 feet and two putts. Pretty routine, although his mouth was full of cotton, his stomach was churning and his knees were knocking. Geiberger had been a professional golfer for 18 years and had won nine PGA Tour events, including the 1966 PGA Championship, the 1975 Tournament of Champions and the 1975 Tournament Players Championship. But he never had felt pressure like this.

"There are always tournaments to win or lose," he says. "If you lose, it's like missing a putt: you always think you'll get another chance. But to shoot 60, or even 59? You realize that chance may never come along again; you'll probably never get the opportunity. It's a once-in-a-lifetime."

WORN OUT: *Al Geiberger looks as though he couldn't walk another step after receiving a plaque for winning the 1975 Tournament Players Championship with a record-breaking 10-under-par 270 at Colonial Country Club in Fort Worth. His seven-year-old son Brent doesn't appear very happy, either.*

The trees seemed to be closing in at the narrow 403-yard ninth hole as Geiberger stood nervously on the tee. He had to put his drive in the fairway, and he did with a perfectly grooved high left-to-right fade that landed gently and rolled within nine-iron distance of the flag. There it was, the chance of a lifetime. A simple nine-iron. "Knock it close, you dummy," he told himself. He did, of course, no more than 8 feet left of the hole. It wasn't more than a 110-yard walk to the green, but Geiberger doesn't remember any of it. He was in a daze. When it was his turn to putt, he says he doesn't even remember stroking the ball. Those who saw it said it was in from the moment it left the blade. Plunk! Birdie! 59!

"I was still in a daze," Geiberger says of his incredible round of 11 birdies, an eagle and only 23 putts. "I guess my first thought was that I was leading the tournament. Then when I realized what I had done, shooting 59, I said, 'Well, you can't shoot 59 and then not win the tournament.' So the pressure didn't stop. It lasted two more days."

Geiberger went on to win with rounds of 72 and 70, beating Gary Player and Jerry McGee by three shots, but for once, winning wasn't paramount. You could ask 100 golf buffs who won the 1977 Memphis Classic and 95 of them probably wouldn't know. But ask them what the lowest score was in PGA Tour history and any fan worth his matching head covers will answer 59 by Al Geiberger. It's Roger Bannister's four-minute mile, Wilt Chamberlain's 100-point game, Don Larsen's perfect game in the World Series. *Sports Illustrated* called it "one of the most significant athletic achievements of the century."

"I'm surprised no one else has done it," Geiberger said last year.

PGA CHAMPION: *A happy Geiberger tosses his hat to the crowd after sinking the last putt to win the 1966 PGA Championship at Firestone Country Club in Akron, Ohio.*

"Initially, I made the comment that if I could shoot 59, anybody could because there are so many really good players out here."

In the last 15 years, it has grown into a seemingly insurmountable barrier, a mental block, if you will, something that every player dreams about, but none—not one of the strong young players, with all the modern technology and immaculately groomed courses—have been able to achieve, until Chip Beck did in the 3rd round of the Las Vegas Invitational, October 11, 1991. Oh sure, there are a bucketful of 62s nowadays. Sand saves are almost as common as birdies, and eagles fly every day. But until David Frost did it in the second round of the 1990 Northern Telecom Tucson Open, there hadn't even been a 60 shot since Sam Snead did it 33 years before.

"There is a huge mental barrier the player has to jump over to get there," says Paul Azinger, a seven-time winner from 1987 through 1991. "It's all mental, and the pressure is unbelievable."

Dan Pohl felt it during the second round of the 1989 Honda Classic. He was 10-under-par at the wind-whipped, par-72 TPC at Eagle Trace course with five holes remaining, including a par-5. He parred in for 62 and shot 75 the next day. "Sure, you start thinking about it; you can't help it," he says. "Once you get to 10-under, you know it is within your grasp, but the pressure is unbelievable. Everybody has pressure when you're in contention to win a tournament, but how many times do you get a chance to shoot 59?"

Two all-time greats, Jack Nicklaus and Tom Watson, never have really come close, never have shot 61 in a lifetime of competition under all sorts of conditions. When asked last year about the possibility of somebody tying Geiberger's record, Nicklaus shrugged. "Why not? It would depend on the course and the conditions, but I'll tell you this: Geiberger shot a legitimate 59. That's a long and difficult course in Memphis." (In fact, three-time U.S. Open champion Hale Irwin was there and shot 73 that day.)

"Shoot 59?" Watson says with a quizzical look. "You have to

make 13 birdies, or a couple of eagles to go with the birdies. That's about 70 percent of the holes you play. Even in a best-ball event at your country club, the average score is about nine-under-par. So think what you'd have to do to shoot 59 on your own ball. It's pretty much beyond the realm of possibility, but it probably will happen some day."

Many say that muscular Mark Calcavecchia, the 1989 British Open champion, is a strong candidate to break 60. While he doesn't say he'll be the one, he does believe it will happen soon.

"I think we'll see a lot more 61s and 62s, maybe even a few 60s," he says. "In the 10 years I've been out here, the quality of play has become so good. If you go out and shoot 70 or 71, you'll get blown out. The guys start off with a different attitude now. They say, 'Hey, I need to shoot 65 to get into the tournament or a 67 to keep from losing ground.' You need to set a goal.

"Yeah, it's going to happen. It will be shot on a day when there isn't a breath of wind and where the fairways are perfect and the greens are perfect and you can reach the par-5s in two. Then, if you get your driver, wedges and putter going, you can go crazy."

That's just the way it was that warm, humid morning in Las Vegas when Beck started on the back nine, as Geiberger had done. After a birdie-par start, Beck reeled off six successive birdies to make the turn in 29. That's when he started thinking about 59. On the back nine, Beck felt he needed to make a 25-foot eagle putt at the par-5 seventh hole. He missed, but sank an 8-footer for birdie at the 191-yard, par-3 eighth and knocked an eight-iron within three feet for birdie at the 408-yard ninth.

"I was shaking," Beck said about his record-tying putt. "The longer I looked at it, the longer it looked."

Some players were quick to point out Beck's 59 came on a 6,914-yard resort course, used as a fill-in for one year. Many said the course and conditions couldn't compare with the rain-soaked 7,249-yard course at Memphis where Geiberger set the record. But the fact is, Beck made 13 birdies, including the last three holes when the pressure peaked.

"I'm a little disappointed," Geiberger says. "I guess I was lucky to hold on to it this long. I've been dodging arrows for years. With all the quality players coming out, the odds were narrowing down. A record is something you can't do anything about. You can't change it, it's just there."

Regardless of Beck's performance, it won't tarnish Geiberger's feat, done back in the days before souped-up balls, graphite shafts and modern agronomy. They break four-minute miles in college now, but Bannister's name lives on because he was the first. Geiberger's round still stands like a magnificent monument in golf history, and—fittingly for one of the game's really nice guys—it served him well as the financial lifeboat that would keep him afloat during his floundering, frustrating forties.

It seemed that no sooner had Geiberger scaled the highest mountain, reached the zenith of his career that day in Memphis, than things started to crumble. Later that year, his father, Ray, died in the crash of two airliners on a runway in the Canary Islands.

The following year, in January, a benign growth was removed along with a section of his colon. He had been bothered by an inflamed colon since 1966. "Ulcerative proctitis is the name," Geiberger explains. "And when it flares up, it is very painful, but you have to live with it."

Living with that and a floundering marriage, which finally crumbled in 1969, Geiberger was winless from another great height—his victory in the 1966 PGA Championship at Firestone in Akron, Ohio—until the 1974 Sahara Invitational in Las Vegas.

After his surgery in 1978, Geiberger returned to the Tour in time for the Greater Greensboro Open in April, but he was ineffective the rest of the year. He never had a top-10 finish and plunged from 30th to 107th on the money list with just $20,477.

FRUSTRATING TIMES: *After winning the 1966 PGA Championship, Geiberger went through a divorce, illness and an eight-year slump before winning again.*

Once more, he bounced back the following year, when he won the Colonial National Invitation at famed Colonial Country Club in Fort Worth. He bolted to the lead with a third-round six-under-par 64, then slipped to a 73 on Sunday, barely holding off Don January and Gene Littler by a stroke. First prize was worth $54,000—the largest check he'd ever won. But it was to be his last victory for eight long, lean years.

That September he had knee surgery for the removal of loose cartilage. The following summer, while he was playing in the Jerry Ford Invitational in Vail, Colorado, his abdominal pain became so acute that he was rushed to a hospital for emergency surgery. A mass of polyps the size of a golf ball was found to be blocking his colon. When he got back home to Santa Barbara, his doctors told him he was tempting cancer. They performed a procedure called ileostomy. It took three operations to remove his entire colon and fit him with an external pouch to eliminate body waste.

"Actually, at the time I was counting my blessings because fortunately it was benign," he says. "Had it been malignant, I would have been gone. I had surgery for the same thing in 1978, but in one and a half years the polyps had grown back and blocked the colon. There was a huge mass there, and once the doctors saw that, they said we had to get it out of there. It was gradually bleeding my system."

Geiberger says he has no reservations about wearing the "appliance," as he calls it, because "I am just happy to be above ground and not below it. That's why three-footers just aren't all that important

HAPPY TIMES AGAIN: *Geiberger waves to the crowd after firing an opening-round 65 in the 1977 Colonial National Invitation at Colonial Country Club. He wound up finishing fourth, but a month later he would achieve golfing immortality by shooting a record 59 at the Danny Thomas Memphis Classic.*

STRUGGLING AFTER SURGERY: *Although he managed to keep his spirits up, Geiberger's game was sagging in the early 1980s after his ileostomy.*

anymore. But at the time, I didn't think I could play golf wearing the appliance. Little did I realize that it's almost easier than what Mother Nature gave you, it's so advanced."

Once at a cocktail party, Geiberger was talking to Otto Graham, the Hall of Fame quarterback and coach who also battled cancer and wears an appliance. Graham told him, "You know, Al, we're the only two guys at this party who can relieve ourselves and have a cocktail at the same time."

A strange quirk of fate gave Geiberger a tremendous boost in his mental approach to his appliance. It was a coincidence that may have reshaped his life—certainly a chance meeting that he'll never forget.

A nurse came into his hospital room, and by chance they started talking about her favorite football team, the San Diego Chargers. The Chargers field goal kicker, Rolf Benirschke, had undergone the same surgery, she told Geiberger, and he wore the same appliance.

"It was like a tremendous weight had been lifted off my shoulders," Geiberger says. "I kept asking her for more details. She knew all about it, of course, and was very interested. I figured right there that if he could play football with it, I could certainly play golf."

Mental rehabilitation started immediately, and he was given a final lift when he talked to Tony Sills, a veteran Tour player who also had had an ileostomy, about a new appliance made by ConvaTec. Later Geiberger and Benirschke became co-chairmen of the National Foundation for Ileitis and Colitis Sports Council. Geiberger still wears a logo and does corporate outings for the organization. "At first," he says, "I really didn't want to talk about it, but then I realized it was no big deal and that I probably could help a lot of people. A lot of people have told me that it has helped them to know that I had the operation and it didn't end my career."

His career wasn't over, but it certainly was floundering. Although his spirits were high and his desire was strong, Geiberger's game never returned to what it had been. From 1980 through 1986, he won a total of $87,473—an average of $12,496 a year.

"I had been losing confidence even before the surgery," he explains. "I had been getting sicker and wasn't playing that well, so even after the operation, I had a lot of doubts that I would ever be a winner again."

On top of everything else, his second marriage was on the rocks and he had four children to support. The divorce was an expensive one—she kept the house in Santa Barbara, and Al moved to borrowed quarters in the San Fernando Valley. This was the lowest point of his career, the dreadful forties. Geiberger calls it his incubation period.

His only financial salvation was the lifeboat he built that muggy June day in Memphis, for he would always be "Mr. 59." It was written on the bottom of his golf bag and under every autograph he signed.

"I had some lean years," he says. "You don't go through two divorces without losing a lot. First you split your income in half, then half of half. I wasn't starving, but for a while I was playing every outing in sight. I'd say yes, then ask, 'How much?' You know the commercial where they say, 'Mikey will eat it'? Well, the agents knew if there was an outing, Al would do it. Fortunately, the 59 thing kept me in the public eye during the quiet years.

"Guys love to ask me about it and I love to talk about it. I play in pro-ams, and all the players are getting strokes, and still the best we shoot as a team is 58. So I guess when you're out there all by yourself, shooting 59 is pretty good. At outings, guys can relate. They might choke to death trying to break 90, but it's all the same, all about pressure."

Most of Geiberger's corporate outings were for around $3,000, but he admits he took some for less. He even worked on a cruise ship, giving lessons to the passengers by hitting balls into a net. During this dismal time, Geiberger found happiness, again, in an unusual way.

He had met Carolyn Spring when he was a young pro and she was the daughter of a member at the local club. She had gone off and married another touring pro, Buddy Allin, but now, in Geiber-

THE DREADFUL FORTIES: *From 1980 until he joined the Senior Tour in September of 1987, Geiberger earned $87,473, an average of $12,496 a year.*

ger's time of need, she was back, living with her mother. She was divorced, had no children and wasn't sure she could have any. When Al's divorce was final in July 1985, they were married. They borrowed money from LPGA star Patty Sheehan to buy a house in Palm Desert, California.

"Santa Barbara was so expensive, and there were ex-wives and ex-husbands all over the place," Geiberger says. "Besides, there were so many golf courses in the Palm Springs area." At age 48, Geiberger was starting over, dreaming once more of making it on Tour, this time the burgeoning Senior Tour. And like many starting on the regular tour, he also was thinking of something else—fatherhood, once more. Carolyn was pregnant.

The birth of Matthew in June was the highlight of 1986, the long last year before Geiberger reached 50 and became eligible for the Senior Tour. He played a few tournaments, but unlike George Archer and J. C. Snead, who never missed a beat from the PGA Tour to the Senior Tour, Geiberger planned to come in "rested and eager, rather than sharp and burned out. I wanted to feel enthusiastic about golf again and I did."

Not until Lee Trevino's opening charge to start the nineties did anyone start his Senior Tour career with the rush Geiberger put on in the closing months of 1987. He was like a starving bear in the woods, gobbling up everything in sight. He had been waiting for a long time, but he even surprised himself with his coolness under pressure and his ability to respond with the crucial shots at the critical times. And by golly, even the putts were falling. It was another comeback, at the best of times.

Geiberger became eligible September 1 and didn't waste a day, entering the Bank One Classic in Lexington, Kentucky, and shooting a 69 in his very first round. It was as though he had never been away. He added a pair of 68s in the next two rounds, and although his five-under-par 205 was eight shots behind winner Bruce Crampton, the tie for seventh and check for $6,900 gave him the feeling of belonging and, more importantly, the confidence that he could compete after such a long drought. In his next two tournaments, he was under par in five of the six rounds and comfortable in his new surroundings. He was back with his old friends, he was playing well and he was making money. He was happy again. But nothing prepared him for what would happen at the richest stop, the $1 million Vantage Championship at Tanglewood Park, just outside Winston-Salem, North Carolina.

This was the big one, the tournament the top players had been pointing toward. First prize was $135,000—the biggest check any of them had ever played for in their lives—and a victory could make the year. The big guns were off and firing. Orville Moody opened with a 66, Dave Hill had 67, Don January shot 68 and Billy Casper was among those at 69. Geiberger straggled in with a two-over-par 72 over the hilly 6,606-yard layout.

The next day turned cold, which didn't help a lot of those creaking, aging muscles. Turtleneck sweaters were the order of the day. Neither Moody nor Dave Hill, playing in the last group, could handle it, staggering in with 74 and 76, respectively. But Gene Littler, who opened with a 70, tacked on a brilliant 67 to take a one-shot lead over 55-year-old Gay Brewer (67-71). Geiberger moved quietly into contention with a 67 of his own.

"When I first got out here, I thought to myself, 'I can't keep up with these guys,'" Geiberger said. "I'm too rusty. I haven't been under the gun in so long, haven't had a chance to win, I don't know how I'll react."

That cool autumn Sunday, with the leaves showing off their finest colors, a huge crowd was caught up in the electricity of Geiberger's putting for the first time in almost a decade. He birdied the first two holes but bogeyed the difficult 430-yard 3rd. Then his putter got hot. He sank a 12-footer at No. 7, rolled in a twisting 20-footer on the next hole, then capped his birdie barrage with a stunning 25-footer in front of the big crowd that surrounded the treacherous,

slanting 9th green. Later he would say, "Those holes set up the championship for me." He also said (and only a genuinely nice guy like Al would even think of this) he felt compelled to apologize to Littler going to the 10th tee. "I had to say something to Gene about what happened on the 9th green," Geiberger said. "The putt had a 5-foot break and I was lagging it up and it went in."

Once he got the lead, Geiberger magically shed the rust of eight years and finished off a brilliant three-under-par 67 to hold off charging Dave Hill, who closed with a 65, by two shots. Littler shot 72 and finished third, a stroke in front of Moody, and still collected his biggest check, $67,300.

"The Senior Tour may have snuck up on some players who didn't prepare for it," Geiberger said at the time. "I've been thinking seriously about it for two years, but I still can't believe it happened."

Later, after the awards ceremony, when the numbing sensation began to wear off, Geiberger was back in the interview area for an encore. He talked and talked, as though he had been away for eight years and had a lot of stories he had been saving.

The next day he was still talking. "I woke up in the middle of the night and just couldn't sleep," he said. "I still can't believe I won $135,000. Instead of counting sheep, I kept trying to figure out how many times $3,800 went into $135,000. That's what I got when I won my first tournament [the 1962 Ontario Open]."

"I was very down the last few years I was playing on the other tour. I was missing the cut a lot and not making any money. You can only get hammered so much. Once you lose that edge, you're in trouble. It's not easy to get it back."

PRIMED FOR VANTAGE: *When he became eligible for the Senior Tour in September of 1987, Geiberger was ready and won the fourth tournament he entered: the rich Vantage Championship in Clemmons, North Carolina, with a first prize of $135,000.*

Once Geiberger got it back at the Vantage, he didn't let go. After an obvious letdown the following week at the Pepsi Challenge, he came back to win the Hilton Head International on the picturesque Harbour Town Golf Links. He took the lead with a second-round 68; then, after making 18 consecutive pars for a closing 71, he beat Jim Ferree in a playoff with a birdie on the second hole to collect $37,500. In just six events on the Senior Tour, Geiberger had earned more money ($197,671) than he had won in his best year on the PGA Tour ($194,821 in 1976).

"[Hilton Head] was another test," he says. "At Vantage, I was never in the lead until the last nine holes. At Hilton Head, I got into the lead after two rounds and had a lot of pressure all day Sunday trying to protect it."

Now on one of the hottest rolls of his life, Geiberger headed for Las Vegas to see how long his luck would run. He started with a solid 68 at Desert Inn, one shot off the pace set by Bob Charles. The next day, Geiberger stumbled to a 73—17 pars and a bogey. "I really felt tired. I just couldn't get anything going," he says. "Being in contention every week was brand-new to me, and it wore me out mentally."

Nobody was more surprised than Geiberger over what happened the next day. He started with five birdies in a row. Was he on the way to another 59, to being the first player on both tours to crack 60? Desert Inn was much easier than the course in Memphis, and he was off to a much better start.

"I started so fast and, looking back, I probably did have more of a chance that day than when I shot 59," Geiberger says. "But the way I started off is not the way to shoot a great round, because then you start choking to death. It really made me appreciate what I did when I shot 59. After making five birdies in a row, I realized I still had to make eight more."

He didn't, falling three short with a still-magnificent 62 that gave him a four-shot victory over Chi Chi Rodriguez, who said afterward,

T I P

"In 1975, I was in a stretch where I was playing very badly. I had a friend of mine, an assistant pro, look at my swing, and he noticed I wasn't 'rotating' when I went through the ball. He said my hands and forearms were breaking down at impact instead of moving together in a counterclockwise fashion through the shot. The rotation places your body more behind the ball and lets your arms rotate through, keeping the club going down the target line longer. I took his advice and went to play at the Tournament Players Championship, which was being played that year at Colonial Country Club in Fort Worth, Texas. As the week went on, I hit the ball better and better, so by the start of the tournament, I felt as though I could hardly miss. I shot 63 in the pro-am, then had four tournament rounds in the sixties and won by three or four strokes. My score of 270 stood as a record at the Colonial for a number of years. In my 30 years of professional golf, there's probably been only three times when I felt as though I hit the ball great and had total control of it. That was one of those times, and it was a very special week for me."

Al Geiberger

"The way Al was hitting the ball, he could have easily shot 59 if he had made a few more putts." The victory boosted Geiberger to 10th on the money list with $235,171.

A two-week break in the schedule didn't cool him off. He came back to finish 2nd behind Dave Hill at the Fairfield Barnett Classic in Melbourne, Florida, then tied for 12th and 7th in the last two tournaments to wind up his whirlwind, three-month blitz 9th on the money list with $264,798.

"I thought I would do OK, but I certainly didn't expect that," he said at the time. "My friends all said they knew what I was going to do when I got out here, but they're not the ones who have to do it. My goals for '87 were to get acclimated, pick up some nice checks. I was hoping to make $50,000 to $60,000. Winning was a secondary goal, but once I won Vantage, got that off my back, my goals moved up.

"I still can't believe my checking account. A year ago, I was juggling, borrowing, calling to say the check was in the mail. Now I send them checks and they must think the comma is in the wrong place. Heck, I had bonuses for winning from Spalding and clothes companies I forgot I had, it's been so long since I've won."

Yes, Geiberger was back on top of the world that fall of 1987, but there was to be one more pitfall, one more downer, the worst one of all.

He started the year full of optimism and played well, winning The Pointe/Del Webb Arizona Classic after starting with a tournament-record nine-under-par 63 and then holding off Orville Moody's closing 65 to survive by a shot. He also had three second-place finishes and was brimming with confidence when he arrived at the Bank One Classic, site of his Senior debut a year ago.

After his opening round and dinner with his 20-year-old son John, who was caddying for him that week, Geiberger went browsing in the mall, just killing time before he returned to his hotel room, where the red message light had been flashing.

The call was one he'll never forget. Come home, quickly. Matthew has drowned.

That stifling 100-degree afternoon in Palm Desert, while his mother was in the bathroom, young Matthew, 2, had walked past his stepbrother Bryan, 11, who was watching television in the living room. Matthew went out the front door (which the usually reliable maid had left unlatched), across the street, around the corner, past a dozen houses, over a wooden footbridge and into an unguarded swimming pool.

His mother found him minutes later and raced home with him to call for help. It was too late. The emergency crew established a heartbeat, which they managed to maintain until Al got home. But the boy's tiny lungs had taken too much water. He was brain dead. The support system was removed and Matthew's life was over.

Geiberger didn't touch a club for five weeks. Carolyn never returned to the house. They moved into a condominium in Al's native Santa Barbara while they waited for their new house—already under construction in Solvang, 35 miles northwest—to be completed. After the tragedy, they considered canceling the project, but there were too many memories in Palm Desert: it was time to get away. It was an extremely difficult time for Carolyn, who underwent a lot of therapy, but finally Geiberger knew he had to get back to work. The Vantage Championship was coming up, with its $1 million purse, and he was defending champion. So he went to Atlanta the week before, to try to play in the more tranquil atmosphere of the Pepsi Challenge. He shot 76 the first round and finished tied for 34th.

The next day he was prepared, almost eager, to talk about his tragedy with the press. He waited on a rainy Monday afternoon until almost 5:30 P.M. for this reporter, who had asked for an interview.

"It's so strange," he said softly. "Here I am coming back to such a high point in my life at such a sad time. I've been mourning for a long time; now I think it's better that I talk about it."

He painfully recounted every detail and went through all the strange circumstances surrounding the tragedy. What if he hadn't shown Matthew the pool a week earlier? What if Carolyn hadn't taken a little longer to get ready? What if Bryan had seen his younger brother walking out the door, or one of the neighbors had noticed the youngster walking down the street alone?

"I've been thinking about all those things, but you finally realize there's nothing you can do, you have to go on with your life. It's been tougher on Carolyn. It was her first child. She never had a babysitter—she rarely left his side. The burden was almost too much; she keeps blaming herself. But life goes on. You have to keep going."

Geiberger, graciously accepting condolences all week from the many friends at the Vantage he had made the year before, kept playing that difficult week.

"There's too much attention on a defending champion," he said. "Last week in Atlanta, I had a chance to talk to the players quietly. I also talked to a lot of the wives. When you experience a tragedy like this, it's important to have good friends. Recovery is such a slow process; you have so many ups and downs. I think I'm ready to play now, and I want very much to win again. But if I do, can I really be happy at such a sad time?"

Geiberger didn't win, but he came close. With 69s on Saturday and Sunday, he tied for second behind Walt Zembriski. "It was difficult," he says. "Golf is a slow game. There is a lot of time to think out there, and my thoughts kept drifting back to Matthew, not on the job at hand. To make myself concentrate, I had to talk myself through each shot, describe each putt. If I was busy talking, I didn't have time for my mind to wander." Although his wife stayed home with friends, Geiberger played the final five events of the year, earning another runner-up check at the Gus Machado Classic at Key Biscayne, Florida, and finishing the year ninth on the money list at $346,735.

The following year, he made $527,033 and set a then–Senior Tour record by earning $1 million in the shortest time—two years, one month. The house was completed; Al Jr. had come along to help fill the void. Once more, everything seemed right.

But in 1990, Geiberger suffered a curious letdown. He cut back on his schedule and it seemed to affect his play. He rarely was in contention on Sundays until his favorite tournament, the Vantage, rolled around. Once he arrived at Tanglewood, he appeared to be revitalized.

After an opening-round 69, he put on a magical putting display Saturday. He one-putted 11 times—including the last five holes—while setting a tournament record and tying the eight-under-par 64 course record that Gary Player set in the 1974 PGA Championship.

"I have so many good thoughts about this place," he said after making nine birdies and a bogey. "It brings back a lot of fond memories and creates a lot of motivation, something I think I've been lacking this year."

When the final round started, Geiberger trailed Charlie Coody by a shot, but he bogeyed two of the first four holes and never mounted a charge. He still had a chance when Coody started to falter down the stretch, but he missed a seven-foot birdie putt at No. 15 and bogeyed the par-5 17th with a bad bunker shot. With a scrambling par at 18 after a bad drive and a bunkered second shot, he tied Bob Charles for second and collected $126,000—the second largest check of his career.

"This will repair a lot of wounds this year," he said. "I just haven't played well. I've tried to figure out why, and after talking to a psychologist, I think I know why. When I lost my son Matthew two years ago, my wife was devastated. She blamed herself and needed a lot of counseling. Because she was having such a tough time, I had to take a strong lead. I pushed, pushed, pushed for a year. Now she's a lot stronger and I think I let down. I stayed strong for a year, played a lot and did well, but this year I seem to have lost my interest and desire. I just didn't have the drive and enthusiasm I usually do.

"I guess eventually the wounds heal a little. You don't ever forget, but you learn to keep plugging along. Let's face it, there's not a hell of a lot else you can do."

CHI CHI
RODRIGUEZ

When the hard times of his forties hit Juan (Chi Chi) Rodriguez, he didn't have a U.S. Open championship like Orville Moody or a 59 like Al Geiberger to fall back on. His biggest asset was his personality—fortunately that was all he needed.

Never a consistent winner on the PGA Tour, Rodriguez had been struggling financially all his life. It started with his indigent youth in impoverished Bayamon, near San Juan, Puerto Rico, where he grew up as one of five children. The family's usual dinner consisted of a shared bowl of beans mixed with corn, and farina, bananas, an occasional pork chop, and black coffee.

"My father worked 28 years in the fields as a laborer, cutting sugarcane with a machete. He never made more than $18 a week and never missed a day," Rodriguez says. "And he was the happiest man I'd ever seen. I had two brothers and two sisters and he would never eat at night until us kids were full. We didn't have a table— we would eat out of our hands—but we were always happy."

With a diet like that, it wasn't surprising that Rodriguez was ravaged by rickets and tropical spruce, which left his bones thin and sensitive to pressure. Doctors thought he would die when he was six, but he surprised them and has been surprising people ever since.

"You can see my hands are a little crooked from rickets," he said one day, holding them out for inspection. "But if you look closely, when I close them, it's a blessing from God because they form a perfect golf grip."

Chi Chi Rodriguez always looks to the bright side. So he was properly prepared when the lean years followed his last PGA Tour victory, the 1979 Tallahassee Open. After all, he had already been tiptoeing on a financial tightrope for six years, balancing an occasional solid performance with his never-ending wit, since winning the Greater Greensboro Open in 1973. Only twice in that span had he made more than $50,000 in official earnings. He needed another talent to market—something to make him different—so he could maintain his lifestyle as a touring pro.

He has no idea where he got it—he's not quite sure how he keeps it—but Chi Chi has a quick-witted sense of humor that television producers would kill for. A loner and devoted family man, he doesn't stay out at night swapping jokes at the bar, and he's really not much of a locker room wag, but when he gets in front of the public, it's as though the little red light has gone on. George Burns used to say that when he went down for a midnight snack and the refrigerator light went on, he'd do five minutes. That's Chi Chi, although he always comes off warm and sincere.

"My name used to be O'Connor, but I changed it for business reasons."

Eddie Elias, who has managed Rodriguez's business affairs for many years, says the biggest drawback during Chi Chi's tough times was that "his heart was too big for his body." During the down times, he was still giving away more than he was making.

"Instinctively, Chi Chi saw he could no longer compete on the regular tour. We were going to open a public relations firm, give exhibitions, get into course design, give speeches. He could have done very well, but he wanted to be out with the people. The thing he enjoyed the most was giving clinics, doing outings, talking and laughing with people. Then when it was over, he'd sign autographs for hours. He made a living doing corporate outings. He has that special flair, the personality, the sense of humor that makes people like him. And he's one of the kindest men in the world.

"One time he did an exhibition for a real estate firm that was hurting. He didn't charge them a nickel. A year later, they gave him $10,000 and a piece of the action. Now he gets something from them every year.

"He was king of the clinics," Elias continues. "I could have booked him 600 days a year and he could have made a nice, comfortable, pressure-free living."

Rodriguez wasn't satisfied with that, of course. The competitive juices that were generated when he was a teenage baseball star in Puerto Rico never stopped flowing. He had a long taste of the competition on the PGA Tour, and he couldn't wait until he was eligible to play on the Senior Tour.

"When I was 45, I knew I couldn't win on the regular tour anymore," he says. "But at that time there was no Senior Tour, nothing to look forward to—not like today, when the players in their midforties keep playing, trying to stay sharp, stay competitive so they can cash in when they hit 50.

"I was very lucky when I met Eddie. When I was on my own, I lost everything I had. When I met Eddie, he said, 'Give me your money and stop worrying. I'll make all the decisions.' He did and now I have CDs, stocks, real estate."

One year, Rodriguez did 106 outings at $3,000 each for a cool $318,000. In 1982, his PGA Tour's winnings were a paltry $7,119, and the next year wasn't much better ($8,190). If it wasn't for his gift of gab, and an amazing array of trick shots he has mastered that delight fans from coast to coast, Rodriguez might never have been able to keep his game sharp enough to become one of the top money winners on the Senior Tour.

"My caddie had the easiest job in the world. He only had to work three days a week. When I made the cut, he used to tell me he already had plans for the weekend."

If Chi Chi would have been as frugal as Charlie Coody, who Lee Trevino said has the shortest arms and deepest pockets on the Senior Tour, he wouldn't have gone through the tough times. But that never has been his nature. His outlandish generosity and sensitivity to suffering began when he first joined the PGA Tour in 1960.

"My first tournament, I won $495 for finishing 16th in Buick Open," he recalled while sitting in the lobby lounge of the PGA Sheraton before the PGA Seniors Championship at Palm Beach Gardens, Florida. "My biggest check that year was $1,400 for finishing 4th, 67-67-76-67, all sixes and sevens.

"There were no Marriotts when I started, no nice hotels like this for us to stay in. We'd share four to a room and eat in diners. It was a tough way to make a living in those days."

Rodriguez made $2,137 his first year and $2,269 the next, but it didn't much matter, he says. "Whenever I got a check, I would just send as much as I could home to my mother. I didn't need it and she did."

One of the biggest shocks and most lasting impressions of his life came when Rodriguez went to visit his mother, Modesta, in New York City while he was stationed in Oklahoma during his army stint. She had divorced his father when Chi Chi was six, and after remarrying, she moved to New York.

"I couldn't believe my eyes when I found the house," he recalls. "I was naive. I thought she was doing fairly well to be living in New

York. In Puerto Rico, we saw all these people from the States and they all seemed to have money. But I found her in this tiny apartment. That night there was a rat in the living room, and I told her I would work as hard as I could to get her out of there. All the way back on the train to Oklahoma, I thought about getting a home for her in Puerto Rico. It was a dream I never forgot."

That dream was fulfilled when Rodriguez won his first tournament: the 1963 Denver Open, where first place was worth $5,300. He took the money and bought a modest home for his mother in Puerto Rico, and she lived there until she died in 1987 at age 73.

"It was malpractice," Chi Chi said. "She had a kidney problem and they didn't treat it properly, but I couldn't sue. I would never sue a hospital or a doctor. Doctors make their living taking care of people, and hospitals do a lot of good for a lot of people. I would never cause them any trouble."

When Rodriguez won the Texas Open in 1967, he wanted to donate $5,000 of his $20,000 purse to the victims of tornadoes that had ripped through Illinois a week earlier. A few months later, Elias asked where the money had gone, and the local people said there wasn't an organization to take care of it, but the money was still there. Rodriguez told them to form a group and keep the money.

At the 1987 Silver Pages Classic in Oklahoma City, Rodriguez set a Senior Tour record by making eight consecutive birdies during a second-round 65 en route to a three-shot victory. He then donated $10,000 of his $37,500 prize to the victims of a recent tornado in Saragosa, Texas.

Once, in Japan, Rodriguez won a tournament and wanted to give $14,000 to a local orphanage. The city didn't have one, but a year later he got a letter saying that one had been created and was handling six children.

"All I was doing was spending money. I was making $30,000 to

$40,000, but I was spending $100,000. Things got so bad the IRS sent me a get-well card."

Rodriguez, married to Iwalani, a native Hawaiian, for 26 years, has no children of his own (she has a daughter, Donnette, by a previous marriage, who lives in Hawaii). But he always has had a soft spot in his heart for kids. In 1979 he cofounded the Chi Chi Rodriguez Youth Foundation in Clearwater, Florida, a counseling and education service for abused, troubled and disadvantaged children. The foundation is run by Bill Hayes, a former golf pro who became a social worker. Every year about 600 kids go through the program, working at Glen Oaks municipal course; they're taught course maintenance and shop management, but mostly they learn how to accept responsibility, deal with other people and stay out of trouble.

"I'm very proud that so far we've had 28 of our kids graduate from college," Rodriguez said while relaxing in the locker room at Tanglewood before the final round of the 1990 $1.5 million Vantage Championship. "Winning a lot of golf tournaments does something for my ego, but seeing those kids grow up and be successful means more to my heart. Sometimes when I get there I'm so tired, I want to lie down, but then somebody will say, 'The kids are waiting,' and when I get to them it's like the Fountain of Youth. When they touch me, I feel like Clark Kent. I love those kids."

There is a judge in Florida who, instead of sentencing kids to reform schools or jail, sends them to Rodriguez's youth foundation. Chi Chi says that the rehabilitation rate has been 99 percent.

"All most of these kids need is a chance," he says. "We give them hope and encouragement, something most of them never had. Now, we have colleges who will accept them, give them a chance,

DETERMINED YOUNGSTER: A *lean, hungry and determined Chi Chi Rodriguez joined the PGA Tour in 1960, but he had to wait three years before his first victory.*

110

because of our past success. It was tough at the beginning, but because we've helped so many kids, now we've got judges and college administrators on our side."

As if all this isn't enough, Rodriguez has set up a hotline on which any troubled kid can call him any night. If he doesn't get calls, he's on the phone initiating them.

"It's worth more to me than winning a hundred golf tournaments," he says. "When I talk to these kids on the phone, some of them call me Daddy, some Uncle. And it's such a happy moment for me when I get there and they gather around me and massage my shoulders."

Iwalani, who always has traveled with Chi Chi, has learned she must share his time with the kids.

"The Clearwater kids are very important to him," she says. "They call him at all times and he'll talk, give them guidance and support, right in the middle of a tournament. That's pretty special."

No one questions Rodriguez's sincerity or generosity anymore. Doug Sanders probably put it best a few years ago when he said, "Chi Chi feels so lucky, is so proud of what he's done, that he has to give something back. The sword dance, the jokes, the hat, the bright clothes, the way he helps kids and everybody else, it just comes down to saying, 'Look at me. You didn't think I could make it. But I did. In spite of everything. Now let me share it with you.'"

Nobody on the Senior Tour had it tougher growing up. Rodriguez's parents were separated when he was six, and the five kids lived with their father. Whoever first said that "charity begins at home"

FIRST WIN: *Rodriguez gives it a full body twist as he watches his winning putt at the 1963 Denver Open drop on the 18th green at the Denver Country Club. This was his first professional victory.*

could have been thinking of Chi Chi's dad. That's certainly where Rodriguez learned to be so generous.

"I remember when I was seven," Chi Chi says, a smile creeping across his lips. "My father had a banana tree, and about three o'clock in the morning, some guy came into our yard to steal some of the bananas. My father saw him, woke me up and brought me outside. He grabbed the machete away from the man. Then he cut some bananas down, gave half of them to the guy and told him, 'Next time you want something, come to the front door and ask for it.' That was really a compassionate thing to do and it always stuck in my mind."

Rodriguez will sit in a locker room and spin stories for hours about his father's compassion. Obviously it made a vivid impression, and he has made a constant effort to follow the example. Late in life, his father inherited 16 acres of land but wouldn't accept it. He said he wouldn't take anything that he hadn't earned with his own sweat.

Iwalani recalls the time she and Chi Chi stopped in a grocery store late one night to pick up something for breakfast. "These two guys came in and were looking around," she says. "Chi Chi went up to them and said, 'Hey, you guys look like you could use $20. Go ahead, take it. I don't want you to rob me and get in trouble.' That's the way Chi Chi is. If he can help somebody stay out of trouble, he'll do whatever he can."

Iwalani was a dancer at the Hawaiian pavilion at the 1964 World's Fair in New York. After the fair was over, her agent told her she could make a lot of money dancing in Puerto Rico. At first, she said, she didn't want to go, but finally she agreed, and that's where she met Chi Chi. "I was headed back to Hawaii," she says. "I really had to be talked into it. I guess it was fate."

Chi Chi insists that his wife travel with him, and he's always been devoted to her. "There have been a lot of cloudy days, a lot of rainy days, and she's always been with me," he says. "Now that the sun is shining, I want her to enjoy every day. I've been married to

ON THE VERGE OF VICTORY: *Rodriguez lines up his final putt before winning the 1967 Texas Open at San Antonio.*

the same woman for 26 years. I believe for every successful man, there's a successful woman. Look at all the great golfers. They all stayed married to one woman: Nicklaus, Palmer, Player, Snead, Hogan, Watson, all of them. That should tell you something."

Rodriguez says he loves his wife and golf so much that there is precious little time for hobbies or social diversions.

"I've only been to about five bars in my whole life," he says. "The only time I ever got drunk I was 13. I was working at the Dorado Beach golf shop. It was late and I was mopping the floor in the clubhouse. I asked the bartender for a Coke, and I guess he thought it would be funny to see how I reacted to some crème de cacao. He mixed it in with the Coke. I didn't know what it was, but it sure tasted good. He asked me if I wanted another and I said sure. I guess by the time I finished my work, I must have had five or six. When I got home, I passed out under a grapefruit tree in the front yard, and the fire ants ate me up. I didn't even feel it. Finally about 4 A.M., the roosters started crowing and I woke up. I was all eaten up by the ants. I went to the bathroom and got sick all over the place, then I went to bed. A little while later, my father woke me up. He told me to go in the bathroom and see if I liked what I saw. 'If you don't,' he said, 'don't do it again.' I've never been drunk since."

He says his hardworking father, who died in 1963 at age 73, only drank once a year, on New Year's Eve, when he would give his sons a shot of rum to ring in the new year.

As a teenager, Rodriguez was a better baseball player than a golfer. His first taste of golf was as an eight-year-old forecaddie at the now defunct Berwind course. His first attempt at playing was using a club made from the branch of a guava tree to hit a ball shaped from a tin can.

"I was never a kid," he says. "I started working when I was eight

HELPFUL AID: *Rodriguez looks to encourage his shots in any way he can.*

years old, making one dollar for eight hours. Then I became a caddie and got thirty-five cents for 18 holes."

On the one day a week the caddies were allowed to play, he competed intensely against his colleagues. He had an old pair of size 13 shoes a member had given him, and he had to stuff paper in them because they were so big. He put stones or broken glass in his pocket and jingled it so everyone thought he had a lot of money. He told his friends that some day he would beat Sam Snead and Ben Hogan.

"They all laughed at me," Rodriguez recalls, his narrow eyes lighting up at the memory and the knowledge that he showed them, that he had made it big. "There had never been a touring pro from Puerto Rico. They told me I was a hound dreaming about pork chops."

Although he was only five foot seven and never weighed more than 120 pounds, Chi Chi was no easy mark in this tough neighborhood. He was a battler and had plenty of opportunities to sharpen his skills as a fighter. He doesn't remember all of his fights, but he recalls his last one.

"We were in a movie house one night, and the toughest kid in town kept throwing popcorn at me. I kept telling him to stop, but he just taunted me. He asked me if I wanted to go outside and see who was toughest, but I looked around and he had six friends with him. I didn't like the odds. I didn't even stay around for the end of the movie. About two weeks later, I was walking by this baseball game and that guy was pitching. I walked right out to the mound and knocked him down with one punch. He never knew what was coming. He got up and chased me all the way to my house. I finally got there, slammed the gate and ran up to my room. My father was home, and later he asked me what happened. When I told him, he said, 'If you don't want to fight, don't fight,' and I never had another one."

As a baseball player, nobody laughed when fireballing Juan Rodriguez took the mound. That's when he took the name Chi Chi, after a hustling third baseman, Chi Chi Fores, who wasn't the best player on the team but tried the hardest.

CELEBRATION: *Rodriguez, a showman from the time he first joined the PGA Tour, does a little dance after sinking a long birdie putt in the third round of the 1966 "500" Festival tournament in Indianapolis.*

"I was a damn good pitcher," Rodriguez says. "I could throw a sharp screwball, and my fastball was almost 90 miles per hour. My dad always said he wanted me to be a baseball player, so I played as much as I could, although I liked golf a lot better. I used to play with Roberto Clemente and Juan Pizarro. We played for the same teams. Actually, Clemente was our pinch runner in Class A ball. Our manager must have been a genius. Roberto Clemente pinch-running for Chi Chi Rodriguez.

"There were a lot of good baseball players in Puerto Rico in those days, but a lot of them were killed in Korea. They would lie about their age to get into the Army because it was a better life than they had in Puerto Rico. They were 15, 16, and went to Korea and never came back."

After dropping out of school in the 11th grade and working various golf jobs, Rodriguez saw a way out, an escape from the poverty he had grown to accept. At 19, he decided to follow his friends into the Army.

"I knew I had to be in special services, either baseball or golf," he says. "I went over to the baseball field there in Oklahoma, and there was a guy named Darryl Spencer batting. He must have been hitting the ball 400 feet. I thought, 'I could probably get that guy out, but if he ever hit me with a line drive, he'd kill me.' Besides, there must have been 30 guys trying out for pitcher, so I figured my chances were better in golf."

Given a chance to work on his game at better facilities than he had ever seen, Rodriguez fine-tuned his skills and won the post championship at Fort Sill, Oklahoma. His last stop in the Army was Fort Dix, New Jersey, where he was to be discharged.

"I was a PFC and knew I'd pull KP when I got there," Rodriguez says. "I had $45 to my name and wanted to fly home to Puerto Rico, so I went to the golf course, looking for a game. The post champion was there, and I said I'd play him. I said I'd stand on my head, and

HIS TRADEMARK: *Rodriguez shows off his familiar matador routine after sinking a birdie putt on the 18th hole at the 1971 Memphis Classic.*

whatever fell out of my pockets, I'd play for. I needed $55 for the plane fare. He was a sergeant and I was a PFC weighing 117 pounds. If I lost I would have had to stay on base and pull kitchen duty for who knows how long. It was getting late, so we decided on nine holes. I birdied the first five, collected my money and made the plane."

When he returned to Puerto Rico in 1957, Rodriguez got a job that he still says was the most gratifying he ever had. He went to work in a psychiatric ward for $80 a month. He said helping people who couldn't help themselves gave him more satisfaction than winning a golf tournament. But he was itching to get back to the game he had learned to love, so he went to the new Dorado Beach resort to look for a job. It was there he eventually met one of the men who helped change his life.

The late Ed Dudley was the head pro, and he offered to teach Rodriguez the business. But the first time they played, Chi Chi was so nervous he shot 89. Then Dudley said he was bringing in a young assistant from Florida. Rodriguez pleaded—said he'd shine shoes, pick up range balls, do anything for the job—so Dudley hired him as the caddie master.

Rodriguez made $300 a month, working seven days a week from 7 A.M. until the last golfer left. He ran the pro shop, picked up practice balls on the range, was the shoe shine boy, did anything that had to be done—and he never missed a day in two years. Dudley was eventually replaced by Pete Cooper, and Rodriguez's life would never be the same.

Cooper, whom Chi Chi calls the greatest player ever to come out

HEADED FOR VICTORY: *Rodriguez rips another arrow-straight drive down the middle of the 16th fairway during the final round of his one-shot victory over Gary Player at the 1986 Digital Seniors Classic in Concord, Massachusetts.*

123

of Florida, won eight Florida Opens, four Florida PGA championships and the 1976 PGA Seniors Championship. He became more
than a boss and a teacher—he became Rodriguez's surrogate father.

"He gave me my first steak," Rodriguez says. "They say red meat
is bad for you, but I probably eat it five, six times a week. I never
saw a lion or a tiger look sick.

"Pete also taught me the ethics of the game. I remember one
time we were playing and I spit on the green. He hollered at me, 'If
you spit in my office again, I'll fire you. Spit in the rough or on the
fairway, but the green is my office.' "

Cooper, now 77, also changed Rodriguez from a local hustler
in the caddie yard to a potential Tour player, changing his grip and
making him hit 50-yard wedge shots to a rock-hard green until his
hands bled.

"Chi Chi was the caddie master when I got to Dorado in 1959,"
Cooper recalls. "I brought him out and let him play and give lessons
every day. He was just a little ol' country boy who showed quite a
bit of personality. He had a pretty good swing and, after changing his
grip, he was on the right track. I probably made him hit 5,000 balls
with his wedge. Also, I watched him deal with people. He was very
friendly and easy to get along with, but he didn't back down to anyone,
either. I liked that. He had guts."

"That green was harder than Idi Amin's heart," Chi Chi says
with a laugh. "But it made me a better player. That's when I started
thinking about going on the Tour. But when I mentioned it to Pete,
he just laughed and said, 'You can't even beat me.' And I couldn't,
but I kept working. The next year he came back to Dorado and we
played 16 times. I beat him every time. That's when he told me,
'Pack your bags, son, you're ready.' "

Rodriguez had the talent, but he also had the same problem he
grew up with: lack of funds. Laurance Rockefeller, one of the owners
of Dorado, had accepted Chi Chi as his friend; he invited the young

golfer to his house and introduced him to other members of the famous banking family. So, when Rodriguez needed a backer, he called, hesitantly, and asked if he could come by.

"He said, 'Sure, come on over, we'll talk,' " Rodriguez says. "I was very, very nervous. We talked for 10 or 15 minutes and he really put me at ease. He knew what I wanted, but he wanted me to ask him. Finally, he said, 'Well, Chi Chi, what's on your mind?' I told him I needed $15,000 to go on Tour. He laughed and I was really scared. Then he said, 'I thought you were going to ask for $25,000.' He told me there was no problem and he wanted me to go first-class. He said if I needed more, just let him know. I tried to thank him a hundred times and he always said, 'Don't mention it.' "

Traveling with Cooper in his old Pontiac, Rodriguez hit the road in 1960. In his first two years, he only had one top-10 finish. With total earnings of a paltry $4,406, he says, many nights he and Cooper ate hamburgers and slept in the car.

Even though there wasn't much to smile about in those days, Chi Chi always maintained a happy face. He had never been able to resist the impulse to make people smile, he always enjoyed spreading laughter and happiness, even when he wasn't playing well. Even then, he bantered with the crowds, took deep bows after good shots, and started a routine performing a little tango and putting his hat over the hole after sinking a birdie putt. That didn't exactly ingratiate this skinny little nobody with his fellow pros, most of whom had been weaned at country clubs and, particularly during that era, were doing their best impressions of Ben Hogan.

"In the beginning, when I first did my thing, a lot of people looked down at me, especially the pros because most of them had patterned themselves after Hogan," Rodriguez says. "A lot of guys misunderstood me. I never did anything to show people up or upset anybody. I just did it to have a good time, to have people enjoy themselves because I was enjoying myself."

Gene Littler, the U.S. Open champion in 1961, admitted that "We weren't quite ready for Chi Chi and his act. We were a pretty serious bunch. I guess he was just ahead of his time."

Although he didn't have that many opportunities to display his birdie routine, Rodriguez began attracting crowds with his antics. He was encouraged to tone them down until Arnold Palmer asked him to do them after they played together in the 1964 Masters. A few years later, wisecracking Lee Trevino arrived on the scene, and after Trevino won the 1968 U.S. Open, entertainment suddenly was in. The Hogan era was over and Chi Chi could go back to being natural. He thanks Trevino to this day for that.

Once he joined the Senior Tour, Rodriguez was a familiar figure with his snap-brim panama hat (he packs 10 for every tournament), fancy clothes and sword dance. "I pretend the hole is the bull. A birdie stops the bull, so I draw my sword, stab it, then wipe off the imaginary blood and thrust the sword back in my scabbard. Crowds seem to enjoy it."

The Senior Tour started as low-key competition with a heavy dose of entertainment, so Chi Chi fit right in. He drew crowds, and that's what the seniors needed. And in contrast with his performance on the regular tour, here he was a winner—boy, was he a winner. In 1986, his first full season, he won three times, had seven seconds and was in the top 10 in 23 of his 24 starts. Golf was fun again and the money started rolling in.

One of Rodriguez's biggest financial boosts in the lean years just before he became eligible for the Senior Tour came from his friend Jack Nicklaus, about whom Chi Chi coined the phrase "He's a legend in his spare time."

TROUBLE AHEAD: *Bending down to avoid some low-hanging limbs, Rodriguez keeps his eye on a fading fairway wood shot.*

"I was really down," Rodriguez says. "I played a round with Jack at Pebble Beach, and afterward he said he'd like to sign me to play MacGregor [clubs]. I was shocked and told him, 'I'm in the twilight of my career; what do you want with me?' I was very happy with Northwestern; they had been very good to me. He insisted and offered me twice what Northwestern was paying me. It meant so much to me that Jack thought I could still play. It gave me confidence to keep going."

Elias went to Nat Rosasco at Northwestern, who told him he didn't want to lose Chi Chi, but if MacGregor was offering that much, he would release him. So, when Chi Chi joined the Senior Tour, he had a 10-year deal, giving him the kind of security he had always strived for, the type of deal most of his chief rivals enjoyed, the kind that makes it easier to fire at the pin on Sunday afternoons.

His first victory came at the prestigious Senior Tournament Players Championship at Canterbury Golf Club in Cleveland, where he beat Bruce Crampton by two shots with a 10-under-par 206. Two months later, he rallied with a final-round 66 to edge Gary Player by a stroke and win the Digital Seniors Classic in Concord, Massachusetts. In September, he added a third victory at the United Virginia Bank Seniors at Hermitage Country Club near Richmond with a tournament record 14-under-par 202.

The following year, 1987, was one that Rodriguez never will forget. All the dreams, all the hopes, all the hard work, all the tough times were rewarded. It was the end of the rainbow. He won seven times, including threee in a row and four straight that he entered. He was unstoppable, finishing No. 1 on the money list with a then–Senior Tour record of $509,145. During one white-hot stretch, he set a record with eight consecutive birdies.

His most important victory came first, at the PGA Seniors Championship at PGA National in Palm Beach Gardens, Florida. He overcame a six-shot deficit on the final day, passing leader Dale Douglass,

Harold Henning, Bobby Nichols, Bob Charles and Gary Player with a five-under-par 67.

"The Senior Tour was like being born again," Rodriguez said after winning the Vantage at the Dominion by three shots over Butch Baird in San Antonio. "My career has completely turned around. Three or four years ago, I had very little confidence. Now I go into every tournament expecting to win."

One of the most cherished moments of his career came at the end of the season, when he was honored by President Reagan and given the National Puerto Rican Coalition Life Achievement Award.

"Winning tournaments is fun and the money is nice, but something like this, to be honored for representing my country, is something I'll cherish to my grave," he said. "Winning means more than money because now that I have become successful, kids will listen to me more, and I want very much to be a good role model. My father was a very good role model, but nobody ever heard of him. I feel very fortunate to be in a position to set a good example for kids."

After finishing 2nd and 1st on the money list the previous two years, Rodriguez slipped to 10th in 1988. He won the Doug Sanders Kingwood Celebrity Classic in Houston by overtaking John Brodie and Bobby Nichols with a final-round 69. Then he became the first player on the Senior Tour to win the same tournament three years in a row when he won the Digital Seniors Classic by a shot over Bob Charles.

Honors for golf's most popular goodwill ambassador continued to pour in. Rodriguez was given the Fred Raphael Award for distinguished service to the game and the Old Tom Morris Award by the Golf Course Superintendents Association. The highlight was the Bob Jones Award for distinguished sportsmanship—the highest award given by the United States Golf Association. And he never lost his humility or sense of humor. When presented a symbolic sword at a banquet at the Waldorf-Astoria in New York, Chi Chi, never at a loss for words, held it up and said, "This is what we hitchhike with in Puerto Rico."

The following year, Rodriguez woke up one morning and couldn't move his neck without a sharp pain running to his shoulder. It didn't go away for six months. It was diagnosed as anything from a calcium deposit to a pinched nerve to a disk problem, but all Chi Chi knew was he couldn't swing without pain. So what did he do? Kept playing, of course.

"My mother always said if I was a woman I'd be pregnant all the time, because I don't know how to say no."

After trying to play several weeks in pain, he withdrew from the Southwestern Bell Classic after an opening-round 76 and skipped the Kingwood Celebrity Classic in Houston, where he was the defending champion.

"I have a headache 12 hours a day," he said before the Senior Tournament Players Championship at Ponte Vedra, Florida. "It's so difficult to concentrate when you're hurt. This game is tough enough when you're healthy. But I don't know how to say no. I'm still doing clinics and outings and trying to play when I can."

It was a difficult year, with only 10 top-10 finishes in 24 starts, but one day in September, the pain went away as mysteriously as it had occurred. Rodriguez came back after a 30th at the GTE Northwest Classic, two weeks off, then a 33rd at GTE North Classic in Indianapolis to win the Crestar Classic near Richmond with another one of his come-from-behind charges. He closed with a 4-under-par 68

POPULAR PICTURE: *One of the most popular players on the Senior Tour, Rodriguez always has time to sign an autograph or pose for a picture.*

to win by a shot over Jim Dent and Richard Rhyan at 13-under-par 203.

Once he regained his health, Rodriguez, 54 at the time, made still another comeback, winning three times in 1990. He edged George Archer and Charlie Coody by a shot at 12-under-par 204 in Las Vegas, where he said, "This is the first time in Las Vegas where a 12 beats an 11."

He blew away the field in the Ameritech Open at Grand Traverse Village, Michigan, winning by seven shots with a 16-under-par 203. Three weeks later, he won the Sunwest Bank/Charley Pride Classic in Albuquerque, New Mexico, by two shots at 11-under-par.

Before the 1991 season, Rodriguez said he was going after Trevino. Sure, Lee had dominated 1990 with seven victories and $1,190,518 in official earnings, but Chi Chi said, "As great as Lee is, it's tough to stay on top for long. Last year was his year; this is going to be mine."

Strong words for a player approaching his 56th birthday, but then he's always believed that he's destined for a long life. "My grandfather lived to be over 100 and so did my grandmother," he says. "I'm only middle-aged. I'm going to live to be 120. Hey, if I'm off five years one way or the other, I'm not going to sweat it."

Playing like a youngster, Rodriguez came out of a sick bed—where he battled the flu for two days with "three gallons of water and dozens of aspirin"—to win the rain-shortened GTE West Classic in Ojai, California, shading Bruce Crampton and Gary Player by a shot with a pair of 66s.

Two weeks later, he edged Mike Hill and 61-year-old Don January by a stroke with a final-round 69 at the Vintage ARCO Invitational in Indian Wells, California, boosting himself to No. 1 on the money list for the first time since he finished on top in 1987.

Rodriguez won for the third time in eight weeks when he passed Gary Player down the stretch, shot 66 and won the Las Vegas Classic

T I P

"I used to work at a psychiatric clinic as an orderly when I was a young man. Every time a mentally ill person got nervous, the first thing the doctor would tell them is to take a deep breath and let it out. They also teach you this in martial arts as a way of relaxation. It also carries over onto the golf course as well. When you are nervous and in the pressure-packed situations of a tournament, take a moment to stop, take a deep breath and let it out. This relaxes the entire body and enables you to swing smoothly at the ball."

Chi Chi Rodriguez

by three shots over Player and Walt Zembriski. "Winning is a habit and I have that habit now," he said after winning at Las Vegas for the second year in a row.

The following week, he won again, outlasting Jim Colbert in a four-hole playoff at the Murata Reunion Pro-Am in Frisco, Texas. His fourth victory of the year boosted his earnings to $395,703, almost $150,000 more than second-place Trevino.

"Believe it or not, my putting has gotten better," he says. "Your putting is supposed to get bad as you get older, but mine has gotten better. One reason, I think, is because the level of competition out here has gotten better. With Trevino and Nicklaus playing, they're very hard to beat. That's why I feel better when I beat them once in a while, because on the other tour I couldn't beat them at all. So, as I'm getting older, I'm trying to get even."

Rodriguez has gotten even—gotten even with life, which dealt him such a lousy opening hand. He's got a full house now—several of them, in fact: one each in Dorado Beach, Puerto Rico, and a quiet retirement development in Naples, Florida. Now he doesn't sleep in his car or take trains halfway across the country to see his mother. He has a private plane and two full-time pilots. He also has his youth foundation in Clearwater, Florida, he has financial security and, most important, he has earned the respect and admiration of his peers. He's also enjoying himself.

"I have fun," he says. "Somebody said it's only fun when you win, but I have fun when guys like Al Kelley and Rives McBee win because I know they need the money. When I see people happy, that's my fun."

Chi Chi says he hasn't changed, but little things have changed. His only concession to age is the dye he puts on his hair ("Why not? President Reagan does it"). And he never wears blue jeans, not even around the house ("I worked all my life to get out of tennis shoes and blue jeans and now I'll never go back").

Yes, Rodriguez is fiercely proud of what he's accomplished, rising from a poverty-stricken broken home to become one of the best-known golfers in the world, one closing in on $4 million in official earnings.

"I've never felt guilty about my success," he says. "I'm a nice guy. I've worked hard and I deserve what I have. God gave me a second life and I used it well."

GARY PLAYER

Like all the pros, Gary Player had his lean years in his forties, too. But the quintessential positive thinker just doesn't like to talk about it. Despite his incessant compulsion for physical fitness, his unflagging determination to be the best, his constant battle against aging, he suffered through seven and a half years without a victory.

In fact, after winning the 1974 Danny Thomas Memphis Classic, Player struggled through three winless seasons before he caught lightning in a bottle during one torrid stretch in April of 1978. It was as though he suddenly recaptured his youth, regained that flair for performing so well under pressure, aroused the instincts of his championship years.

There was no indication of things to come when Player arrived at Augusta National that year. In his three previous tournaments, he tied for 28th at the Tournament Players Championship, 45th at the Sea Pines Heritage Classic at Hilton Head, then 19th at the Greater Greensboro Open in North Carolina.

The gritty little South African, then 42, gave no hint that he was on the verge of one of golf's hottest streaks when he opened The Masters with a pair of 72s and trailed co-leaders Lee Trevino and Rod Funseth by five shots. Hale Irwin and Gene Littler were a stroke back at 140. On a bright, sunny Saturday, Hubert Green, in his prime at the time, took the third-round lead with a seven-under-par 65, which left Player and his quiet 69 still seven shots behind and seemingly out of contention.

That's when it started—a stretch of golf that Player will never forget, a streak surpassed only twice in the history of the PGA Tour. It began with a sizzling final-round 64, including a six-under-par 30 on the back nine that, at the time, tied The Masters record. After his spectacular run of seven birdies on the last 10 holes, Player finished far ahead of the leaders and had to wait nervously as Tom Watson (69) and Funseth (69) made their charges at the fading Green. They had their chances on the final green, but Watson made bogey and Funseth missed a birdie putt.

Most Masters aficionados vividly remember Green sagging over his putter after his three-footer to gain a playoff slid past the cup to the right on the 18th hole. A laser-accurate eight-iron that put him in birdie range had sent thousands scurrying to the 10th hole to await the playoff. Certainly, it was a putt Green never will forget, but he is quick to point out that he didn't lose the green jacket on the last green. At the famed 11th hole, he boldly went for the pin and knocked his approach shot into that foreboding pond on the left, the same one that drowned Raymond Floyd's dream of becoming the oldest Masters winner in the 1990 playoff with England's Nick Faldo.

"Everybody saw me miss the putt on 18," says Green, who can smile now when he recalls that dark day. "But where I really lost the tournament was on 16. I had a short putt there, and if I would have made that, I could have two-putted from three feet to win at 18."

So while the spotlight was on Green, the 1977 U.S. Open champion who had won two weeks earlier at Hilton Head, Player headed for Bobby Jones' cabin to collect his third green jacket.

"Whenever I'm trailing in a tournament going into the last day, I always think back to that '78 Masters," Player says. "Knowing I needed a 30 on the back nine and going out and shooting it, well, you can't do much better than that. It proves that anything is possible in this game if you keep trying, that you're never out of it, that anything can happen."

Surprisingly, that was only the beginning. The following week, at the MONY Tournament of Champions at La Costa Resort in Carlsbad, California, Player, the last one to qualify for this elite winners-only event, opened with a 70, then added a 68. But he still was four shots behind Spain's dashing newcomer Seve Ballesteros, who had won his first PGA Tour event, the Greater Greensboro Open, two weeks earlier. Player seemed out of it when he skied to a 76 in the third round and once again was seven strokes off the pace. And once again, he caught fire in the final round, shooting 67 while Ballesteros blew to a 79, giving Player his second straight victory.

Nowadays, players on the PGA Tour rarely win back-to-back although their game is at a peak and their confidence is sky high. Most claim there is a tremendous letdown after winning, while a few, like Fred Couples, are honest enough to admit that after picking up that big check on Sunday, they don't even want to get out of bed on Monday morning.

Player wasn't done yet. The following week, at the Houston Open, he set a tournament record at the Woodlands with an opening 8-under-par 64. His second-round 67 left him a shot in front of Andy Bean, who shot 65, and Bob Murphy. Bean, a three-year veteran who would go on to win 3 tournaments that year, added a 66, and his 18-under-par 198 was the year's lowest score on the Tour to that point and three shots ahead of Player. But Player would not be denied. He fired a final-round 69, and when Bean stumbled in with a 73,

HAPPINESS IS A BIRDIE AT 18: *Gary Player*
birdied seven of the last 10 holes, including
the 18th, for a 64 to win his third Masters
in 1978 at Augusta National.

140

Player had become only the 10th player in PGA Tour history to win 3 consecutive tournaments. (Jackie Burke won 4 in a row in 1952 and famed Byron Nelson holds the record—the one sports record that it can safely be said will never be broken—winning 11 consecutive tournaments from March through August of 1945. His total winnings during that streak: $30,250.)

Player had a good chance of tying Burke's mark the following week at the New Orleans Open, where he started 69-67-69 to tie for the lead. At last, his final-day magic ran out. With the world watching, with a media blitz surrounding his attempt to win 4 in a row, with the pressure building with every putt, he shot 72. He would never win again on the PGA Tour.

In 1979, he cut his schedule back to 12 events and, fighting a balky putter, missed the cut five times. The highlight of the year came at the U.S. Open at Inverness Club in Toledo, Ohio, when he bolted from out of the pack on the last day with a three-under-par 68. But alas, he started nine shots behind the eventual winner, Hale Irwin, not the seven he had managed to make up at The Masters and Tournament of Champions the previous year.

No, it was over for Player, no matter how many push-ups he did, how many miles he pedaled on his exercise bike, how many sit-ups (300 a day, he says) he agonized over. He, undoubtedly, was the best-conditioned 45-year-old on the Tour, but he wasn't challenging those young flat bellies anymore.

"The two things that go when you get older that you have no control over are your eyes and your nerves," he says. "When you get older you lose your depth perception. It hurts you more with your chipping than your putting. If you're 40 to 50 feet off the green, sometimes it's difficult to gauge just how far you are from the pin. When you have a full shot, your caddie tells you the yardage, but on the short chips, you have to trust your eyes.

"Your eyes can play tricks on you on long putts, too, but when you miss the short one, laddie, that's nerves. We all go through that, too. You can't help it. When you're young, you think you're supposed to make all the eight-footers. Then, when you get older, you realize how easy they are to miss, because you've missed so many by then that it's sickening."

Player obviously never had any trouble putting once he finally took up the game, which was at middle age compared to today's youngsters with their cut-down clubs, country-club lessons, and junior standards.

The youngest of three children, he was born in Lyndhurst, a suburb of Johannesburg, South Africa, on November 1, 1935. He worked hard as a kid growing up in Booysens, a poor neighborhood on the outskirts of Johannesburg. His house was actually over a gold mine called Robinson Deep, where his father was the mine captain. Working some 12,000 feet under the ground, the elder Player never made more than $200 a month in his life. When young Gary was 8, his mother died of cancer at age 44, but not before she set an example of never complaining, of always looking to the bright side, that Player, an eternal optimist, never forgot.

To get to school in those days, Player took a trolley car to the middle of Johannesburg, then walked about a mile to catch a bus out of town to King Edward VII School. It took an hour and a half each way. When he got home, the house was empty, and he had to wait for his father and sister, Wilma, to come home from work.

"My early life was filled with adversity, but thanks to my father's example, I turned it into a positive experience," Player says. "It gave me the drive to succeed. I became, and still am, an extremely hard worker. So many people who are successful come from poverty, and I must say, it was the key to my development as a player and a person."

Player's father had to quit school when his father died at an early age, and he worked in the mines all his life. He did manage to play

YOUNG AND AMBITIOUS: *Player came out of Johannesburg, South Africa, at age 17 determined to become a world-class player.*

APPREHENSIVE: *Player and his wife, Vivienne, seem lost in their thoughts as he heads for the first tee at the 1958 Kentucky Derby Open in his first full season on the PGA Tour. He went on to win, his first of 21 Tour victories.*

enough golf, however, to maintain a single-digit handicap, but it didn't impress young Gary, who said he thought it was a silly game and didn't even try it until the day before his 15th birthday. Reluctantly, he agreed to join his father that day and then, incredibly, parred the first three holes. After that he was hooked, and he played as often as he could, frequently with the son (Bob) and daughter (Vivienne) of the head pro, Jock Verwey. There was only one diversion from his obsession for the game—Vivienne.

When he finished school at age 17, Player turned pro and shortly thereafter began a traveling experience that made Ferdinand Magellan look like a local hitchhiker. There just wasn't enough competition or events in South Africa to keep him busy and financially solvent. Player knew if he was going to achieve his burning desire to be the best golfer in the world, he would have to leave his native land, broaden his horizons and prove himself on foreign soil.

His first trip was to Egypt, where he won a match play tournament. The next year he won in Australia and then beat the best British players in the Dunlop Masters at Sunningdale, England. After he started reaping some financial rewards for all his practicing and traveling, he decided to ask Vivienne to marry him. He says today it was the single best decision he ever made in his life. He also admits that one day when they were playing, Vivienne, who once carried a two handicap, beat him in a head-to-head match.

"I was determined not to let that happen again," he says with a grin. "That's when I decided that we'd have six kids."

In 1957, Player made his first trip to the United States to play in The Masters at age 21. After he won the South African Open the previous year, his father wrote to Bobby Jones and Clifford Roberts in Augusta, Georgia, praising his son's ability but explaining that he was not financially able to send his son to the United States. However, if an invitation to The Masters were extended, he would pass the hat and try to gain the necessary funds. Jones' reply was typically succinct. It read, "Pass the hat."

The following year Player joined the PGA Tour full-time. His first check was for $26 for finishing 16th, but by May he had his first victory in the Kentucky Derby Open, and he went on to win $18,591 that year. He also won the first of seven Australian Opens. Perhaps his most memorable day, however, came at his first U.S. Open at Southern Hills Country Club in Tulsa, Oklahoma. He used his excellent physical condition and stamina to pass several challengers in 95-degree heat on the double-round final day and finish second to Tommy Bolt.

That was the day long remembered by fans of Bolt, nicknamed Thunder because of his terrible temper. Bolt didn't join the PGA Tour until he was 32, after 4 years in the Army and 10 in the construction business. After finishing the Open at three-over-par 283 and winning for the 11th time, Bolt, then 40, claimed he had changed—that he had tamed his temper, that he was through throwing clubs and tantrums, that he had found peace of mind.

"I just decided that golf wasn't worth breaking a blood vessel over, so I relaxed. I'm a different man," he said. He started carrying a card that he would quickly and proudly show; it said, "God grant me the serenity to accept the things I cannot change, the courage to change things I can and the wisdom to know the difference."

One week later, Bolt stepped off a plane in New York on his way to the Pepsi Cola Open and allegedly threw a punch at a tournament organizer, Frank Shields—Brooke Shields' father—although he now denies it.

"I had won the Open, then went right to the Buick Open and led for three rounds before shooting 74 in the final round," Bolt related. "I was exhausted and flew to New York. I was looking for a ride to the hotel, but nobody was there. I knew Mike Souchak and Jack Burke had been picked up, and there I was, the U.S. Open champion, without a ride. I went over to Shields and asked where my ride was. He acted kind of smart, I thought. I started to punch him in the nose. Some words were exchanged, but he needed punching."

WINNER'S REWARD: *Player gets kisses from his wife, Vivienne (right), and Kentucky Derby Festival queen Pat Travis after his first PGA Tour victory at the 1958 Kentucky Derby Open.*

147

So much for serenity. He went on to run his career victory total to 15, and long before there was a Senior Tour, he won the 1969 PGA Seniors Championship and five National Seniors Association titles.

Bolt was one of the pioneers of the Senior Tour after combining with Art Wall to finish second in the 1979 Legends of Golf in Austin, Texas, behind Julius Boros and Roberto De Vicenzo. In 1980, when the Senior Tour began with two events worth a total of $250,000, Bolt and Wall teamed up again, and this time they won the unofficial better-ball event. He continued to support the Senior Tour throughout the 1980s, although his official earnings for the decade were only $31,175. At age 70, he teamed with Sam Snead to finish sixth in the Legends' Legendary Field at Onion Creek and earn $11,000 in unofficial money.

"If the Senior Tour had started in 1970 instead of 1980, I'd be a multimillionaire," Bolt says. "I won all the Senior tournaments in the sixties. I won the first one I entered when I was 52."

For Player, the 1958 U.S. Open was just a preview of many magnificent performances in the major championships, which he has always put so much emphasis on, even now on the Senior Tour. After his runner-up finish, this relatively unknown young South African made a bold statement to the national media.

"I have set four goals for myself," he said unabashedly. "I want to win the U.S. Open, The Masters and the PGA Championship, and I want to be the leading money winner on the Tour. I don't expect to do them all in a single year. This is a long-range goal."

This seemingly impossible goal for a youngster with one PGA Tour victory was achieved in a mere seven years when Player won

SAND MASTER: *Player displays the form that has helped him save pars all over the world. He says he maintains his touch by practicing in the dunes on his ranch in South Africa.*

the U.S. Open at Bellerive Country Club in St. Louis, beating Kel Nagle in a playoff. Player had won the 1959 British Open at Muirfield and thus became only the third player in history—after Gene Sarazen and Ben Hogan—to win the four major championships. (Jack Nicklaus later became the fourth.)

In his goal to win the three majors in the United States, the 1961 Masters was the first step for Player, who was treading on Arnold Palmer's sacred turf. The popular Palmer was the defending champion—having won at Augusta National for the second time in three years—and an overwhelming favorite as the reigning U.S. Open champion as well. Player had been improving at Augusta since his baptism in 1957, and the previous year he had tied for sixth, but few thought he had a chance to unseat the King.

On a gray, drizzly first day, Palmer, firing at the pins on the soft greens, opened with a 68 to share the lead with Bob Rosburg, who chipped in for a birdie at No. 5 and sank a 100-foot putt on the 14th hole. Player quietly posted a 69 to start a chase that would not end until Monday evening in one of the most dramatic conclusions in Masters history.

With the skies clear and windless on Friday, Player intensified his pursuit. Playing two holes ahead of Palmer, he sent a message loud and clear through the pines as thunderous applause followed his birdies on the 9th, 13th and 15th holes. There was one moment when Palmer, who had answered with birdies of his own at the 9th and 13th, was lining up a 25-foot birdie putt at the par-3 16th. Suddenly another huge roar came from the 18th green, and it was obvious that Player had done it again. Seemingly unrattled, Palmer coolly rolled in his birdie, and his gallery exploded. At day's end, Player had shot 68, Palmer 69; they were tied for the lead at seven-under-par 137. Rosburg was next at 141. It was a two-man battle.

During that duel, Player made one of what for him would be hundreds of spectacular sand shots, the kind that earned him the

BRITISH OPEN CHAMPION: *Player used his masterly skill with fairway woods to win his first of three British Opens in 1959 at Muirfield, Scotland.*

CHASING PALMER: *In a rainy first round, Player blasted from a bunker and birdied the par-5 second hole en route to a 69, one shot behind leader Arnold Palmer in the 1961 Masters.*

reputation of being the best bunker player in the world—although this one wasn't from a trap. His four-wood tee shot to the 220-yard, par-3 4th hole drifted close to a bunker to the left of the green. The ball wound up in high grass with a lot of sand left from a previous player's explosion shot, about 75 feet from the hole.

"I didn't know whether to chip it or try an explosion from that lie," Player says. "I finally decided to explode and play for a bogey." The shot rolled up within inches of the pin for a tap-in par.

On Saturday, Palmer had two birdies before Player teed off. "Here I am out on the putting green and I'm already two shots down," Player says. "I was frightened stiff."

He didn't show it once his turn came. He also opened with birdies on the first two holes, and when Palmer faltered with bogeys at the 4th, 5th and 7th holes before making a birdie at the par-5 8th, Player charged to a four-shot lead. Despite three straight bogeys starting at No. 11, Player stayed steady, came back with birdies at the 15th and 16th and finished with 69 and a four-shot lead.

Midway through the fourth round Sunday, the skies opened up, drenching the course and making it unplayable. So young Player now had another night to toss and turn, another day to live with his four-shot advantage over the popular American hero.

He said at the time that it was the longest 24 hours of his life, but he never showed a hint of nervousness as he opened with two birdies for the third round in a row. "That was the key to winning," he would say later. "I birdied the first two holes three times. That puts you in the right frame of mind, gives you the confidence to play the rest of the round aggressively."

There weren't any more birdies in Player's bag that day, however, and when he made a double bogey on the par-5 13th, which yields so many birdies, his four-shot lead was wiped out.

"I'll have nightmares about that hole the rest of my life," he says. Trying to keep his drive away from the woods on the left, he pushed it into the pine trees on the right. His best opening was to the adjacent 14th fairway, where he could still reach the green with his third shot. But for Player to make the shot, the huge gallery would have to be moved, and there just didn't seem to be any place for all the people to go. The marshals tried and Gary pleaded, but it wasn't working.

"I should have sat down and waited," he says. "Even if it had taken an hour, I should have waited for the crowd to move, but I was getting edgy. My four-shot lead was cut in half, and I was too excited and worried about the delay to think clearly."

Instead, Player tried to hit a two-iron back to the 13th fairway, but he hit it too hard, hooking it into the ditch on the left, where he had to take a penalty drop. Shaken, he hit a three-iron to the back of the huge, undulating green and nervously three-putted for a double bogey seven. His lead was gone.

Although he was still tied, his troubles weren't over. He also bogeyed the par-5 15th and now trailed Palmer by a stroke. Leaking oil, as they say in Georgia, Player had to scramble for pars at the final two holes, exploding out of a bunker at 18 and sinking the pressure putt for par.

When he came off the 18th green after his 74, young Player seemed on the verge of tears, certain he had given away the championship he wanted so much. The large white scoreboard clearly showed that Palmer was leading by a stroke and playing the par-5 15th, where birdies were plentiful. Player and Vivienne then went to Clifford Roberts' clubhouse apartment to watch what he felt surely would be a painful experience.

Palmer missed his birdie at 15, but he still had his stroke lead on the 18th tee. A par and he would have his third Masters title in four years. After a booming drive, he had a seven-iron to the green, but he pushed it into the same right-side bunker that Player had escaped from. The ball settled in a depression, but it was nothing that should have caused the horrid shot that Palmer pulled: he skulled it across the green, through the crowd and down a slope toward a TV tower. Suddenly, instead of dreaming of victory, Palmer had to get down in two just to force a playoff. Player, watching with Vivienne and Roberts, was suddenly on the edge of the couch.

Palmer, with the crowd's urging still echoing in his ears, hitched his pants one more time, then carefully pitched 15 feet from the hole. Slowly, he walked from one side of the green to the other, studying the tantalizing putt from every angle. Finally, there was nothing left to do but wiggle into that familiar, knock-kneed stance, stare at the hole one more time and stroke it. He winced as the ball slid by on the left. In Roberts' apartment, a stunned Player watched in disbelief. He had won after all and at 25 became the first foreign player to slip on the coveted green jacket.

Player went on to achieve another of his goals that year when he won two other events, the Lucky International and the Sunshine, and finished No. 1 on the money list with $64,540. Oddly, it would be the only time in his long, successful career that he would top the money list.

"Once I did it, that wasn't very important to me anymore," he says now. "I wanted to be a world-class player, to win all over the world, not concentrate on one tour. Also, I wanted to spend more time with my family. My children were growing up and I hated to be away from them for long periods of time. I'm sure, if I had moved to the United States or played a full schedule, I could have won the money title again. But I made a decision early in my career to concentrate on major championships, and that's what I did."

Player's next major championship after his Masters triumph came the following summer. He won the PGA Championship, at Aronomink Golf Club in Newtown Square near Philadelphia, by a stroke over Bob Goalby. While he had made his mark at the 1958 U.S. Open and the 1961 Masters, Player had never distinguished himself at the PGA Championship, playing only in 1961 and finishing tied for 29th at Olympia Fields near Chicago.

He certainly wasn't enthusiastic about his chances when he arrived in Philadelphia after having missed the cut at the British Open at Royal Troon the week before. He said he was tired of traveling, was disappointed in his game and needed to get home.

He started with a lackluster 72 and trailed unknown leader John Barnum by six strokes, but he moved into contention on Friday with a near flawless 67. That put him in a second-place tie with Cary Middlecoff and George Bayer, just a shot behind Doug Ford. After Saturday's 69, Player had the lead by two strokes over Bayer and Bob McCallister. Ford trailed by three and Goalby by four going into the final round.

While the other contenders faded, Goalby, a two-time winner that year, made a charge. Player still had a three-shot advantage after 13 holes, but Goalby sank a 20-footer for birdie at No. 14 and made another birdie at the par-5 16th to draw within a stroke. After they both parred the 17th, Goalby put his approach inside Player's on the final hole. Player lagged within 2 feet, then, after watching Goalby's attempt for a tie slide past, tapped in his winner.

It had been 15 months since his last victory, that emotionally draining triumph in Augusta, and Player seemed more relieved than elated with his first of two PGA Championships. He said later that he had started to have doubts about his game, and that victory gave him the confidence that he could still win major championships.

Player's only U.S. Open championship came in 1965 at Bellerive in St. Louis—the first time the Open would be played over four days, instead of concluding with a 36-hole final on Saturday. The previous year, at Congressional Country Club in Bethesda, Maryland, just outside of Washington, D.C., Ken Venturi had almost collapsed from heat prostration playing 36 holes in saunalike conditions. Also, television was becoming a major financial contributor and, naturally, it

ANOTHER FAST START: *Player tees off on the second hole in Saturday's third round. He birdied the first two holes three times en route to his first Masters triumph in 1961.*

wanted a Sunday show. Although most of the players quietly agreed—heck, welcomed the change—there was the predictable handwringing from the purists wailing that they were deprived of one of the greatest days in sports—the 36-hole U.S. Open final. Everyone else breathed a sigh of relief.

Although it ended with an 18-hole playoff, the 1965 U.S. Open was robbed of a lot of its glamour when both Palmer and Nicklaus were victimized by the huge greens. Palmer, struggling through his worst years of the sixties, three-putted his way to a pair of 76s and missed the cut. Nicklaus, The Masters champion who would go on to win the money title for the second straight year, barely made the cut after an opening 78 and never was a factor.

Kel Nagle, a 44-year-old Australian who won only once on the PGA Tour (1964 Canadian Open), jumped out with an opening 68, then fell back with a 73 to trail Player by one at the midpoint. Player increased his lead to two shots with a methodical 71 in the third round, and he seemed to have the coveted championship wrapped up with three holes remaining on Sunday after Nagle double-bogeyed the par-4 15th hole. Then, as in his Masters victory, disaster struck.

At the 218-yard, par-3 16th hole, with a mammoth green and huge bunker in front, Player hit his tee shot into the sand. He played out to about 15 feet, but he ran his first putt three feet past and then hung his comebacker on the lip.

Just then a deafening roar went up from the par-5 17th green, where Nagle had birdied. Suddenly, the tournament was tied. Both players parred in, so a championship that traditionally had its climax on Saturday was now moving to Monday.

A foreign player had not won the U.S. Open since 1920, when Edward "Ted" Ray survived near gale-force winds and a back-nine collapse by 50-year-old Harry Vardon to win at Inverness in Toledo, Ohio. But there would be a foreign winner at Bellerive.

It was anticlimactic, as are many U.S. Open playoffs—such as the duel between Billy Casper (69) and Arnold Palmer (73) the following year at the Olympic Club in San Francisco, or the dud at Winged Foot in 1984 that featured Fuzzy Zoeller (67) and Greg Norman (75). Nagle never gave himself a chance, spraying the ball all over the lot on the front nine and falling five shots back at the turn. Player cruised in with a 71 to win by three.

In 1962, Player had said that if he ever won a U.S. Open, he wouldn't accept the prize money, and he remained true to his word. The purse, thanks in part to the added television revenue, had increased, and first place was worth a whopping $25,000. At the presentation ceremony, Player donated $5,000 to cancer research and gave the other $20,000 to the U.S. Golf Association for the promotion of junior golf.

"I always felt so fortunate to have the opportunity to play golf in the United States that I wanted to give something back, to express my gratitude," Player said. "I think the United States has a wonderful program for junior golfers—something I would like to see in my country—and I will do whatever I can to promote it. This was just a small token of my appreciation for being allowed to support my family by playing golf in this country."

Strangely, it would be four years before Player would win again in the United States, and in his three winless seasons, his earnings totaled a mere $134,161. He still was winning abroad, however, adding 2 more of his 13 South African Open titles, 2 of his 5 World Picadilly match play championships and, most important, a 2nd British Open championship. In 1968 at Carnoustie, Scotland, he started poorly with 74-71, but after a late-night session on the practice range (it stays light in Scotland until 10 P.M. that time of year), he came back, making Nicklaus a disappointed runner-up for the second year in a row.

When Player won his third British Open title, outlasting Peter Oosterhuis at Royal Lytham in 1974, he became the first player ever to win this prestigious championship in three decades. The distinction is perhaps the strongest endorsement of his relentless devotion to physical fitness.

At 17, when Player started down the trail of professional golf in 1952, he weighed 150 pounds. Before the 1990 PGA Seniors Championship at Palm Beach Gardens, Florida, he said he weighed 152, but that he had added two inches to his waist and now had to order size 32 slacks.

It's been said that he is the original hard body, that grown men suck in their guts in his presence. He says he has the metabolism that allows him to eat heavily at times, but never at night.

"I don't follow a special diet," Player says. "I believe in eating well, but staying away from fatty foods and too much sugar. I like high-fiber foods like whole grain bread, cereal and fruit. I enjoy poultry and fish, salads, steamed vegetables and baked potatoes. I drink decaffeinated coffee and tea, plus lots of water.

"The foods I try to avoid are fried and fatty foods such as pork, bacon, butter, cream. These foods can make you fat and take away energy. Oh, I'll occasionally have red meat, say once every 10 days or so, and sometimes on the road, I'll treat myself to bacon and eggs, but not very often."

It must be interesting when Player and his good friend Chi Chi Rodriguez go out for dinner. They were born eight days apart in 1935; they are both very healthy, very trim—but their eating habits are as similar as those of Willie Shoemaker and Wilt Chamberlain.

While Player is having flounder, steamed cauliflower, salad and a special herbal tea that is tannin- and caffeine-free, Chi Chi is finishing up a rare steak and french fries, heading toward his 10th cup of coffee of the day and another cigarette.

Oddly, the smoker and coffee drinker is a virtual teetotaler, although he might sip a scotch or two at the end of a tough day. Player admits to an occasional whiskey or beer; he says there is scientific evidence that moderate drinkers may live longer than those who don't drink at all.

In addition to carefully watching his diet, Player is a fanatic about exercise, and he religiously sticks to a schedule of 1 hour a day, 5 days a week, no matter where in the world he happens to be sleeping. He starts with about 30 minutes on an exercise bike, then does stretching, followed by 300 sit-ups. He also was into yoga for a while.

Another thing that helps keep Player so fit is his work on his horse farm in Blair Atholl near Johannesburg. When he is home, he still shovels manure and lays cement.

"When I go back to my ranch, I need to recharge my batteries by doing different things," Player says. "I want to work in the stables. I want to ride, to put up fences and cut hay. I love nature. I think one reason why I'm so productive and playing so well on the Senior Tour is because I've been closely associated with nature. I draw a lot of strength from it, and it gives me a philosophy that is unbeatable."

After he struggled through a victory drought of more than seven years, it was obvious that Player was primed and ready for his Senior Tour debut. With his November 1 birthday, the 1985 season was drawing to a close before he became eligible. The Quadel Seniors Classic in Boca Raton, Florida, was the last event of the year, and Player was primed.

After an opening-round 73, which left him seven shots behind co-leaders Dan Sikes and Ken Still, he served notice that he was back with a brilliant second-round, eight-under-par 64. That left him five shots behind Still, but now the leaders were looking over their shoulders and, sure enough, Player put on one of his patented charges, shooting 68 to win going away. Still ballooned to a 75 and Sikes, who was second, shot 76.

The Senior Tour. Player had been waiting, as everyone in his generation had, for the chance to play tournament golf again, to compete, to test his skills and his nerves under pressure. Many of the

SKILLED IN THE SAND: *Known as one of the world's best bunker players, Player blasted out of the sand by the 18th green and made par to win the 1961 Masters by a single stroke over Arnold Palmer and Charlie Coe.*

players had doubts when they first started playing competitively again, but not Player, the master of positive thinking. He knew, because of his physical and mental discipline, that he was going to win again, early and often. And after his smashing debut, the other players knew it too. They never doubted his physical condition: they knew that he was the youngest 50-year-old in golf and that he would probably still be winning after most of them had retired to the couch.

"Gary is one of golf's greatest self-made champions, and also one of the healthiest and happiest men I've ever known," says Nicklaus. "You can never shake Gary. You could make a big putt on a pivotal hole and he'd just knock it in on top of you."

Player, like Nicklaus and other great champions, always had placed his emphasis on the major championships. He continued that thinking on the Senior Tour. The first major he played was the PGA Seniors Championship at Palm Beach Gardens, Florida, the second event on an ever-growing schedule that had reached 28 tournaments worth $6,300,000 in total prize money by 1986.

Like a man possessed, Player came out firing the first day, carding a four-under-par 68 and following it with another 68 to bolt into a seven-shot lead over Lee Elder. After winning his debut in the last event of the previous year and now cruising with a seven-shot lead, Player thought this Senior stuff was a stroll in the park. He quickly found out that these old guys can still compete. When he slipped to a third-round 73, Elder shot the best round of the day, a 69, to cut Player's lead to three strokes. But Elder ran out of steam—couldn't do better than 71 on Sunday—and Player had another of what he calls major championships.

"I always get pumped up for majors," Player said afterward. Asked what he considered major championships, Player said, "The Senior PGA, the U.S. Senior Open, the Senior British Open and the Senior TPC [Tournament Players Championship], which is our own players championship."

The next year, Player closed with a pair of 69s to win the Senior Tournament Players Championship at Sawgrass Country Club in Ponte Vedra, Florida, by a stroke over Chi Chi Rodriguez and Bruce Crampton. After winning the U.S. Senior Open three weeks later in a six-shot runaway at Brooklawn Country Club in Fairfield, Connecticut, the subject of major championships came up again. Let's see, he had 9 before joining the Senior Tour, now 3 more—why, he might just catch Nicklaus' seemingly untouchable record of 20.

"Majors?" Nicklaus said. "How can you call those majors? Greg Norman wasn't playing. Curtis Strange wasn't playing. How can it be a major championship without the best players in the world?"

Player's answer, when told of Nicklaus' statement, was light but carried a sting. "At least I don't count my amateur titles," he said, in reference to Nicklaus' two U.S. Amateur championships—a tournament that, in the days of Bobby Jones' Grand Slam, was considered a major championship.

Now Nicklaus was responding, via the media, saying that "it was you guys [reporters] who called it 20. I've always said I have 18 major championships and 2 U.S. Amateur titles. Gary would count the Bangkok Open, if you let him." In the locker room, the other Senior players chuckled at the banter of the two superstars without taking sides. They kind of enjoyed seeing Nicklaus put on the spot, but they didn't actually appreciate the way Player was popping off about his accomplishments. Still, they agreed they profited from the media coverage that resulted from the spat.

"If Gary wants them to be majors, that's fine with us," said Al Geiberger. "We'd all like to win another major championship, and all the publicity is good for the Senior Tour."

Player was at it again in 1988, when he had his best year as a senior—winning 5 times in 20 starts, adding a pair of seconds, posting three third-place finishes and ending up second on the money list to Bob Charles with $435,914.

The PGA Seniors Championship again attested to Player's physical condition and stamina. He started five strokes behind Charles after an opening-round 69 and was still five back after two rounds. Then the usually unflappable Charles bogeyed three of the last five holes Saturday for 78 and matched that ugly number again Sunday to finish tied for 11th.

When the other contenders also started to falter in the gusty winds, Player played relentless, nearly error-free golf. He never led until he made the turn on Sunday, then sunk two birdies down the stretch for 70 to win by three over Rodriguez.

"It was very, very tough to make birdies in this wind," Rodriguez said. "But that's why Gary Player won. He's such a great player. I don't feel like I lost; I just got beat by a great player."

Player was at his best during the U.S. Senior Open at Medinah, where again conditioning and fitness made the difference as the 72-hole test was played in oppressive heat and humidity. The pressure was on him as defending champion from the moment he arrived at the famed Chicago course, which would host Hale Irwin's dramatic U.S. Open playoff victory over Mike Donald two years later.

As in the PGA Seniors, Player started slowly with a 74, and once again he was back in the pack after two rounds, trailing Billy Casper by four shots. As the scores started rising with the temperatures, Player posted a steady third-round 71 and moved into a tie for the lead with Charles at one-under-par 215.

With four holes to play, Charles held a three-shot lead, but he bogeyed three holes in a row and three-putted the treacherous 17th green. He needed a par on the final hole to join Player in an 18-hole playoff Monday.

"I was very disappointed after blowing it when I had it in my pocket," Charles recalls. "You should be able to hold on when you have a three-shot lead, but it shows you how hard those closing holes are."

Player took control early in the playoff, sinking a 12-foot birdie putt on the third hole, which Charles bogeyed. He increased his lead to three shots on the next hole when Charles missed another green. Player hit the first 11 greens, missed only 2, and was in command all day while shooting a bogey-free 68.

"Under the circumstances, it was one of the finest rounds I've ever played," Player says. "In our profession, this tournament means so much. There is nothing worse than finishing second in a major. When you finish second, only your wife and dog remember."

When the 1990 PGA Seniors Championship came around, there was a new look and an old controversy. Nicklaus had arrived on the scene, having reached his 50th birthday January 21, and again the subject of Player's "major championships" was brought up. By now, Gary was claiming 6 on the Senior Tour, giving him 15 lifetime.

"Certainly I count 'em," Player said Tuesday on the practice range. "These are how I measure my career, not how much money I've won. Those money records will be broken every year, but major championships stand forever."

Then he probably put the entire matter in the proper perspective, when asked if the Senior Tour had to have major championships. He stopped whaling his one-iron, looked inquisitive and said, "Laddie, must we not?"

In one of the most dramatic events in years, a flashback to the 1970s when they were all in their prime, Player, Nicklaus and Trevino battled head-to-head on the final day.

SENIOR PGA CHAMPION: *After falling five shots behind Bob Charles after two rounds, Player rallied to win the 1988 PGA Seniors Championship at PGA National Golf Club in Palm Beach Gardens, Florida.*

T I P

"Norman von Nida from Australia was a wonderful bunker player. We used to play closest to the hole for a pound a shot out of the bunker when we were young pros. He taught me how to hit the long bunker shot, one of the most difficult shots in golf. His advice to me was to make certain that you get a full shoulder turn on a long bunker shot. If you have a distance of 30 to 40 yards from the sand, you cannot make a short swing. You must get the club back, and the shoulder turn helps to accelerate it through the ball to get the distance needed. In my first British Open at Muirfield, Scotland, in 1959, I had a long bunker shot on the ninth hole and knocked it out about 2 inches from the cup. I'll always remember it as the key shot that led to my victory that year."

Gary Player

The previous afternoon, Player openly showed how much this tournament meant to him, the pressure he felt. It was The Masters or the U.S. Open all over again. Age has not mellowed this intense competitor a morsel. After his third-round 65 put him five shots in front of Nicklaus and six ahead of Trevino, Player was a bundle of nerves while going over his round with the press.

"I shot 74 [in the first round] and came back with 65," he started off. "Nicklaus shot 78 [in the second round] and came back with 67. It shows anything can happen on this golf course. I don't really consider a five-shot lead a safe lead. You can make double bogeys real quick out here."

Earlier Trevino, who had shot 70, told the media he was going to have fun on Sunday. "There's only going to be one winner, and I'm not going to lose any sleep if I don't win," he said. "The sun's going to come up the next day. I'm still going to have money in my pocket, my wife and little girl. So I'm just going to go out and have fun."

Later, when jocular George White of the *Orlando Sentinel* innocently asked Player if he was going to have fun in the final round, Player exploded.

"Fun? Fun? You think this is fun? You think taking a lead out against Nicklaus and Trevino is fun? That's work, mister. I'll tell you what fun is. Fun is pitching hay, feeding my horses, digging ditches on my ranch. That's fun. It won't be fun tomorrow. There's a tremendous amount of pressure out here, and having a lot of pressure on you isn't fun."

The next day, Player again showed how tense he was when playing with Nicklaus and Trevino, even after all these years. On the second hole, he jabbed at a three-foot birdie putt—poking it two feet past—then missed coming back. Three putts from three feet. But he bounced right back with a birdie on the par-5 third hole, and although he only shot 73, it was enough to hold off his two rivals and win by two shots over fast-closing Chi Chi Rodriguez, who fired a 66. Nicklaus had 72 and Trevino 71.

After two rain delays, it was so dark when the talented trio finished that they couldn't see their shots land and photographers were using automatic flashes to get Player's winning putt. Hopefully the negatives were salvageable, because it would be his only victory of the year.

"I was a little like Ray Charles playing those last three holes. I couldn't see a thing," Player said. Then, before a hasty departure back to Johannesburg, he added, "The trophy is nice, the check [$75,000] is nice, the car is nice. But to win this tournament against two players like Nicklaus and Trevino is something I'll cherish for the rest of my life."

Then it was back on another airline—Player claims to have flown more than 8 million miles and sat in airplanes for almost three years of his life—for another few weeks at the ranch. Now he could have what he calls fun: working in the stables, cutting hay and going for walks with his longtime foreman and companion, Willie Betha, who was no youngster when Player brought him to his ranch in 1964.

"Willie has a richness because of his closeness to nature that to me is so far beyond a man who has $10 million in the bank but lives in a big city and inhales smog and pollution every day," Player says. "He's one of the happiest people I know because he loves what he's doing, his body is in great shape and his productivity is good. I've learned a lot from Willie."

Those who were paying attention must have learned a lot from Player, who may be too intense for his best public interest, but who remains one of the great role models in all of golf with his fierce competitiveness and diligence in physical fitness. He is truly one of the world's all-time self-made success stories.

And it just keeps rolling along. Player started his sixth full season on the Senior Tour as though he was a 50-year-old rookie, winning the Royal Caribbean Classic in record-smashing style. A closing 68 in heavy wind and rain down the stretch enabled him to hold off his three chief rivals—Trevino, Rodriguez and Charles—by two shots and set a tournament record of 13-under-par 200.

"Gary doesn't lose tournaments in this situation," Rodriguez said. "You have to take it away from him with birdies. He's really amazing, a 55-year-old man with a 40-year-old body."

After claiming his 157th career victory (nobody knows where that figure came from), Player said, "I've tried to take good care of my body. You can't walk into a drugstore and buy another one.

"Winning on the Senior Tour is just as difficult, just as exciting and rewarding, as [winning on the regular tour] ever was," he says. "Maybe even more so, because I know it's coming to an end. I figure I have six more years at the most.

"I want to get to be 60 years of age and have the young guys on the PGA Tour say of me, 'Isn't Player incredible?' I hope I'm as fit and playing as well when I get to be 60. That's a goal I really want, and the beauty of it is that it will keep me going for a long time."

THE HILL
BROTHERS

W hen Dave Hill started on the Senior PGA Tour in 1987, he owned 13 Tour victories and that was all.

"I was $265,000 in the hole," he says. "Divorce will do that to you. I was a nice guy. I gave her everything I had. And she was real nice. She let me have everything she didn't want."

When Mike Hill joined the Senior Tour two years later, he was running a little nine-hole golf course in Brooklyn, Michigan. His wife, Sandy, was teaching school and taking care of three children, and he says he had $16,000 in the bank.

By the end of 1991, Dave had earned $1.5 million and his younger brother had passed him, topping $2 million in Senior Tour earnings in just three years.

"It's a fantasy world," Dave said before the $1.5 million Vantage Championship in Clemmons, North Carolina. "Here I am at 53, playing in a golf tournament with a first prize of $202,500. Hell, I'd be out here if the total purse was half that. I bought some land and this is the only way I know how to pay for it."

The Hill brothers weren't raised in country club surroundings. They didn't teethe on a nine-iron, have their first lesson before the first grade and spend their high school days being chauffered to tournaments all over the state. No, the Hill boys grew up in a three-story colonial brick home on a 60-acre farm in Jackson, Michigan. They had cattle, pigs and horses, plus corn and vegetables. They learned all about farming and hard work from their father, who, in addition to the chores around the farm, held down a full-time job at the post office during the day and worked at a building-supply factory at night. He literally worked himself to death, dying at 58 after a protracted illness long before his boys reached the lofty status they enjoy today.

Fortunately for the Hill boys, the farm was adjacent to Jackson Country Club. They didn't play much as kids since they weren't allowed to play at Jackson and had to wait for a ride down to Al Sharp Public Course from their father. But they knew where to make a little money. The sixth hole at Jackson backed up to the Hills' farm; the boys would sit in a large maple tree and watch the players hit to the green. If the shots missed the green to the left, the ball would go into the woods. If the players couldn't find it, the Hills would wait until the players moved on to the next hole, then they'd scramble down and get the ball. When they had a full pail, they'd give it to their father, who would sell the balls at the post office.

Dave had a speech problem. He stuttered badly until the eighth grade from nervousness and was teased a lot in school. That made him a loner and also very combative. He says that his younger brother, Mike, who never saw a fight he didn't like, usually came to his rescue.

Dave's older brother, George, now an attorney, started caddying first because Dave wasn't allowed until he was nine. Then he had a chance to start playing on Mondays, caddies' day. Once he picked up a club regularly, Dave was a natural. Like Chi Chi Rodriguez, Walt Zembriski and others who started as caddies, the Hills learned

TWO OF GOLF'S MOST SUCCESSFUL
BROTHERS: *Both Mike (left) and Dave Hill
seem happy after Dave won the 1969 Buick
Open in Grand Blanc, Michigan.*

176

the game mostly from observation, watching older players and trying to imitate their swings. Soon Dave was competing in peewee tournaments and doing well, but it was only one of the sports he enjoyed. Although he never got very big, he played football and basketball, but he was known more for his hot temper than for his talent.

"My competitive spirit certainly was better suited to football and basketball," Dave says. "When I get mad on the golf course, which is frequently, I feel mean and want to fight, but I can't. Not that I'd ever whip anybody. I've probably had 400 fights in my life and haven't won one yet."

After high school, Dave stopped by the University of Detroit, but his heart and mind were always wandering to the golf course. He turned professional at age 21, but he made only $1,655 that year. After that one summer of seasoning, however, he blended right in on the PGA Tour, moving up to 46th on the money list. In 1961 he won the Home of the Sun Open in Denver. From then on, Hill, rated one of the best ball-strikers in the game, was a permanent member of the top 60 money winners.

Mike had avoided competing directly against his older brother when they were youngsters, and they went their separate ways after high school. When Dave went off to play on the PGA Tour, Mike joined the Air Force and spent 42 months in the service. He played very little golf before returning home and enrolling at nearby Jackson Junior College. From there it was on to Arizona State, but he came back home and returned to what he knew and loved best: farming.

"I didn't choose to compete with Davey when we were growing up," Mike says. "I didn't play junior golf; I played baseball and basketball. I guess I knew I wasn't as good as he was, so I went off in other directions. There was no rivalry. He could always beat me."

THE OTHER HILL: *Early in his career, Mike Hill always seemed to be chasing his older brother Dave, who already was a big winner.*

When Mike came home from college, he got various jobs that included driving a beer truck, hauling tires and working on the farm. Unlike his outspoken, controversial brother, Mike is the strong, silent type. He never backed down from a fight, and after being in the Air Force, then tossing tires and beer kegs around, he was built like a bull. Some of his fights around the Jackson beer halls are still legendary.

When Mike was 27, Dave came home from the Tour and told him to get a life, try the PGA Tour. He pointed out all the money there was out there (although he hadn't won a tournament that year, Dave finished 35th on the money list and earned a whopping $26,857).

"Davey told me I was wasting my time," Mike said while reminiscing before the 1990 U.S. Senior Open at Ridgewood Country Club in New Jersey. "I decided he was right. I was going nowhere doing what I was doing."

So he wiped the rust off his golf clubs and started practicing. It took him three tries at the Qualifying School before he finally earned his card in the spring of 1968.

The Hills made quite a team that year. Dave, who by now had won three times, was 48th on the money list with $34,036. Mike was 55th at $30,892, and he was very satisfied with his first year as a touring pro. It sure beat the hell out of lugging around cases of beer and tires.

Throughout his 14-year career, however, Mike never outgrew being "Davey's younger brother," and a rather large chip developed on his shoulder.

While Davey was making quips ("The golf swing is like sex in one respect: you can't be thinking about the mechanics of the act while you're performing") or popping off ("I tell the lady scorekeepers that if they can hear me cuss, they're standing too close; they've got to realize they're not at a church social"), Mike was answering questions like "Have you ever beaten Dave?"

In 1969, Dave was on top of the golf world. He won three tournaments—the Memphis Open for the second time in three years, the Buick Open and the 1VB Philadelphia Golf Classic. He finished second to Frank Beard on the money list with $156,423 and won the coveted Vardon Trophy for low scoring average with 70.344 for 90 rounds.

Meanwhile, Mike was struggling, barely making cuts and getting tired of hearing Davey this, Davey that, while he was packing his bags. He finished the year a frustrated, angry man, 97th on the money list at $16,239, wondering if maybe the old farm wasn't so bad after all. There, at least people left you alone.

"I learned to deal with it, though, accept it for what it was," Mike says. "I'm not like Davey. I've never run down anybody's golf course. I've never run people down."

While Mike brooded and seemed to be on the defensive, his older brother had no problems expressing his opinions on any subject or person that happened to come up. Once, when someone groaned that Gary Player was discussing wheat germ again, Hill shot back, "He runs, he lifts weights and eats health food. That's all well and good, but I get tired of hearing him brag about it. So what if he has the most perfect bowel movement on the Tour?"

Another time, on one of his favorite subjects, Hill expounded, "Doug Sanders has said he likes to have sex and a hot-tub bath every morning, then he's loose and ready to go. Of course, if Sanders had scored half as often with women as he claims he has, he'd be dead."

Golf finally got exciting for Mike in 1970 at the Doral-Eastern Open in Miami, where he was tied with Jim Colbert at three-under-par 139 after 36 holes. Mike came back with his second successive 69 to take a three-shot lead when no one else challenged, and then he shot a final-round 71 to win by four.

"Mike was as tight as I've ever seen anyone in that final round," says Bob Green, the Associated Press's longtime golf sage. "This was his chance. It was more than winning; it was getting out from under, although he must have known he'd always be 'the other Hill.' "

Mike won again in 1972, the first year the San Antonio-Texas Open was played at Woodlake Golf Club. He came to the tournament needing a high finish to boost him into the top 60 money winners and an exemption for the following year. He handled the pressure of a charging Lee Trevino on the final day to win by two strokes. For the year, however, he again was overshadowed by Dave, who won Monsanto and finished 18th on the money list at $98,464, compared with 33rd for Mike.

Mike's most rewarding year financially came in 1974, when he closed with a flourish, finishing second at San Antonio, tying his brother for second at Las Vegas and winding up fourth at the Southern Open to hike his season's earnings to $76,802. He appeared headed for an even better year in 1975 before his motorcycle accident on the farm. He fell and the kickstand tore into his right leg just above the knee, sidelining him for 12 weeks.

Although he threatened on several occasions after that, he didn't win again until the 1977 Ohio Kings Island Open at the Jack Nicklaus Golf Club in Mason, Ohio. His second-round 65 gave him a one-shot lead over Ben Crenshaw, but after Mike's 72 on Saturday, they were tied going into the final round. With Tom Kite reeling off birdie after birdie en route to a 62 in front of him Hill knew what he had to do and did it, shooting a nerve-wracking 64 that gave him a one-shot victory—his last and most impressive of a 14-year PGA Tour career.

"It was really a moral victory to win after five years," he says. "When you're on the downside and you can turn it around, it means something. It showed that I still had some heart."

After his Kings Island victory, Mike never cracked the top 100 on the money list again, and he dropped off the Tour when his brother did in 1982. Then it was back home, back to farming. He had gone full circle without causing much of a ripple, and he said he was

MIKE'S FIRST VICTORY: *Victory finally came to Mike Hill at age 31, when he rolled in this winning putt at the 1970 Doral Open in Miami.*

181

SANDRA APPROVES: *While his wife, Sandra, admires the biggest check of his career at that point, Mike Hill gives his victory speech at the 1977 Ohio Kings Island Open in Mason, Ohio. He beat Tom Kite by a stroke to earn $30,000.*

content to spend the rest of his life farming with his wife and three children.

Dave was just the opposite. Often there were tidal waves in his wake. The biggest, of course, came at the 1970 U.S. Open at Hazeltine Golf Club in Chaska, Minnesota, just outside of Minneapolis. Some say, facetiously, that the championship was won on the first hole. A gusting 40 mph wind that ripped tents, bent trees and even partially uprooted a section of the huge scoreboard greeted the golfers that day. With the gale at his back, somehow Britain's Tony Jacklin, obviously more used to these conditions that the Americans, managed to hold his shot to the first green and run in a birdie putt. He went on to be the only player to break par that day, and his 71 gave him a two-shot lead he never lost. The carnage was staggering. Jack Nicklaus shot 81, Gary Player 80 and Arnold Palmer 79. Jacklin was off and running, and nobody could catch him. Dave Hill came closest, finishing seven shots back at even-par 288. It was during his futile chase, with writers desperate for any angle, that Hill served them up a fat one that they blasted all over the country for days.

Following the second round, Hill was asked what he thought of the course, designed by famed architect Robert Trent Jones. Here's just a sampling.

- "It looks like a man destroyed a beautiful farm."
- "What it lacks is 80 acres of corn and a few cows."
- "Just because you cut the grass and put up flags doesn't mean you have a golf course."
- "The man who designed this course had the blueprints upside down."
- "Either of my little boys could build a better golf course. So could my wife and she doesn't know anything about golf."
- "If I had to play this course every day for fun, I'd find me another game."

Hill was fined $150 for his remarks by the U.S. Golf Association. His statements angered Hazeltine members and didn't exactly thrill Robert Trent Jones, either. But the insults still live in infamy, and whenever there is criticism of a U.S. Open course, someone is bound to say, "Wonder what Dave Hill would think of this goat yard?"

Surprisingly, in the summer of 1990—a year before the U.S. Open returned to Hazeltine—Reed MacKenzie, a member of Hazeltine's board of directors and general chairman of the 1991 U.S. Open, played a round with, he says, "two gentlemen who are very important to the history of Hazeltine." One was Rees Jones, Robert Trent Jones' son, who has redesigned the course. The other was Dave Hill.

ANOTHER TROPHY: *The Buick Open trophy was the second of three Dave Hill won in 1969, when he finished second on the money list with $156,423.*

"I not only made Hazeltine famous, it made me famous," Hill says. "Twenty years later, people are still talking about it. They still come up and ask me, 'What was the name of the place you called a cow pasture?' "

Obviously, the many severe doglegs, which have been eliminated, didn't present too much of a problem for Hill in 1970, but he says now it was a mater of total indifference that enabled him to shoot even-par.

"I really didn't give a damn," he says. "That's probably why I did so well, because I didn't care. I was hoping I'd miss the cut so I could go home after two days."

If Hill had missed the cut, there wouldn't be much to remember Hazeltine for—certainly not for a foreign player winning wire-to-wire with Nicklaus, Player and Palmer on the sidelines. For it was after he made the cut and was in contention that Hill was invited to the press tent and given a stage for his candid comments.

"That Saturday, there was a lot of mooing in the galleries," Hill says. "All my comments did was put pressure on me, more pressure than the fact that I was playing in the U.S. Open."

Hill recovered in time to win his favorite tournament, Memphis, for the third time and finish 10th on the money list. He earned a spot on the second of his three Ryder Cup teams in 1973, then started reducing his schedule—although he maintained his spot among the top 20 money winners for three more years. After his 1973 Ryder Cup performance, he took the rest of the year off to have knee surgery for removal of cartilage that had bothered him for some time.

"After I had knee surgery, one of my smart-assed fellow pros said, 'How's that going to help his head?' " Hill says. "I'm crazy, but I have an advantage over most people: I know it."

He returned in 1974 to win at Houston. From four shots back, he passed the four co-leaders with a sizzling 7-under-par 65, on the second round of a 36-hole final caused by Friday's rainout.

The following year he finished seventh in The Masters and PGA Championship, but he complained about his game, about his consistency, right up to his last tournament of the year, the Sahara Invitational in Las Vegas. There he strung together rounds of 68-66-67-69, then beat Rik Massengale on the first hole of a playoff and said, "My game is so bad, it's embarrassing. I haven't hit but four good shots all week."

A major milestone was reached in 1976, after Hill won his 13th tournament, the Greater Milwaukee Open. Six weeks later he tied for 22nd at the PGA Championship and became the 11th player to earn more than $1 million on the PGA Tour.

He knew how to win and how to celebrate. At the World Series of Golf one year, Trevino, who didn't back away from any tequila in those days, came up to Hill and said, "Baby, I counted 14 beer bottles in there with your fingerprints on them. That must have been some party."

During the 1988 Tournament of Champions at La Costa, where Hill would win by a shot over Miller Barber and Al Geiberger, Hill was talking in the lounge one evening; the subject, unsurprisingly, turned to drinking—which players were good at it and who couldn't handle it. Names like Frank Beard and Larry Mowry were thoroughly discussed, then someone asked Hill if he ever took a drink before playing. His response was classic: "You wouldn't expect me to go out there *alone*, would you?"

Between 1977 and 1981, Hill won only $63,290 as the steady downhill slide picked up momentum. So it was back to the farm for the Hill boys in 1982. And just as the good times were better for Dave, the bad times were worse. He had divorced his first wife in the early 1970s, married Sandi and moved to Denver. There were good times—plenty of vodka and tonics—and some not so good times.

"In 1982, I moved back to Jackson and bought some property," Dave says. "I had just gone through another divorce and didn't have any money, gave her everything. I was doing some corporate golf,

DAVE WINS BUICK: *Dave Hill waves to the crowd after sinking the winning putt at the 1969 Buick Open at Grand Blanc, Michigan.*

maybe 40, 42 days a year, probably making $85,000 to $100,000, which was basically just enough to pay the bills. I sure as hell wasn't banking any. The only dealings I had with the bank is when they wanted their money."

Two of Hill's first caddying clients turned out to be lifelong friends and generous benefactors.

"I started caddying for Al and Bob Glick at Jackson Country Club in 1956 when they were just starting Alro Steel," Dave says. "Now they've got 28 warehouses. They would always ask Mike or me to do outings for them."

Mike said he'd rather make $2,000 or so a day doing an outing than travel on the Tour and beat his head against the wall. He would go down to Florida—to the Glicks' plants in Orlando, Clearwater and Boca Raton—play golf with 6 to 10 customers and come home.

It was during this time that Mike made his retirement investment and achieved a goal he had dreamed about for 20 years—he bought a golf course. Well, not exactly a golf course, but a piece of land, perhaps something like the farm terrain that Hazeltine was built on. Anyway, he knew what he wanted to do with it.

"Some guys buy CDs. I bought land, about 300 acres," he says. "I didn't have the money to build on it right away, but I knew what I wanted: my own little golf course, a place to hang my hat."

Eventually, Hill's Heart of the Lakes was a reality. It wasn't much, a 2,800-yard nine-hole municipal course in neighboring Brooklyn, Michigan, but it was all his.

"I always wanted to run my own course," he says. "I bought it as a retreat. Now, with my winnings from the Senior Tour, I have been able to build the back nine: it's about 3,300 yards. When I finish playing, I'd still like to run it. I top-seed, fertilize and aerate the greens. That's part of the fun, watching it grow, develop. That's what I think about when I think about retiring."

So while Mike was running his little nine-holer, his older brother was regrouping, looking for something to do with his time. In between

HOW THE MONEY ROLLS IN: *Dave Hill reached a milestone in 1976, when he won for the 13th time and became the 11th player to earn more than $1 million. Ten years later, he was $265,000 in debt.*

golf outings, he decided to become a gentleman farmer, much to Mike's chagrin.

"I had to have something to do," Dave said with a shrug in the locker room one day at the Vantage Championship. "So I decided to farm with Mike. I'll tell you, I didn't think I could do that much hard work. Mike's only love is farming. I don't know shit about it. I just drive a big tractor for him.

"One of the funniest things that happened was one day, I had the tractor by myself. I'm cruising along, then I see I'm low on fuel, but what the hell, I'm in the middle of a field, I still had five gallons. Well, don't you know, I ran out of gas. Here I am out in the middle of nowhere. I found an extra gas can, but I couldn't get the son of a bitch started. Finally, Mike comes out. He's really pissed off that I

DAVE'S FAVORITE TOURNAMENT: *Dave Hill knocks in an 18-foot birdie putt on the fifth hole en route to an opening 67 and his third Danny Thomas Memphis Classic victory in 1970 at Memphis, Tennessee.*

can't start the thing. He said to leave it until the grapevines grow over it. To this day, the only thing I know about tractors is that they break down."

Fortunately, the Senior Tour was on the horizon. Although Dave hadn't worked on his game, he said he felt confident that once he got out there, got back in the routine, he could hold his own as he had done on the regular tour, when he was among the top 60 money winners for 17 consecutive years. He married Joyce and hit the road in 1987.

It didn't take him long to shake the cornstalks out of his hair and the hay off his shoes. Once he pulled that old baseball-style Wilson cap down around his ears, he was all business. He became eligible May 24 at the Silver Pages Classic in Oklahoma City; he shot 71-71-72 to tie for 29th and earn $1,887. The next week, at Denver Champions of Golf, he shot a final-round 69 to tie for 13th and pocketed $4,925. Then he let everyone know he was a force to be reckoned with the following week, when he shot 69-69-68 to finish 5th and earn $9,457 at the Senior Players Reunion at Bent Tree Country Club in Dallas. After a week off, he strung together three successive 69s for 4th place at the Greater Grand Rapids Open and picked up $14,800. That added up to $31,069 in four starts—more than he won in four of his last five years on the regular tour, and certainly more than he would ever earn planting corn.

"I wasn't really surprised," he says. "I had never been a practicer away from the course, anyway. I worked real hard on my game when I was at tournaments, but when I was home, I'd rarely touch a club. I figured these were the same guys I'd played against on the regular tour, and once I got my swing down, I figured I'd do all right."

That was just the beginning. After taking the month of August off, Dave came back strong, closing with a 69 to finish third, a stroke behind Gary Player and Bob Charles, at the PaineWebber World Invitational in Charlotte, North Carolina, and earned $18,750.

At the rich Vantage Championship, he fired a final-round 65 to get the second-place check of $81,000—the largest of his career.

"I can't believe it," he said that Sunday. "To be playing for this kind of money, to play under these ideal conditions and be treated so well. Well, it's more than any of us old guys deserve."

The Vantage is where Al Geiberger started his memorable rookie streak. Beginning with the Vantage, his first victory since the 1979 Colonial National Invitation, Geiberger won three of four starts before Dave Hill stopped him at the Fairfield Barnett Classic in Melbourne, Florida. Hill took the lead from Bobby Nichols with a second-round 66 at Suntree Country Club, then held off a charging Geiberger (who tied for second with Lee Elder) with a closing 68.

Dave wrapped up his sensational rookie season with a pair of 68s and a third-place finish at the GTE Kaanapali in Maui, Hawaii. That gave him $232,189—more than $75,000 better than his best year on the regular tour.

In 1988, Dave enjoyed his best year in golf: winning four times, finishing third on the money list with $415,594 and finishing second to Bob Charles in the race for the Byron Nelson Trophy for best stroke average at 70.40. He closed with a rush, finishing in the top five in 8 of his last 11 starts.

In the opening event, the winners-only Tournament of Champions at La Costa, Dave had the easiest victory of his career. After he opened with a 68 and added a 72 and 71 to match the numbers of Miller Barber, who started with a 69, heavy rain and hail fell on the plush resort just outside of San Diego. The fourth and final round finally was canceled at 4 P.M., with the scores reverting to the 54-hole totals.

"You win some, you lose some," Hill said afterward. "If you're out here long enough, everything will happen to you. I would have liked to play the last round with a one-shot lead—that's what's fun, to see how you hold up—but I'll tell you, it ain't no fun playing in hail."

At the Syracuse Classic in August, neither rain nor storm nor

IN TOP FORM: *Dave Hill enjoyed his best year in 1988, when he won four times on the Senior Tour and was third on the money list with $415,594.*

gloom of night could have kept Hill from winning after he fired a tournament-record 64 in the second round to build a three-shot lead over first-round leader Doug Dalziel. A final-round 68 in hot and humid weather gave Hill a five-shot victory over Bobby Nichols and Butch Baird. The following week he shot 64 again, but it came in the last round and fell two strokes shy of catching Orville Moody at the Greater Grand Rapids Open. Still on a roll, Hill finished with a

T I P

"At the 1989 PaineWebber Invitational at Quail Hollow Country Club in Charlotte, North Carolina, I came to the last hole tied with Bruce Crampton. The 18th hole there is a tough par-4, and I made it even tougher by driving it into a fairway bunker. I had 172 yards, but I hit a little four-iron about 4 or 5 feet from the pin and made the putt to win by a stroke. I was never a very good fairway bunker player, and more often than not I couldn't get the ball over the lip. I started working with Norman von Nida in the early 1970s, and he told me to dig right down to solid footing and make sure to keep my legs quiet. At Charlotte, I lowered my hands, moved the ball back a little bit in my stance and tried to think about Norman's advice. It's a tip I'll never forget— you've got to keep your legs quiet in a fairway bunker."

Dave Hill

65 two weeks later and picked up his third second-place check of the year behind Gary Player at the GTE North Classic in Indianapolis.

After Arnold Palmer won his 10th and last Senior PGA Tour event the next week at the Crestar Classic near Richmond, Hill came back to win for the third time that year at the PaineWebber Invitational in Charlotte, North Carolina. He opened with a pair of 68s to take a one-shot lead, then fought off Bruce Crampton's 66 with a closing 70 to win by a stroke.

Hill's fourth victory in 1988 came in the season-ending Mazda Champions at Dorado Beach in Puerto Rico, where he teamed up with Colleen Walker to breeze to a four-shot victory over host pro Chi Chi Rodriguez and gallery favorite Jan Stephenson. Hill and Walker combined for a 12-under-par 60 in the first round for a three-shot lead and never lost it. The $250,000 first prize was a fitting climax for Hill's greatest year.

There was a little more money ($488,541) but only two victories in 1989. At the Bell Atlantic/St. Christopher's Classic in Malvern, Pennsylvania, Hill was tied with Jim Dent, who was making his Senior Tour debut, after two rounds. Dent faded to a 71, but Rodriguez came on with a 67 to tie Hill. Then Dave won the playoff with a par on the third extra hole when Rodriguez made bogey.

In August, fortune smiled on Hill again at the Rancho Murieta Senior Gold Rush near Sacramento, California, when Orville Moody missed a 1-foot birdie putt on the 70th hole and lost by stroke. But Hill still had to make a tester on the last hole after leaving a 35-foot lag putt about 5 feet short.

"That wasn't any fun; that was work," he said afterward over a light beer. "This is a job for me now. We could go out right now with a six-pack and a cart and we'd have a pretty good time. But once you start playing before 30,000 people under all that pressure, it's not fun."

That's when Hill started talking about retirement again, and oddly, it was his last victory.

"I'm looking forward to farming now," Dave said, referring to his 330-acre cornfield about two miles from his brother's spread. "All you do is plant corn, then go out every day and see if it's come up. You can't screw that up.

"But you have to make it while you can on the Senior Tour; between 50 and 55 you gotta grind, play 30 tournaments a year and stash it away. It's a full-time job. It will be nice when I have enough where I can pick and choose, play 12 to 15 events. I'm counting the days. I'd rather be farming, drinking, playing cards and chasing Momma around the house—if I've still got the energy."

For Mike, it was 13 long years between his final victory on the regular tour at Kings Island in 1977 and his victory at the GTE Suncoast Classic at Tampa Palms in February of 1990.

He had several opportunities the previous year, when he won more money than any rookie ever had: $453,163. He was second at the Digital Classic by two shots to Bob Charles after opening with a 65. He came in third at the Sunwest Bank/Charley Pride Classic after closing with a 65.

"There were times I felt I was playing pretty well," he says. "But it just didn't happen. I played every week just trying to get into the top 10, because I figured sooner or later somebody would stub their toe and it would be my turn to win."

It was his turn at Tampa, although it didn't seem like it at the beginning of the week when he had muscle spasms.

"I would have gone home if it wasn't for the Centinela [Hospital] Fitness Trailer," he says. "Rob [Mottram] really did a good job of relaxing my muscle and getting me ready to play. Those guys do a fabulous job. I don't think the Senior Tour could exist without them."

After starting 68-69, Mike had a two-shot lead over Larry Mowry and Dale Douglass, but it was the irrepressible Lee Trevino who posed the biggest challenge. Although Hill had built a four-shot lead with four holes to go, it was a real struggle down the stretch. He bogeyed the 15th hole, pushed a drive into the woods and bogeyed the 16th. His lead was sliced in half.

"After that drive I got to thinking, 'Damn, am I ever going to hit another good shot?' " he says. Then came the moment of truth at the par-5 17th. Hill was facing an eight-iron third shot from 130 yards, and suddenly a nightmare flashed back from a year ago. From almost the same spot, Dave, who had a four-shot lead, hit two shots in the water for a triple bogey. He eventually lost a four-way playoff to Bob Charles.

"I thought about it," Mike admitted afterward. "I didn't want to repeat what Davey did. Nobody should have to go through what happened to him. All I knew was I had to get it somewhere where I had a chance to make birdie."

He dropped it five feet from the hole, and although he missed the putt, the pressure was off. He parred the par-3 18th hole, easily clearing the water in front of the green, and was met with a big hug from Dave, who had shot 71 to tie for 10th.

"It's great that we can both compete out here and root for each other," Mike says. "I know I can help him and he can help me, and it won't be bullshitting like you get from some guys. I hesitate to go to anybody except my real good friends for any advice. If I'm having a problem, I'll always go to Davey first.

"This really takes a load off," Mike said after his victory at Tampa. "Now, maybe some of my peers will see that I'm capable of winning."

If there were any doubters, they were eliminated when he shot 15-under-par at the GTE North Classic, then beat Bruce Crampton with a birdie on the first playoff hole.

"I knew I could be a winner," Mike says. "I played practice rounds with Davey, Lee and Gary and compared our games. There wasn't that much difference."

Mike went on to win again a month later at the Fairfield Barnett Space Coast Classic in Melbourne, Florida, where Dave had won his first Senior Tour tournament in 1987. This time, Mike was the last-round charger, overcoming a six-shot deficit in the last eight holes to overtake Bob Charles.

"When I started the last day, I didn't think I had a chance," Mike recalled the next week while tuning up for the $1.5 million Vantage Championship. "After nine holes, I was still six back, but then I birdied 10 and 11. I was playing with Davey and Gary Player, and as we were walking off the 11th green, Davey saw Charles hit into the water. He turned to me and said, 'If you make some birdies, you can win this thing.' "

With that sort of incentive, Mike started firing at the pins. He knocked an eight-iron 2 feet away at No. 16 and a pitching wedge 18 inches away on No. 17. After two-putting from 15 feet on the 18th hole, he waited to see what Charles and Dale Douglass were doing. Charles had become completely unraveled after his triple bogey on the par-5 11th, and he three-putted the 15th. Douglass birdied the 17th to catch Hill, but Charles' attempt to join the playoff failed when his 15-footer on final hole lipped out.

"This was the biggest lead I've ever blown in my life," said Charles, the leading money winner on the Senior Tour the two previous years. Hill easily won the playoff on the first hole with a two-putt par when Douglass ran a 40-footer 5 feet past and missed coming back for a bogey.

"I like to think I'm a pretty good Sunday player," Hill said at the Vantage. "My last four Sunday scores have been 68-64-69-64. I think I can play on Sundays as well as anybody."

He certainly made his case at the Security Pacific Classic in Los Angeles in early November, where he fired a blistering eight-under-par 63 to catch Player and win by a stroke. Hill had eight birdies, including four in a row, starting at No. 8. He sank a 20-footer and three 15-footers.

"I can't ever remember putting that well," he said. "This was my lowest final round on the Senior Tour. This has been a fairy-tale year. It's hard to imagine that I won four times after winning only three times my whole career. It's something I never would have dreamed of."

T I P

"When I won at Kings Island in 1977, I had actually played badly all year. I was home the week before, and I sat down and tried to figure out why I was hitting duck hooks and pull hooks. I decided to try and emphasize more of a one-piece takeaway with my swing. I thought possibly it would slow me down and help my tempo. I worked on that for two or three days and then went down and won the golf tournament in Ohio. I now try to work on something different every week that will help me play better. I think many amateurs in our pro-ams will roll the club away and break their wrists too quickly on the backswing. If they will take the club away with the hands, arms and shoulders together, they will get better extension, have a much smoother tempo overall and have more time to hit the golf ball. It should make them much better players in the long run."

Mike Hill

His biggest dream was yet to come. Five weeks later, at the Hyatt Dorado Beach course in Puerto Rico—the picturesque site where he teamed with Patti Rizzo to win the 1989 Mazda Champions—Mike Hill achieved the greatest victory of his life. It happened in dramatic fashion at the brand-new $1 million New York Life Champions, a season-ending event that brought together the top 30 money winners on the Senior Tour. Jack Nicklaus didn't show up, leaving 29 players on hand to play for a first prize of $150,000.

When Hill opened with a 69, it didn't look as though it would be his week. Besides, all the attention was focused on whether Lee Trevino could surpass the $1,165,477 that Greg Norman had won on the PGA Tour and become the No. 1 money winner. Trevino started with a 68 and trailed Dale Douglass and Al Geiberger by three. Then Hill put together one of his best rounds of the year, an eight-under-par 64 to tie Douglass, a stroke ahead of Rodriguez. Trevino added another 68 and was three shots back.

"I'll need a 65 to catch those guys," Trevino said, then went out and shot precisely that. It caught them but didn't pass them, and they finished in a three-way tie at 15-under-par 201. All three reached the green on the first playoff hole, with Trevino apparently having the edge, only 15 feet away. Douglass was about 20 and Hill at least 40.

Then Hill climaxed his greatest year by rolling in his 40-footer for a birdie. After watching Douglass and Trevino miss, Hill had his fifth victory of the year and earnings of $895,676, breaking Bob Charles' record of $725,887 set in 1989. Yet once again, Hill was overshadowed. The headlines the next day weren't about his second-round 64 and his 40-foot birdie putt. They focused instead on the runner-up: Lee Trevino had earned $95,000 and passed Norman to become the first Senior Tour player to win more money than the leader on the regular tour.

It was left for Trevino to add a fitting tribute to Hill's dream year. "Mike has a tremendous amount of drive and determination, and he strikes the ball as well as anyone on the Senior Tour," Trevino said. "Besides me, I think he made the biggest impact of anyone on our tour this year."

The next year was even better for Mike. Once again he won five times, starting with the Doug Sanders Kingwood Celebrity Classic, then adding the Ameritech Senior Open, the GTE Northwest Classic with a tournament record of 198 and the inaugural Nationwide Championship. He climaxed his greatest year with a successful defense of the $1 million New York Life Champions in Puerto Rico, coming from behind to beat Jim Colbert by two shots with three successive birdies starting at the 13th hole.

After hitting a 134-yard nine-iron within 8 inches of the cup for a clinching birdie on the final hole, Mike said, "This is, by far, the biggest thing that has happened to me in golf."

By winning the $150,000 first prize and another $150,000 for a season-long Vantage bonus pool, he became the second senior to reach the $1 million mark, finishing the year with $1,065,657. That topped regular tour leader Corey Pavin's $979,430 and made Mike golf's number-one money winner in 1991.

Yes, at long last, it is Dave who now is clearly "the other Hill."

Still, the feisty younger brother wasn't completely happy. "It bugs me when people ask me why I'm playing so well now," Hill said. "Like all of a sudden, I'm a good player. I won 3 times on the PGA Tour and had 10 or 11 seconds, so I must have been doing something right. Hey, it's a hell of a lot easier out here once you've made some money. Money frees up your swing. I don't have any pressure anymore. It's like in poker: if one guy has $30 to play with and the other has $300,000, who do you think is going to win?"

So now Mike had enough to put the finishing touches on his pride and joy, Hill's Heart of the Lakes. He can relax and enjoy his peak years on the Senior Tour with the knowledge and satisfaction that he can go back to farming whenever he chooses.

"I love it at home, but you've got to strike while the fire's hot," he says. "To do well out here, you have to play regularly. You can't come out every three weeks. My muscles will get screwed up from farming and I'll start shooting 74, 75. I don't want that. But you can't play every week or you'll go brain dead and wind up just going through the motions.

"That's what makes farming so nice. It's tranquil; you can get on that old tractor and ride all day without anyone messing with you. Growing corn is like mining gold: you just sit there and watch it come up. I like to watch things grow. All you need is a bunch of money."

When asked how much it takes to run a successful farm, Dave quickly interjects with one of his favorite jokes.

"Did you hear the one about the farmer who inherited a million dollars? His friends asked him what he was going to do with the money, and he said, 'Oh, I don't know. Guess I'll just keep farming until it's all gone.' "

JIM DENT

Twenty-five years ago, Jim Dent's job was carrying trash out of his friend's bar on Crenshaw Boulevard in Los Angeles. The PGA Tour wasn't even a dream. He loved golf, but qualifying for the Tour seemed out of the realm of possibility for a muscular black man who had never had any formal training in the game and certainly didn't have the financial backing to go on the road.

Dent was working nights for his friend, Mo Stephenson, so he could play golf during the day at the various public courses in the Los Angeles area. He was single, without responsibility and, seemingly, without a future.

By the end of the 1991 season, after just 31 months on the PGA Senior Tour, he had a wife, two teenage children and $1.5 million in official prize money. He also has a contract with Cadillac, a clothing deal with Bullet Golf and many offers to do clinics and outings worth at least $150,000 annually.

"The Senior Tour is the greatest thing since heaven," he says. "Not in my wildest dreams did I imagine making money like this. I thank the PGA Tour every night before I go to sleep for doing this for us."

Because of his background (growing up in a broken home as part of a large family), his lack of lessons, poor practice facilities and no financial support, it took Dent a lot longer than most players to learn how to win. He always could hit the ball as far as anyone, but he never learned the short game, never developed the soft touch around the greens that is essential to winning on the PGA Tour. As a result, he played 18 years and never won, never really came close.

Once he got professional help and started working on his chipping and putting conscientiously, his overall game improved immensely. During a 15-month period, beginning with his victory in the 1989 MONY Syracuse Senior Classic June 25 at LaFayette Country Club in Syracuse, he won six titles. He was Rookie of the Year on the Senior Tour in 1989 and among the top 10 money winners in 1990 and 1991 with annual earnings of more than $500,000.

Back in Los Angeles, the biggest thing that had ever happened to him was receiving $25,000 for winning the Queen Mary Open, one of three local tournaments he entered every year. That was the highlight, but there were plenty of lowlights. Mostly, though, it was the same old routine. Dent would get up at five-thirty every morning to be ready when Stephenson came by to pick him up and take him to Compton Community College. There they could go out to the track and football field and whale away at golf balls from seven to nine o'clock before classes began and the physical education courses took over the field.

"He would stand at one end, and I'd stand at the other with my shag bag, and we'd hit balls back and forth," Dent recalls. "Not a lot of finesse, but it was sure fun to see how far I could hit it. After a while, though, it started me thinking about hitting the driver and

BIG BOOMER: *"Not a lot of finesse, but it was sure fun,"* Jim Dent says of his early days of driving balls at Compton Community College in Los Angeles.

making it do something: left to right, or right to left. I couldn't just keep pounding it."

At six foot three and 225 pounds, Dent could pound it with anybody, and he could always find a game when he left Compton in the morning and headed to the many public courses in the area. One of the courses he frequented was Rancho Park on West Pico Boulevard, where the Los Angeles Open was played from 1956 to 1972. It was there in 1969 that Charlie Sifford, one of the black pioneers on the PGA Tour, defeated Harold Henning in a playoff for his second and last Tour victory. (He also won the 1967 Greater Hartford Open, shooting a final-round 64.)

Sifford, whose trademark is keeping a cigar in his mouth while he plays, was one of the originals when the Senior Tour began in 1980. At the age of 58, he won the Suntree Classic in Melbourne, Florida (now the Fairfield Barnett Space Coast Classic). In the other tournament on the two-event schedule that year, the Atlantic City International, he fired a closing eight-under-par 63 but lost to Don January.

Still active on the Senior Tour in 1991 at age 69, Sifford won $96,746 in the Vantage Classics competition for players over 60, plus $65,201 in official earnings. His best year on the Senior Tour was 1985, when he was 18th on the money list with $104,294. In 1990 his career earnings finally topped the $1 million mark. Sifford, a native of Charlotte, North Carolina, who now lives in Kingswood, Texas, narrowly missed winning the 1990 Vantage driving accuracy title for the second year in a row.

"Aw, hell, Charlie hasn't hit anything but an iron off the tee since August," Lee Trevino said with a laugh in the locker room at the Vantage Championship in October 1990 when asked if he could top Sifford's percentage of fairways hit. Sifford just laughed and waved his cigar at the Merry Mex before attacking the buffet table. Finally, his plate overflowing, he turned to Trevino and said, "Hey, whatever it takes. You, more than anybody, should know that. You've played that way all your life."

Trevino said he might have a chance to pass Sifford if Charlie ever went to a wood off the tee, but that he had no shot of ever passing Dent for driving distance.

"That man doesn't play the same game the rest of us do," Trevino said. "And now, damn it, he's gotten a lot smarter, now that he's learned to manage the golf course. He's always had the talent to win. He has a tremendous advantage because he can reach all the par-5s in two. It's like playing against Nicklaus or [Greg] Norman. Now that Jim has improved his short game, he's a threat to win every week."

It wasn't like that, of course, when Dent was knocking around Los Angeles. But the more he played and practiced in the mornings with Stephenson, the more he started dreaming of the PGA Tour.

"Mo started me thinking about the Tour," Dent says. "He told me I wasn't going anywhere, doing anything, working at his bar. That was deadendsville. But when you're single, you don't care. I didn't have to be to work until five o'clock, so I could play every day."

Finally, Dent decided to try the Qualifying School, but he failed three times before finally getting his playing card in time for the 1971 season. At last he had a chance to escape the dreary lifestyle he had fallen into. Finally he had an opportunity to cash in on all that strength, that power, that ability to hit a golf ball as far as anyone he had ever played with.

It was a long way from Augusta, Georgia, one of golf's most famous addresses. He was born and raised there, but he hasn't lived at the home of The Masters since quitting Paine College after a few months of his freshman year. "Augusta is a good place to be from," Dent says, smiling. But it has to have a warm spot in his heart because that's where he first picked up a club—not to swing, but to carry for somebody else. Many players, such as Chi Chi Rodriguez, Dave Hill and Walt Zembriski, got their start in golf from caddying, but all Dent got for his first effort was abuse.

"The first time I caddied, I got a whuppin'," Dent says. "My aunt [his mother died when he was eight] had told me not to. She said if I hung around with caddies, I'd learn how to gamble and drink. You know, a lot of those guys had those brown paper bags in their back pockets, and they were always talking about bettin'."

"But you know how it is. If your momma tells you not to cross the street, not to go a certain place, if you're an adventurous kid, sooner or later you'll go there."

If Dent hadn't decided to try caddying, if his buddies hadn't encouraged him to join them, he might never have gotten inside those ominous white gates that lead to famed Augusta National Golf Club, the immaculate site of The Masters. Blacks were not admitted unless they were working. In those days, the PGA Tour players were not allowed to bring their own caddies; they had to use caddies from Augusta. So there always was work at The Masters.

In 1956, Dent caddied for Bob Rosburg, now a golf commentator for ABC television. "We shot 41 on the back nine Sunday or we might have won it," Dent recalls. In 1958, he caddied for PGA Tour Rookie of the Year Bob Goalby, who would win the coveted green jacket 10 years later when he apparently tied Roberto De Vicenzo but was awarded the victory when the Argentinean signed an incorrect scorecard. Tommy Aaron, his playing partner, had put down four for De Vicenzo for the par-4 17th hole, although Roberto had birdied it, so even though Aaron affixed 65 as the total, the figures added up to 66. In the excitement of the moment, De Vicenzo signed the incorrect card, and although the officials searched for a way out, they finally were forced to honor the rule and award Goalby the championship.

"I remember Dent, I really do. He was a lazy bum and I never would have rehired him," Goalby says with a laugh during a pro-am cocktail party. "No, seriously, he was fine. I remember all my caddies at Augusta. They were all good. They knew the breaks on the greens, and I sure needed help reading those greens."

Golf was a source of income, but Dent admits he had no great love for the game when he was growing up. He was a football player, both offensive and defensive end for Lucy Laney High, which didn't even have a golf team.

"We had a hell of a team," he says. "Our quarterback was a

Lee Trevino

Orville Moody

Al Geiberger

Chi Chi Rodriguez

Gary Player

Jim Dent

Dave Hill

Walt Zembriski

Mike Hill

Arnold Palmer

Jack Nicklaus

great passer. He went to Maryland State. Our star, though, was Emerson Boozer, who went on to play for the New York Jets. We beat a team 73–0 once at homecoming, and he scored six touchdowns."

The more Dent caddied, the keener his interest in golf became. He and his cousin started sneaking onto the 16th hole of Augusta Country Club, which borders Augusta National, late in the afternoon and banging balls around until it got dark. After Dent got his first set of clubs when he was about 15, he used to go to Augusta Golf Course, a municipal layout known as the "Cabbage Patch," every afternoon. Later he met a friend who could get on the Fort Gordon course at a nearby army base, and that was the ultimate.

"There wasn't much television in those days, no golf on at all when I was growing up," he says. "I knew about Charlie Sifford and Peter Brown, but that was about all. If I hadn't caddied at The Masters, I wouldn't have known any of the players. As it was, I got to see all the great players: Snead, Palmer, Player. To have caddied and now be out playing with these guys, don't you think that's a thrill?"

After high school, while some of his teammates were going away to college, Dent went to Paine, a small liberal arts school right in town. He didn't stay long. Dent decided he had had enough of Augusta, so he packed his bags and headed for Atlantic City, where the action was.

He landed a job at the Smithfield Inn on Mays Landing as a waiter, the ideal job because it left his days free, and by now he had fallen deeply in love with the game of golf. He couldn't think of anything he'd rather do than stand up on the tee and launch one of his long, high, booming drives. He impressed people wherever he went and drew the respect he wanted so badly as a young kid on his own.

"I played every afternoon until three or three-thirty because I didn't have to be to work until four-thirty," he says. "I'd play all day, then bus tables at night. I was young; I never got tired."

What he got tired of was working indoors in the summertime. "I got the bug. I felt like I was in jail, working inside and looking

MONDAY QUALIFIER: *Having to qualify for tournaments on Monday taught Dent how to compete. He worked hard to stay on the PGA Tour in his early days.*

210

out the window," he says. "I wanted to be outside in the nice weather. I got lucky: I met a guy, Mo Stephenson, who offered me a job in Los Angeles."

So it was off to Los Angeles, where he would make his home until he finally passed the PGA Tour Qualifying School on the fourth try and went out on Tour in 1971. It seemed pretty easy at first. In his first tournament, Dent made the cut at the Los Angeles Open. The following week, he made the cut at the Bing Crosby National Pro-Am at Pebble Beach, California. "Nothing to this game," he thought. Then he learned how difficult it can be on Tour. At the Phoenix Open, he shot two-under-par 140 for the first two rounds and missed the cut. That first year, he made only $7,101. He had earned more than that carrying out trash.

"My goal every week was to finish in the top 25 because you were exempt for the next tournament. When you were near the cut on Friday, that was real pressure," he says. "If you missed, it was the Monday qualifying route and that was really rough."

Those who came up the hard way, as Dent, Rodriguez, Trevino and others did, had to worry about making the cut to survive, to eat. When your checkbook doesn't have any commas in it and you're facing another week on the road without a paycheck, those three-footers will have your knees knocking. Most of the players nowadays never face that kind of pressure: they start with financial backers, and all they have to do is crack the top 125 on the money list to be exempt for the following year.

Raymond Floyd, captain of the 1989 Ryder Cup team, thinks the old system was better for developing tough competitors. After the United States lost two Ryder Cup matches in a row before tying the European team 14-14 at the Belfry in Sutton Coldfield, England, in 1989, Floyd talked about the days he and Dent, among others, were trying to carve out a living.

"The Monday qualifiers taught you how to compete, how to be

tough," Floyd said. "There would be 120 guys for 10 spots and it was one day only. If you didn't bring your A game that day, you were out of work for a week. You learn a lot about playing under pressure, and I think it made us tougher competitors. Nowadays, the young players have never experienced that. Once they make the top 125, they're set for a year."

Dent only enjoyed that luxury once in his 18-year career. His ultimate goal each year was to finish among the top 60 and be exempt the following year, but the only time he did it was in 1974, when he finished 59th with $48,486. The following year he tied for sixth at his favorite tournament, the Los Angeles Open, but slipped to 69th on the money list. In 1977, he tied for third at the Ohio Kings Island Open, where he closed with a 66 and picked up the biggest check of his career until then: $8,850. He had three other top-10 finishes that year, but he still made just $46,411 and missed the top 60 by 4 spots. In 1979, he had only 1 top-10 finish in 31 starts—a tie for eighth at the Byron Nelson Classic—and plunged to 109th on the money list.

In the next nine years, he only bettered that feeble effort once (82d in1982) and clearly was on the edge of falling completely off the Tour. Even when the rule changed to exempt players in the top 125, he didn't make it his last four years.

Looking back, he was only in serious contention twice, and those were long shots at best. The first time, he tied for second behind Jack Nicklaus at the 1972 Walt Disney World Classic, where Nicklaus was 21-under-par while winning the second of three consecutive Disney titles. The other was that third at Kings Island, when he started the last round four shots out of the lead and trailing four players, including Mike Hill, who won with a closing 64.

It was hardly a career that inspired any sort of hope for the Senior Tour. The old-timers in the locker room already had embraced the motto "If you couldn't beat us when you were young, you ain't going to beat us when you're old."

When Dent bottomed out in 1987, entering only six tournaments and making the cut once—a tie for 36th at the Pensacola Open, near his home in Tampa, Florida—the only alternative was the J. C. Goosie Space Coast mini-tour in Florida. A fellow still has to eat, and with children 14 and 11, what else was Dent going to do?

It was then that Dent's frustrating career began to change. Just as Moody came back from the dead when he discovered the long-shafted putter, so Dent was revived when he finally realized that to be successful, to score, to be a contender, he had to forget about those enormous drives and start concentrating on his short game.

"Hey, I was a big hitter, and long-ballers don't work on their short game," Dent says. "What you do best, you practice the most. What you do the worst, you don't want to practice. You don't see the big hitters in baseball work on their bunting, do you? Did Willie Mays bunt? Did Mickey Mantle bunt?"

It was that kind of thinking that kept Dent out of the top 60 throughout his career, that kept his name off the leader boards, that prevented him from cashing in on his long drives. It provided fathers everywhere with the perfect example to show their young sons: "See, son, he's the longest hitter but he doesn't win. Remember, when you're playing, it's not how far you hit it, it's how straight."

At age 48, Dent hit the mini-tour with all the up-and-coming young hopefuls. He played the Space Coast tour for two years without any great success. But he was living in Tampa, and most of the tournaments were within 80 miles of his house. So he followed the path that Walt Zembriski had taken in the early eighties, one that eventually led to the riches of the Senior Tour for another guy who couldn't win on the PGA Tour.

"It was mostly young kids on their way up, so I guess us old guys sort of stood out," Dent says, smiling. "There weren't many 48-year-olds out there, playing out of the trunks of their cars. So I put up $300 to play 36 holes and the purse was $25,000. You could pick up

$5,000 if you won, but it was a tough league. I shot 131 once and lost. But it kept you in shape and kept you competitive and that's what you needed."

Playing only two days a week, Dent had plenty of time to kill, and that's when he made the commitment that changed his life. He finally decided that, well, perhaps a little chipping practice wouldn't hurt. Come to think of it, Mantle did lay down a few drag bunts, didn't he?

"I had five days with nothing to do, and as I sat and watched those purses grow on the Senior Tour, I thought, 'Those courses are so short; maybe I should work on my short game.' It wasn't doing me any good to hit the longest drive if I couldn't hit the greens with my second shot and then couldn't get up and down. Even on the mini-tour, making pars wasn't good enough."

With Homero Blancas, a deft chipper who was Rookie of the Year on the PGA Tour in 1965, willing to help, Dent began his reclamation project. Blancas had won four times on the Tour, including a memorable one-shot victory over Lee Trevino and Gene Littler at the 1970 Colonial National Invitation in Fort Worth, Texas. He had also played on the 1973 Ryder Cup team. He, too, was counting the days until his 50th birthday, but until then, well, why not help the big guy who couldn't seem to get the ball near the hole?

"Homero really helped me a lot," Dent says. "And I watched Phil Rodgers around the greens. Pretty soon, I got to where I thought I could chip pretty good. And, of course, as soon as I started chipping better my putting came around."

Now Dent was ready for the Senior Tour. He looked out there and knew he could hit it farther than anyone, but hey, he could do that on the other tour, and what did it get him? So as he prepared for his new career, he continually thought about his short game. The long game would take care of itself.

His long-awaited debut came at the Bell Atlantic/St. Christopher's Classic in Malvern, Pennsylvania, on May 10, one day after his 50th birthday. He shot an opening-round 69 and followed with another to share the second-round lead with Dave Hill, a shot in front of six players. On the final day, Hill shot 68. Dent had 71 and collected $21,800.

"I didn't win, but I proved to myself that I could play out here," Dent said at the time. "I didn't play badly the last day; Davey just played better. And hey, it has been a long time since I won $20,000." In fact, it was his biggest paycheck ever. He was on his way.

The following week, at the NYNEX/Golf Digest Commemorative, Dent was two-over-par, but that just got him a tie for 32nd at the 6,545-yard Sleepy Hollow Country Club in Scarborough, New York. The courses were shorter, but he was learning that chipping and putting were the name of the game. The next week the putter was working, and Dent tied for 5th at the Southwestern Bell Classic in Oklahoma City. Again he let down in the final round, following a 69-70 with a 74. He was playing well and making good money ($12,800), but he was not yet ready to win.

After two weeks of finishing back in the pack, Dent fired a final-round 62 in the 16-hole (2 holes were damaged by water) Northville Long Island Classic, and he was brimming with confidence when he drove to upstate New York for the MONY Syracuse Classic. A first-round 69 put him three strokes behind leader Dick Hendrickson, and even a 68 on Saturday left him five shots back. Then, the guy who had faded in the final rounds the first two times he got in contention came up with a sizzling 64 to pass a host of players, including Gene Littler and Phil Rodgers, to win by a stroke over Al Geiberger with a 15-under-par 201. It was the best final round by a winner all year. First prize was worth $45,000, giving Dent more money in one week than he had won in any year since 1984. He had arrived.

"I thought I could win out here, and that proved it," Dent says. "I worked so hard to get ready that I kind of anticipated it. I figured if I was going to do anything on the Senior Tour, it would have to be early in my career. I had my son James with me, and it was really gratifying to win with him there."

A month later at the Newport Cup, Dent won again, once again coming from behind on Sunday, this time with a six-under-par 66 to make up three strokes on Harold Henning and two on Hendrickson. First place was worth $41,500. In the span of four weeks, he had won more money than he had in any year on the PGA Tour. A tie for 2nd with another promising rookie, George Archer, at the GTE West Classic in December, and a tie for 11th in the season-ending GTE Kaanapali Classic in Maui, Hawaii, boosted Dent's winnings to a whopping $337,691, placed him 12th on the money list and earned him Rookie of the Year honors.

As 1990 approached, the long-hitting Dent—who hadn't seemed to lose any distance from his days on the regular tour, but now had confidence in that elusive short game he could never master—was a force to be reckoned with. But the year started with a disaster, a shocking experience he found difficult to forget.

With three holes to play in the opening event of the year, the Royal Caribbean Classic at Key Biscayne, Florida, he had a five-shot lead over Lee Trevino and seemed destined to start the season with a victory. Then he completely unraveled.

At the 16th hole, he hooked his drive to the edge of a hazard, had to chip out and made bogey. He three-putted the 17th hole for another bogey. Meanwhile, Trevino had made two birdies, and Dent's lead had shrunk to a single shot going into the par-5 finishing hole. His driver, his best weapon, cost him again. He snapped his drive into the water, made double bogey and lost when Trevino made a routine par.

"I just collapsed the last three holes and paid the penalty," Dent says. "It was one of those things you see other people do and think, 'I'd never let that happen to me,' but it did. I've just got to forget about it—you can't think about spilled milk—but as hard as you try,

THE SHORT GAME: *As the Senior Tour approached, Dent knew he had to polish his short game if he was to be successful. With the help of Homero Blancas, he did.*

you can't completely get it out of your mind, either. But I came back the next week at Tampa and finished 10th."

A month later, Dent got another test under pressure, and this time he was up to the task. Despite gusty winds that kept the other contenders from making a charge, Dent shot a final-round six-under-par 66 to overcome a three-shot deficit and win the Vantage at the Dominion by three over Harold Henning.

"Give Jim credit," Henning said afterward. "He did today what he didn't do a month ago. He made the shots when it counted."

In one torrid stretch, Dent overtook the leaders and pulled away. He sank a 15-foot birdie putt at the par-3 5th hole, then eagled the 6th with a 350-yard drive and a nine-iron to within 2 feet. He also birdied the 9th, 10th and 11th holes, chipping in from 40 feet at No. 10, to take a three-shot lead that he protected very well this time.

"Once I got to 10-under-par with the birdie at No. 9, I told myelf this was my tournament to win or lose," he says. "Then I birdied the next two holes. Anytime you win, it makes up for the one that got away, but I'm glad Lee didn't show up and I didn't have to beat him."

There was added pressure at the MONY Syracuse Classic in June. Dent played the role of defending champion for the first time in his life, and he was the favorite because of the course's five par-5s. Nicklaus couldn't have played it better.

Dent opened with a 66 to tie Mike Hill, Larry Mowry and Walt Zembriski, a shot behind Dick Hendrickson, who at six foot seven and 270 pounds is one of the few players who dwarf Dent. In the second round, Dent added a 67 and moved into a tie with Hill at 11-under-par 133. George Archer, playing ahead of Dent, made a charge Sunday, shooting 65 and missing a 12-foot birdie putt on the last hole. Dent held him off with a 66 thanks to a red-hot putter.

"If it wasn't for my putting, I would have finished behind Archer," Dent says. "I haven't had a putting round like that under pressure."

Dent attributed his putting that week to being paired with Jack Nicklaus at the Senior Players Championship the week before in Dearborn, Michigan. Nicklaus put on one of the great putting exhibitions of his glorious career that week to win going away with a

T I P

"In my rookie year on the Senior Tour, I was at the MONY Syracuse Senior Classic in Syracuse, New York. Coming down the stretch on the final day, I was faced with a difficult second shot that would have been hard to get close to the flag due to the position of the pin. My goal was just to put the ball somewhere on the green and give myself an opportunity to make a birdie. I hit the shot 40 feet from the pin and holed the putt that won the golf tournament. My advice is, in certain situations, just get the ball on the green and give yourself a chance. Amateurs tend to want to always try to get the ball close to the hole on every approach shot. The putt will go in from anyplace. Just be patient."

Jim Dent

WINNER AT LAST: *Dent puts a hat on his happy son, Jim, Jr., after shooting a final-round 64 to win the* MONY *Syracuse Classic.*

record-breaking 27-under-par 261. "I picked up something from watching him. I'm not sure what, but I've putted great ever since."

Trevino was playing with Nicklaus in the last round at the Senior Players Championship and doing his best to catch the Golden Bear. But after Nicklaus sank another long birdie putt, Herman Mitchell, Trevino's big-bellied, longtime caddie, said, "Forget it. The only way we got a chance to win is if he don't sign his scorecard."

Two weeks later, at the U.S. Senior Open at historic Ridgewood Country Club in Paramus, New Jersey, Dent had the chance of a lifetime to win a major championship. As a rookie at the U.S. Senior Open the previous year, he had tied for third with Dale Douglass at four-under-par 284 while Orville Moody was outdueling Frank Beard at Laurel Valley in Ligonier, Pennsylvania, so he felt confident he could do well.

Dent started with a solid 68 to tie local favorite Walt Zembriski, Charlie Coody, Ken Still and former stockbroker John Paul Cain, a shot behind the front-running Trevino. A second 68 cleared away some of the debris, leaving Dent alone in second place, still a shot behind Trevino.

Back at the hotel that night, Dent stepped out of his room into the hall and, with his keys back on the dresser drawer, the door began swinging shut.

"I saw it closing and tried to yank the chain. I caught my finger in the door and split it open," Dent says. "It took 10 stitches to close it up. But it didn't bother me the next day; they numbed it up for me."

Playing with his right forefinger bandaged, Dent hung on with a 72 as the pressure tightened Saturday. Trevino slipped to a 73, but two great champions, Nicklaus and Player, responded as they usually do in major championships. Nicklaus holed a 23-footer for birdie at No. 2 and a 45-footer from the front fringe for an eagle at the par-5 fourth; he was off and running toward a 67. Player wasn't as flashy, but his four birdies in a bogey-free round gave him a 68 and a chance at his second major championship of the year. He had outdueled Nicklaus and Trevino to win the PGA Seniors Championship in April at Palm Beach Gardens, Florida.

So going into the final round, Nicklaus stood at 9-under-par 207, a stroke in front of Player, Trevino and Dent. After a rain delay early in the afternoon, Dent birdied the second and third holes and was tied with Trevino at 10-under, two shots in front of Nicklaus and Player. Dent missed the green and bogeyed the par-3 fifth hole, but he came back with a birdie at No. 6 and was still two ahead of Nicklaus and Player, a shot behind Trevino.

"I was really playing good until the eighth hole," Dent says. "I was 2-under and had a little seven-iron to the eighth green. I missed the green, chipped within four feet and missed. Then on the next hole, I drove into the rough, flew the green with my second shot and made another bogey. That was it. I had six bogeys in the last 11 holes. I don't know what happened."

What happened was that Dent's past caught up with him. Nicklaus, Player and Trevino have been battling each other in major championships for 20-some years. When the pressure felt like 40 fathoms, they had been there. Dent hadn't. This wasn't the Syracuse Classic; this was the U.S. Senior Open.

"Sure, I thought about being the first black man to win a U.S. Open. I thought about it at Laurel Valley the year before," Dent says. "I'm not into that sort of stuff, but I think it would be great. It would mean a whole lot to me because it might get more black kids interested in golf, bring more of them to the golf courses. That's what would be important to me."

Undaunted by his 10th-place finish, Dent stayed strong and came back two weeks later to win the Kroger Classic at the Jack Nicklaus Sports Center in Kings Island, Ohio. Once again he was chasing Trevino, and this time he caught him with a final-round 66.

Dent opened with a 67 and trailed Trevino and Dave Hill by two when Saturday's round was rained out. On a clear, breezy Sunday,

Dent started like a whirlwind, making birdies on the first four holes. Trevino bogeyed the third hole to fall two behind Dent, and he never rallied, shooting 71.

The Sports Center course brought back memories to Dent and showed just how far he had come since his frustrating days on the regular tour. It was at this same site 13 years earlier that Dent had battled Mike Hill down the stretch, shooting a final-round 66 and still losing to Hill's 64 in the 1977 Ohio Kings Island Open. Ironically, Hill and Dent were paired in the final round again and Dent remembered back. He should have: his third-place check of $8,850 was the biggest of his PGA Tour career.

Now first prize was $90,000—more than double what Dent made in some of his best years on the regular tour. The victory put him over the top. He had said that his goals for 1990 were to win two tournaments and make more money than he had as a rookie. Now he had three victories. A fourth win, when he came from six shots back with a final-round 65 at the Crestar Classic near Richmond in late September, would boost his season's earnings over the $600,000 mark and nudge him ever so close to the magical million-dollar plateau, which he passes with a season's earnings of $693,214.

"I told Mike before we started that maybe things will turn around a bit this time," Dent said. They certainly have for this former Augusta caddie, who had struggled for so long and faced so many frustrations before.

Now this onetime trashman with bulging muscles is having a new home built in an affluent Augusta suburb, buying some duplexes in Atlanta for investment purposes and financially securing the future of his children.

"They say good things come to those who wait," Chi Chi Rodriguez once said, "but not unless they're working while they're waiting. It took Jim a long time, but once he started working it really paid off."

WALT
ZEMBRISKI

W alt Zembriski was toiling, as usual, high above the busy streets of New York when he saw one of those horrid flashes, an instant nightmare he'll never forget. His friend, Red Dalton, with whom he had just had a sandwich 20 floors below, was falling to his death.

Zembriski saw death several times during his eight years of walking the high beams as a steelworker in New York, but he had steady work, the money was good ($13 an hour) and that's what his wife wanted him to do. Besides, it gave him time to play golf in the afternoons.

Golf. That was the real passion in his life. That's what he lived for, dreamed about, but not when he was straddling those narrow steel beams.

"You can't be daydreaming up there," he says. "You get up at six in the morning and you never know what's going to happen by the end of the day. But you have to have your mind on your work.

And there's no place to sit on your ass. That eliminates a lot of guys right there.

"I'll never forget that day when Red fell. We had been talking at lunch, and he was talking about getting his grandson a pony. We talked a lot about his grandson and by two o'clock that afternoon he was dead. I don't like to talk about it, but I'll never forget it."

A lot of memories from those years on the high beams are still etched in Zembriski's mind. He remembers the Indians who walked seemingly without fear when the wind whistled through the steel structures and everybody else adjourned for cocktails.

"Those Indians, they'd walk around up there like it was nothing. Wind, cold, nothing bothered them," Zembriski says. "They were the best damn workers—they were fast, they got things done—but they drank so damn much, you never knew if they were going to show up or not. They'd get paid and you wouldn't see them for two or three days. Half the time they'd spent the weekend in jail, then they'd come back to work Monday like nothing ever happened. They were good guys, but you didn't want to go drinking with them. They were wild, I mean crazy."

While his pals hit the saloons after work, Zembriski hit the links. Unless it was raining, he'd get to the local public course by three-thirty in the afternoon and play until it was dark. He could never get enough practice. "I could usually get a game, then after 18 holes when the other guys went home, I'd go hit balls. When it got too dark for that, I'd go to the putting green. A lot of guys needed beer after a day on the high beams. I needed golf. That was my relief."

Zembriski went to amazing lengths to play on Saturdays. "You would have to get in line Friday night to get a decent tee time," he says. "We had a foursome and we'd take turns. Once a month, I'd have to stay in line out in the street all night. You'd get a six-pack and a blanket and wait for the sun to come up. I used to get there about midnight, and sometimes you could steal a couple of hours of sleep. As soon as the sun was up, my buddies would come. Still, it was really crowded, took us more than five hours to play. We used to carry a deck of cards and play gin rummy while we waited on the tee."

One day made the Z man, as the players call him, give all this up, one day he realized the money wasn't that good, the free time to play golf wasn't worth the danger.

It was breezy that day, and he was on the top floor of an apartment-house steel skeleton in Passaic, New Jersey, standing on a narrow beam. Suddenly, he saw a craneload of lumber swinging right at him.

"They were carrying it too low and it wasn't balanced right; it was swinging out of control. I jumped on the lumber, dug my fingernails into the wood and hung on for dear life," he says, his voice rising naturally although it happened long ago. "I was real lucky. It was six floors down. In my years as a steelworker, five guys I know got killed. When something like that happens to you, it really makes you stop and think."

It didn't take long for Zembriski to decide it was time to climb down, to get his feet on the ground and keep them there. It was at his wife Gloria's insistence that he had given up his brief, unsuccessful career on the PGA Tour to take up a steady job. But now, after eight years of walking the beams, they were divorced anyway, so he decided to follow the sun, head for Florida, to the carefree life where he could play all the golf he wanted. He had beaten the odds so far, and he wasn't going to take any more chances.

"She was the kind of person who wanted me to work eight hours and come home, stay around the house all weekend," he says. "That wasn't me. That wasn't what I wanted to do. I wanted to play golf."

Golf seeped into his blood as a youngster. Life wasn't easy. Everyone in the family worked. Following in the weary footsteps of his father, Zembriski started as a caddie at the Out of Bounds Club in Mahwah, New Jersey, about 12 miles from Ridgewood, where his father once caddied for Babe Ruth.

"Dad said Ruth was really a long hitter, as you might imagine," Zembriski says. "But he always had that bottle in his bag and never really scored that well. Tipped good, though, and Dad said he was a real friendly guy.

"My five brothers, we all caddied and played when we could. That's how I learned how to play, watching all their swings. I never had any serious instruction. You just picked up what you could from watching others. I guess I really started off hitting rocks with an old six-iron my dad brought home. Scotty Phimister, the pro at Out of Bounds, showed me a good grip and told me to hit the rock as hard as I could. The club was about three miles away and I'd walk over to the course every day. I had a 6-iron hidden and would bring a couple of balls and beat 'em to death."

It was fun at the Out of Bounds Club, but the big money was down the road at Ridgewood, so Zembriski hitchhiked down Route 17 and made $3 for an 18-hole loop. If he couldn't get a ride in time, he'd shell out for a bus ride. Finally, he bought a green 1949 Ford for $200.

"I used to have a caddie swing, a flat hook, so George Jacobus, the club pro at Ridgewood, raised my hands on the club and got me to stand up more," Zembriski says. "But the big thing was they let me play a lot of golf. Late in the afternoons, all day Monday—I loved to play. I learned a lot playing there. It was the first real tough course I played."

A couple of old caddies, Don Powell and Harry Lake, who worked during Zembriski's heralded homecoming at the 1990 U.S. Senior Open at Ridgewood, say they remember the skinny, shaggy-haired kid from Mahwah, remember how accurate he was with his iron shots, remember his unbridled enthusiasm, remember that he shot 68 or 69 almost every Monday and held the Monday course record.

After a while, Zembriski was promoted to club cleaner. That's a promotion? "Sure," he says, smiling. "Club cleaners get paid when it rains. Caddies don't make no money on rainy days."

In 1966 the New Jersey State Amateur was played at Ridgewood, and the former caddie and club cleaner, back from his stint in the Army, made a lasting impression. Although he had never survived the first round of this event in the past, Zembriski stunned the state's best players with a three-over-par performance for 120 holes. In the 36-hole final, he overwhelmed Andy Kunsaw nine and eight in a match he still vividly recalls to this day.

"I remember where the pin was placed on the 10th hole, where I won," he says. "I remember it was about 25 feet from the right side, tucked behind a trap."

That memorable triumph put some funny thoughts in Zembriski's head. Was he that good? The age-old question that gnaws at every golfer now was bugging him: how good could he be if he devoted more time to the game?

So he went to the PGA Tour Qualifying School and earned his playing card on the first try. He was on the Tour, but there was a problem. He couldn't win. He couldn't even cash a check. After two long, frustrating years, he hadn't made a dime. He was flat broke.

"I lost my sponsor," he says with a grin. "My father-in-law was paying my expenses, but when his daughter wanted me to get a job, that was the end of that tune."

Zembriski's favorite story about his struggling days on the PGA Tour came after the second round of the 1978 U.S. Open at Cherry Hills in Denver, Colorado.

"I was stretched out on the bench in front of my locker when Tom Weiskopf came by," Zembriski says with a smile. "Our lockers were in the same row—Watson, Weiskopf, Zembriski, Zoeller. Quite a lineup, huh? Anyway, I was wearing one of my best outfits because I didn't know if I was going to be around on the weekend.

"I had on red pants and a white shirt. Well, that was the same colors as the locker room guys. When Weiskopf saw me, he said, 'Locker, will you open mine, please?' I looked up and said, 'I'm not the locker room guy. I'm in the tournament. And I believe I've got you by a shot.' I did, too. I made the cut, but that was it. That was my highlight."

So it was back to the real world. The best-paying job Zembriski could get was walking those high beams, and that's where he spent the next eight years. His only scar from all those harrowing experiences is on his right thumb, where it was sewed back on after being smashed by a steel beam, but he says, "It doesn't affect my swing, so it's no big deal."

When he got down to Florida, Zembriski got work cleaning swimming pools, working on the maintenance crew of an Orlando course—whatever it took to get out on the golf course in nice weather when the day's work was done. There was no such thing as the Senior Tour in those days—it wasn't even a glimmer in Commissioner Deane Beman's eye—so there was no goal for Zembriski, no dreams of the riches he would one day possess. He simply decided he'd rather hit iron shots over lakes in sunny Florida than tote iron beams 20 stories above the grimy pavements of New York.

"I guess the most I made in one year on the mini-tour was about $40,000," Zembriski says. "The Space Coast events were Monday and Tuesday. Those purses would be $4,000 to $5,000. Then on Thursday and Friday, there was the Northern Florida PGA. I could usually average $800 to $1,000 a week. But they were all within driving distance of my apartment in Orlando, so I could go home every night. There weren't a lot of expenses."

His biggest expenses were entry fees. Once, he borrowed $1,200 to enter four tournaments and ended up winning $1,250. After paying back the loan, he had cleared $50 for the month, but he kept playing, every week, every tournament. Without his family, there was nothing else he'd rather do.

"I played two tournaments a week, played out of the trunk of my car, changed shoes in the parking lot," he says. "At first, I played shitty. I was scared, I guess. I wasn't even thinking about winning. I knew I could make money, but damn, in the back of my mind, I knew if I didn't, I'd have to get a job. I didn't want to go back to what I was doing. I wanted to play golf. The mini-tour hardened me a lot. If it wasn't for golf, I'd be working construction somewhere. I still have my union card.

"It was great experience. I was playing against all these young kids: Paul Azinger, Mark Calcavecchia, Jeff Sluman, Bob Tway. The only difference was they had a dream. They were heading for the Tour. I never dreamed there would be a Senior Tour for me."

By 1983, when the Senior Tour had grown to 18 tournaments, it caught Zembriski's eye. Suddenly, at age 48, he started thinking beyond the Space Coast tour to all the amenities, the huge purses and the fancy courses that he saw every weekend on television on the PGA Tour.

By the time Zembriski reached his 50th birthday, March 24, 1985, he was itching to try the Senior Tour. He worked hard on his game that summer and got a tremendous boost when he qualified for the U.S. Senior Open—his first experience playing against the top players. He led for two rounds at Edgewood Tahoe Country Club in Stateline, Nevada, before tying for fourth as Miller Barber came on to successfully defend his title. "I didn't win, but that taught me I could play with the big boys, I could compete," Zembriski says. "After that, I couldn't wait for the Senior Qualifying School."

When the grueling, pressure-packed six-round qualifying tournament came in the fall, he was ready. He set the pace in the early rounds and finished third at three-under-par 429. In the closing weeks of the 1985 season, he got his first taste of big-money pressure when he was involved in a four-way playoff with Orville Moody, Dan Sikes and Lee Elder at the Lexington (Kentucky) Citizens Union Seniors before losing to Elder's birdie on the fourth extra hole.

Zembriski began his first full year on the Senior Tour in fine fashion, finishing fifth in the Treasure Coast Classic at Fort Pierce, Florida, after being two shots back of wire-to-wire winner Charles Owens following the second round.

Players are fond of saying that you have to lose before you can win, and Zembriski endured that painful experience at the Senior Players Reunion in Dallas, where he had a one-shot lead going into the final hole, then snap-hooked his drive into the water and finished third to Don January. With two strong finishes near the end of the year (tied for fourth at the Cuyahoga International at Hilton Head, South Carolina, and sixth at the Shearson-Lehman Brothers Classic at Delray Beach, Florida), he finished 19th on the money list with $103,551 and was on his way.

The following year he nearly doubled his earnings and again came close to that elusive first victory. He sank a 12-foot putt on the last hole to finish second at Denver, one shot behind Bruce Crampton. He also had a fourth at the MONY Syracuse Classic and a fifth at Grand Rapids, Michigan.

Still living his Spartan existence in his one-bedroom apartment in Orlando, Zembriski now had reached the comfort zone financially. He didn't have to worry about how much prize money he would collect every week. Now his big concern was winning. He knew how to win: he had won 10 times on the mini-tour. He was confident he could win, but he just hadn't been able to put it all together at the right time.

The big breakthrough came in 1988 at the Newport Cup in Rhode Island when he fired a second-round 65 to take a two-shot lead over Charlie Coody. Then the third and final round was rained out.

"Some people called it a fluke, but I didn't care," he says. "Everybody says they don't like to win sitting in the clubhouse, but not me. I'll win in the men's room, if that's what it takes. A win is a win, and after a while nobody will remember anyway."

The highlight of Zembriski's career came three months later at the prestigious $1 million Vantage Championship in Clemmons, North Carolina. Before the biggest crowd he had ever played in front of, he passed a faltering Lou Graham, then coolly held off defending champion Al Geiberger and Dave Hill to win by three strokes with a two-under-par 278 at the difficult Tanglewood track. He was the only one to better par for 72 holes over the tight, hilly 6,606-yard layout.

"I knew even-par would be a good round," he said after his final-round 70, in which he made two birdies on the front side to take the lead, then was able to win with a two-over-par 37 on the back. "Not too many people are going to shoot low numbers when there is that much money on the line.

"Never in my wildest dreams did I envision something like this. I just kept playing and practicing. The mini-tour toughened me up, got me use to competing, to the pressure. But I never in my life faced anything like this. My knees were shaking. I looked at my caddie and told him to hold me up. But he was shaking, too."

Zembriski insisted he never thought about the money—the Senior Tour's largest first prize of $135,000—coming down the stretch, that he wasn't even sure how much first place paid, that he just wanted to win. If that was true, then he had become the consummate professional. Don't let the players fool you. They know the prize money; they know the difference between second and third. But by the time they reach the Senior Tour, most of them are financially secure, and victories are what they really care about.

"When we're all dead and gone, nobody will care how much money we made," says Billy Casper, who won a now seemingly unreachable total of 51 tournaments on the PGA Tour, another 9 on the Senior Tour and more than $3 million in combined winnings. "The only thing people will remember is the tournaments we won. It seems like when you go back to a town where you've won, the people never forget you. That's what we all play for out here. You've heard it a million times: nobody remembers who finished second."

The morning after his victory at the Vantage, Zembriski drew a few chuckles at the Premier Cup (now Vantage) Player Draft at the Convention Center in nearby Winston-Salem, when he showed up in the same light blue pants, blue shirt and white baseball-style hat he wore during Sunday's round. "Obviously, he wasn't planning on staying an extra day," said Kathie Watson, a fun-loving RJR public relations manager. "Maybe now he'll be able to afford a new outfit—and maybe get a haircut."

For the first time in his life, Zembriski started thinking about a financial advisor. For a guy who always lived month to month, winning $348,531 in a single year was mind-boggling. Asked what he was going to do with the $135,000 prize money, he paused, as if the thought never had occurred to him. After a minute, he said, "I've got to think of what I need. I got me a Cadillac and last year I bought a condo, so I've really got everything I want. But I guess I'll need some advice on CDs and stuff like that."

The only change in his lifestyle the next year was a slightly lighter schedule. Now he could afford to take a week off, something he rarely did in his first years on the Senior Tour.

"This year I played in every tournament but one [32 out of 33]," he said of his hectic 1988 schedule. "I didn't go to Albuquerque. They tested the atom bomb there, didn't they? That's enough for me."

There was a change in his status, of course. Suddenly, he was

ON TARGET: *Zembriski had his driver on laser beam at the 1989 GTE West Classic at Ojai Valley, California, where he shot 64-68-65 to beat George Archer and Jim Dent by two strokes.*

among the elite. He was a two-time winner who got better pairings—he wasn't among the dew sweepers anymore. He also started getting invited to pro-ams and corporate outings. He no longer was an unknown with that white Wilson hat pulled down around his ears.

"We all knew he could play," says Geiberger. "He's always been a very good iron player and he putts well. It was only a matter of time before he started winning. He was just behind a lot of us because he didn't play much on the other tour. Some guys never catch up, but Walt's a hard worker and now it's paying off."

Orville Moody, another who came up the hard way, was one of the first to appreciate Zembriski's talents and perseverance. He had seen plenty of guys like him during his 14 years of playing golf in the Army, and he knew Zembriski had the guts to survive on the Senior Tour.

"Walt's game is accuracy," Moody says. "He drives the ball straight and keeps it in the fairway. He's a strong iron player, and he's a terrific putter. He'll win a lot out here."

Zembriski waited almost until the end of the 1989 season to win again, this time at the GTE West Classic at Ojai Valley, California. He had come close at the Doug Sanders Kingwood Classic, tying for second behind Homero Blancas, and the Greater Grand Rapids Open, where he tied for fourth.

With just two weeks remaining in the season, Zembriski's putter caught fire. He opened with a sizzling six-under-par 64, the course record at the time at Ojai Valley, to take a lead he never lost. A second-round 68 gave him a one-shot lead over George Archer, who tied his course-record 64, and qualifier Al Kelley. As the temperature climbed from an early-morning frost, Zembriski heated up again on the final day, shooting 65 to beat Jim Dent and Archer by two shots. The first-place check of $52,500 boosted his season's earnings to $291,861, 15th on the money list. It was the fourth straight year he finished in the top 20.

With the addition of Dent and Archer in 1989 and Trevino and

T I P

"In the Newport Cup that I won in 1988, my first Senior Tour victory, I wrote the word 'slow' on the top of my glove, right by my thumb. It was a subtle reminder, every time I looked down at my grip, to take the club back nice and slow. That led to a nice, smooth tempo and prevented me from jerking the club back on the takeaway. Look at the glove and see the word 's-l-o-w.' "

Walt Zembriski

Nicklaus in 1990, victories haven't come that easily recently, because Zembriski learned what all the great players before him found out. Once you reach 55, no matter how hard you practice, how much time you spend on the putting green, sooner or later the hands start to shake a little, the wrists get a little loose, the concentration wanes and those four- and five-footers that used to roll in so easily start hitting the lip, skimming the edge, coming up inches short.

"My putting ain't been so good lately," he said of the early months of 1991. "I'm still hitting the ball straight, but I'm missing a lot of putts I used to make."

His best chance of winning in 1990 came at the Murata Reunion Pro-Am at Stonebriar in Frisco, Texas, when he fired a final-round 68 to close within two shots of Frank Beard, who won his first Senior Tour event with a nine-under-par 207. His second biggest check came at the $600,000 Kroger Classic at the Jack Nicklaus Sports Center in Kings Island, Ohio, where he tied for fourth and earned $24,600.

The highlight of his year—and one of his most memorable moments—came at the 1990 U.S. Senior Open, back at Ridgewood, where he had learned the game. Not many people in any profession get the opportunity he enjoyed that wonderful week in June. He was the dishwasher coming back to buy the restaurant, the office aide returning as the CEO, the caddie coming back to lead the U.S Open—for a while.

He started the first round by sinking a 6-foot birdie putt on the par-5 2nd hole, then made another birdie at the par-5 4th when his sand wedge nestled within 18 inches of the cup. He also birdied the par-3 8th after hitting a seven-iron within a foot, and he finished his bogey-free round of 68 by sinking a 12-footer on the 554-yard 17th.

"I was hitting my driver very well," he said afterward. "I hit every fairway and placed the ball where I wanted. Local knowledge is very important here because of the tall trees. You've got to be on the proper side of the fairway to have a good shot at the green. Today I hit the ball better than I did when I was last here, 24 years ago."

HOMETOWN HERO: *Zembriski returned to the course where he caddied to briefly lead the first round of the 1990 U.S. Senior Open after a bogey-free 68.*

Walt Zembriski was back home. The former caddie, the ex–club cleaner, was back, this time playing against Jack Nicklaus, Lee Trevino, Gary Player, the giants of the game he loves so much. And for a while on that glorious day, with a legion of loyal fans cheering his every shot, he was leading the U.S. Open. It was a day of fantasy, of dreams, of his fondest wish.

"If I win here, being so close to home, with all my friends watching, it would be the highlight of my career," he said emotionally. "I've been looking forward to this day since I started playing in February, when I started looking at the schedule. I've been getting ready for a month. I even took last week off to get a good rest and be ready.

"It was such a relief to get off to a good start. I wanted to do

LIVING HIS DREAM: *With a huge gallery of old friends following him, Zembriski made four birdies in the opening round of the 1990 U.S. Senior Open, then faded to a tie for 13th, 11 shots behind the winner, Lee Trevino.*

well in front of all these people. My biggest problem was keeping my eyes straight ahead and concentrating. I told my caddie that a lot of people would be yelling and waving, but we just had to keep our heads down and concentrate. There will be plenty of time to see them after the round."

Alas, the dream was shattered later in the afternoon when Trevino, the dominant player in his first year on the Senior Tour, came in with a 67. But by then, Zembriski had lived his dream, had left the course with his name on top of the leader board.

Zembriski slipped to a 73 in Friday's second round and never usurped the spotlight reserved for Nicklaus, Trevino, and Player the rest of the weekend. Although he continued to hit the narrow fairways, his putter abandoned him, particularly on Saturday, when he took 34 putts during a round of 73. He closed with a 72 for a two-under-par 286, which tied him for 13th, 11 shots behind Trevino.

"It still was a great experience, something to dream about, coming home," he said afterward. "I don't get up here anymore, and it is nice to see that some things haven't changed."

One thing that hasn't changed is Walt Zembriski. He's made more than $1.5 million now in official earnings. He has handsome deals with Wilson and Toyota, as well as with Mark Scot, which supplies him with all the shirts he needs (they're not all blue). He's gained the respect of his peers and the recognition of the golfing public. But the Z man still has the same low-key, unassuming personality he had when he was walking those high beams at seven o'clock on bone-chilling mornings in Brooklyn.

"I'm still the *same guy*," he says. "Nothing's changed. Oh, I'm recognized in airports once in a while, and I sign a bunch of autographs. Sure, I'm living a little better—I bought a condo and a new car—but that's it. I'm just happy with the way I am.

"I still can't believe I'm competing against these guys. But this job is easy. People say there's a lot of pressure, but I look over a six-foot putt and that's nothing. I'd rather have a tricky putt for par than be balancing on those high beams. Now that's pressure.

"Oh, I know it's going to end. It's like a peak. When you get to 55, 56, you start going down the other side, but they got these Super Seniors, you know, for guys who turn 60, and I got my eye on that. Hell, I'll play until I'm 75, if there's something there. What else am I going to do?"

ARNOLD PALMER

H is grin was so wide and his eyes were so lit up that his deeply tanned face almost burst as Arnold Palmer shook a reporter's hand with extra vigor, squeezed hard and exclaimed, "Damn right!"

He hadn't won a major championship, not even a Senior Tour title, but Palmer's triumph in the 1990 Senior Skins Game at Kohala Coast, Hawaii, was just as satisfying. The question he was responding to was "Does it still feel good to beat Jack Nicklaus?"

This had been Nicklaus' debut as a Senior Tour player, just eight days after his 50th birthday, and it was the first reunion of golf's famed Big Three of the 1960s—Palmer, Nicklaus and Gary Player—plus the irrepressible Lee Trevino. It was a game of chance, luck and timing, this Skins format where the first six holes were worth $15,000 each, the second six $25,000 and the final six $35,000. If two players tie, the money carries over to the next hole. A friendly little game among golf's greatest Senior players, except the rivalry was just as intense as when the Big Three battled at Augusta for Masters titles, oh so many putts ago.

"This gives me the reinforcement I need," Palmer said. "I work my butt off every day, exercising, riding a stationary bike, doing Nautilus, and sometimes I wonder why I'm doing it. But when you have a day like this, it's all worthwhile. This is my most satisfying day in golf since—well, you have to go back to the last Tour event I won, the 1973 Bob Hope Classic. I beat Nicklaus that day, too. We played in the last group."

Palmer had gone through a lot of putters and a lot of frustrations since that victory in Palm Springs, California, 17 years earlier, and he let it all hang out that night. There was probably more champagne consumed on his flight back to Orlando, Florida, than the entire New York Giants drank following their Super Bowl triumph over Buffalo.

Palmer's victory in the Skins came when he knocked a nine-iron within three feet on the 378-yard 16th hole, then rolled in the birdie putt to win seven skins worth $215,000. That gave him a total of $240,000 to $140,000 for Nicklaus, $70,000 for Trevino and nothing for Player.

"This is the biggest check I've ever won, by far," Palmer said, dating himself instantly. "At 60, this is the first time I've gotten into modern golf. I sure don't feel that old and I hope I don't look that old. As long as I can still hit it with these guys—and I'm swinging pretty good right now—I'll keep going. I guess it's desire. I know I still love to play, and the galleries are so great. When I hear those people cheer, well, it's one of the greatest feelings in the world."

No one has heard more applause and encouragement from galleries over a prolonged period than Palmer, who won his first major championship, the U.S. Amateur title, in 1954, edging Bob Sweeny 1-up at the Country Club of Detroit in Grosse Pointe Farms, Michigan. He joined the PGA Tour the following year and won the 1955

Canadian Open. (That still is the only trophy—a battered little cup, still not engraved—in his office at Latrobe, Pennsylvania). He won at least one championship every year until 1972, winning 60 times to trail only Sam Snead (81), Jack Nicklaus (70) and Ben Hogan (63) on the all-time victory list.

One of the greatest achievements of the Senior Tour—the one accomplishment for which golf fans everywhere should be eternally grateful—is that it extended the career of Palmer at least another decade and gave that many more thousands of fans the opportunity to watch this intense competitor play the game that he loves so much. Yet at the Senior Tour's infancy, no one fought it any harder. No one resisted growing older more than Arnold Daniel Palmer, who has been playing golf since he was 3 years old, and at 62 still wants to play every day.

Palmer properly is credited with lifting the Senior Tour out of its incubator period, propping it up on his broad shoulders and carrying it through its adolescent stages. But when it was first conceived, he didn't want any part of it.

"When I first approached 50, I wondered if I really wanted to play with those old guys," says Palmer. "What was the challenge? My plans were to get my businesses in order. Then I saw the intensity out there. I played in a few tournaments and finished fifth or sixth and didn't like it. I didn't like getting beat, so I went back to practicing and working on my game. It's the only way to survive out here. The nerves tingle, the adrenaline flows, the excitement is still there. The pressure is just as great to win as it was on the regular tour. It still gets me excited when I'm in position to win."

Palmer went through the same withdrawal symptoms from the PGA Tour in 1980 as Jack Nicklaus would in 1990. Both superstars doggedly insisted to the end that they could still compete on the regular tour although they hadn't won in years. In 1981, at age 52, Palmer played in 13 PGA Tour events, and in 1983, he won $16,904 in limited appearances. The following year, he played in 11 PGA Tour events and 15 on the Senior Tour.

His resistance to the Senior Tour came from a burning pride in the fact that he never asked a favor or gave one while competing on the golf course. A deep-seated traditionalist who fiercely objects to any hint of relaxing a rule or making an adjustment to compensate for advancing years, Palmer wanted every Senior Tour event to be 72 holes from the back tees, no quarters asked, none given. He often complains that the courses are set up too easy, even after shooting 75.

When he showed up at the 1989 Tournament of Champions after a two-year absence, he found that several tees had been moved up so the seniors were playing the course at 6,715 yards compared to 7,022 for the PGA Tour winners. He was outraged. After he mistakenly hit from the back tee markers on one of the early holes and was assessed a two-stroke penalty, he said, "Tomorrow I'll wear a skirt if they want me to play from those tees. Let's play the whole golf course."

At age 62, he still refuses to ride a cart, which most of his younger competitors have been doing for a decade. Although he's been plagued with putting problems for years and has tried thousands of different putters, he steadfastly rejects any suggestions that he use the long-shafted putter that saved Orville Moody from bankruptcy, turning Moody from the self-confessed worst putter on the regular tour to one of the best on the Senior circuit. Palmer still is one of the longest hitters, ranking second in driving distance in 1988 with a 262.2-yard average, yet he probably could improve on that if he went to metal woods, which 85 percent of the seniors use. No, Arnie's going down with what brought him—with what his dad, Milfred "Deacon" Palmer, taught him more than a half century ago.

Palmer still has a home in Latrobe, among the heavily wooded foothills of the Allegheny Mountains in western Pennsylvania some

50 miles from Pittsburgh. He was born and raised just a stone's throw away, in an old green frame house near the fifth hole at Latrobe Country Club. His childhood home still sits there—now gray, weathered and empty. But Palmer hasn't gone far. He and his wife of 38 years, Winnie, live in what was originally a three-bedroom white house with black shutters just steps away from his office building and a workshop on six acres of land. They sit on a ridge overlooking the country club—which he bought in 1971—and his old house.

Deacon Palmer was on the construction crew that built Latrobe Country Club, and when it opened with nine holes in 1921, he was given a job on the grounds crew. Five years later, he was promoted to greenskeeper; during the tough times in 1933, when the club couldn't afford a course superintendent and a head pro, he was asked to take over both jobs. He kept them until his death in 1976.

By the time Deacon, a strict Scotch-Irish man with a hard set of rules, became the pro, his son Arnie was four years old. Deacon used to take him on the tractor, put him between his knees and ride him around the course. He also got some old wooden clubs and cut them down for his son, who immediately showed more interest in playing than working. Arnie worked in the pro shop for a while, but after he closed it several times in the late afternoon so he could go practice, his father had to find another job for him. Arnie then did a lot of caddying and developed a real passion for the game, but his father would only let him play the course on Monday, when it was closed to members. Arnie had won a few local caddie tournaments by the time he got to high school, and he was the star of the team as a freshman. He dabbled in baseball and football, but at five foot ten, 150 pounds, he knew where he belonged—on the golf course.

At 17, he won the first of five western Pennsylvania amateur championships. His senior year, Palmer went to the West Coast to play in the Hearst National Junior Championship; there he met Buddy Worsham, whose older brother, Lew Worsham, was the winner of the 1947 U.S. Open. Buddy became his best friend and recommended to the Wake Forest golf coach Jesse Hadock that Palmer be given an athletic scholarship. They lived and played golf together for three years at Wake Forest. Then, one autumn night in 1950, Worsham wanted Arnie to drive over to nearby Duke University with him for a dance. Palmer decided not to go, and later that night, Worsham was killed driving home. A stunned, despondent Palmer dropped out of school a short time later and joined the Coast Guard, where he got his first taste of his second love: flying.

Palmer had been playing in the U.S. Amateur since 1948, when he was 20, but he missed the tournament in 1951 and 1952 because of his military obligations. He received leave to play in 1953 at Oklahoma City Golf & Country Club, and he beat Ken Venturi 2 and 1 in the third round before losing.

The champion that year was Gene Littler, who would go on to win the San Diego Open as an amateur the next year and come within a stroke of winning the 1954 U.S. Open at Baltusrol in New Jersey. He shot 70-69—139 to lead after 36 holes, but then skied to a 76 in the third round and fell three shots behind leader Ed Furgol. After pulling his game together on the pressure-filled final day, Littler needed pars on the final four holes to force a playoff. He parred 15 but bogeyed the par-3 16th. With two par-5s coming up, all he wanted was one birdie. After a par at 17, he hit his third shot into a greenside bunker on the last hole, blasted about eight feet from the cup, then missed the putt.

Littler, winner of 29 PGA Tour events and one of the trailblazers for the Senior Tour, finally got his U.S. Open trophy in 1961 at Oakland Hills in Birmingham, Michigan. Palmer was the defending champion after driving the green on the 346-yard, par-4 first hole at Denver's Cherry Hills in the final round the previous year, then going on to pass 14 players with a 65 to beat Nicklaus by 2 shots. After winning at San Diego, Phoenix, Baton Rouge and the Texas Open

THE FIRST OF MANY: *Arnold Palmer flashes what would become one of the world's most familiar smiles after winning the 1954 U.S. Amateur championship, coming from behind to beat former British Amateur champion Bob Sweeny 1-up in Detroit.*

and finishing second to Gary Player at The Masters, Palmer was heavily favored to repeat. But he never got in the hunt, shooting lackluster rounds of 74 and 75 and falling 10 shots back after two days.

This was to be Littler's year. He started with a 73, then came back with a 68 and added a 72 in the morning round of the final day to close within three shots of leader Doug Sanders. Littler came to the final hole needing a par for a 67 and an even-par 280. He hit his approach into a greenside bunker, made bogey and waited to see how Sanders would finish. Sanders, winner of 20 PGA Tour titles, had to birdie the 18th hole, but after he pushed his drive into some trees and punched to the front edge of the green, his tying chip shot barely missed and Littler was the champion.

Palmer won the U.S. Amateur in 1954, charging from 3-down after 4 holes to beat former British Amateur champion Bob Sweeny, 1-up, taking the lead for the first time on the 32nd hole. Next month, at the Waite Memorial tournament at Shawnee-on-Delaware, Palmer met one of the hostesses at the tournament, Winifred Walzer, whose father was president of a canned goods company. Three days later he asked her to marry him.

Now that he had a wife, Palmer decided it was time to find a career. When he had gotten out of the Coast Guard, a friend had offered him a job as a salesman at his painting supply business in Cleveland, calling on customers in the morning and playing golf with them in afternoon. He started at $500 a month, but after he won the U.S Amateur in August, he got a raise to $750—that was $9,000 a year, plus expenses. But Arnie was itching to get out on the Tour, if he could just get some financial backing. A sporting goods company offered him between $1,500 and $2,500 for three years, plus the use of its equipment, in exchange for his endorsement, so he grabbed that and formally turned pro November 15, 1954.

With some money from his family and Winnie's parents, about

SETS STANDARD FOR SCRAMBLING:
*Palmer ignores a water pump and a couple
of workers to pitch out of a puddle at the 1954
U.S. Amateur championship in Detroit. He
went on to upset Frank Stranahan 3 and 1
en route to winning.*

251

$5,000 in all, he and Winnie bought a secondhand trailer and started following the sun. It wasn't easy. Success did not come overnight; there were a lot of 500-, 600-mile drives with no hope of collecting a paycheck. In those days, the PGA Tour didn't allow rookies to take any prize money for six months, although the players could keep anything they made in the pro-ams. As the defending U.S Amateur champion, Palmer was invited to The Masters, and he started his long, legendary string of appearances at Augusta National (37 in a row through 1991) by tying for 10th and winning $695.83. In June he began collecting on Tour, finishing 25th in the Fort Wayne Open and earning $145. Later, he got that first win at the Canadian Open, worth $2,400. Despite the victory, he won only $7,958 all year and placed 32nd on the money list, but he was on his way.

Although he is one of the few players to successfully defend a British Open championship, and his dramatic come-from-behind victory at the 1960 U.S. Open belongs to the ages, any reflection of Palmer's career should center around The Masters. That was his tournament, his kind of golf course, a majestic layout favoring strong players who draw the ball. It was a gambler's track, sans rough, with opportunities for risks that could be rewarded with eagles. And it was a tournament that always was the center of media attention, that traditionally kicked off the golf season for fans everywhere.

The years from 1958 to 1968 were a decade of dominance for Palmer among the azaleas and pines. In that exciting span, with the lone exception of 1963, he was in contention for a green jacket every year. He won four times; he finished second twice, third once and fourth twice. He owned Augusta National and its zealous fans. Arnie's Army was born there and still lives at every tournament on the Senior Tour.

It was a perfect dramatic setting in 1958 when Palmer challenged for his first Masters title. After three rounds he was deadlocked with the immortal Sam Snead, but destiny seemed to be on Palmer's side.

Snead, the legendary all-time PGA Tour winner, double-bogeyed the 1st hole and was never a threat, staggering in with a 79.

Ken Venturi, who would go on to win four times that year (his second year on the Tour), was paired with Palmer and had made up two strokes to trail by one going into the 155-yard par-3 12th hole. It had rained heavily the night before, and the embedded ball rule was in effect. Both players hit beyond the green onto the bank behind it. Venturi's ball trickled back down to the edge of the green and he made his par. Palmer's shot, however, plugged in the soft turf near a bunker. The newly invoked rule would allow him to lift, clean and place his ball, but the official on the scene wasn't sure. Palmer said later he was determined to wait all day if he had to for a ruling, but he finally agreed to play a second ball. With the embedded ball he made a double bogey five, but with the provisional ball he made par. Still now knowing the outcome, a determined Palmer hit a three-wood within 18 feet of the 475-yard 13th hole and sank the eagle putt.

"It wasn't until the 15th hole that I learned that the rules committee had decided in my favor at 12, that I got a three instead of a five," Palmer says. Obviously shaken, Venturi three-putted the 14th and 15th holes. There were still some anxious moments for Palmer, when Doug Ford and Fred Hawkins lined up birdie putts on the 18th green to tie, but they missed and a legend was born.

The next year it appeared as if Palmer would become the first player to successfully defend a Masters championship. After three rounds he was tied with Stan Leonard, a relatively unknown Canadian who certainly was a candidate to choke. (Leonard fulfilled the prophecy the next day with a final-round 76.) Palmer reached the memorable 12th hole, where he had gotten the favorable ruling in his one-shot victory the previous year. This time, the hole most players call the most difficult at Augusta National was his waterloo: he drowned his tee shot and made six. Even with birdies at the 13th and 15th

holes, both par-5s, he finished with 74 for 284. Still, it looked as though that might be enough. There was no reason to suspect that quiet, unassuming 35-year-old Art Wall would mount any sort of charge. But charge he did, with one of the greatest finishes in Masters history. After starting the day tied for 13th, six shots behind Palmer, the slight bespectacled Pennsylvania native sank a 15-foot birdie putt at 13, a 20-footer at 14 and a third birdie in a row at 15, nearly missing an eagle putt. After a par at 16, he ran in a 15-footer for birdie at 17 and needed only a par at the final hole to beat Palmer. After an approach shot to within 12 feet, he sank the birdie putt— his fifth in the last six holes—for a 66 and a 284.

After winning four tournaments on the winter circuit, Palmer was a heavy favorite at Augusta in 1960, and he responded to his huge, enthusiastic gallery—now officially known as Arnie's Army— by opening with a 67 to take a two-shot lead. Despite a second-round 73, he still was nursing a one-shot advantage, and after a pair of three-putts and a third-round 72, he took the same lead into the final round. But there was a strong group nipping at his heels: Ben Hogan, Julius Boros, Dow Finsterwald and Venturi, once more. Hogan and Boros never made a move, shooting 76 and 75 respectively, but Venturi birdied the 2nd, 3rd and 6th holes to make the turn in 33, and Finsterwald birdied the 8th and 9th for 34. Palmer, playing about an hour behind them, offset his two birdies with two bogeys and was even-par 36. Venturi shot 37 on the back for 70 and 283, a shot better than Finsterwald, who bogeyed 18 from a bunker.

DOWN THE ROAD TO HISTORY: *Palmer intently watches one of his booming drives during a final-round 73 that gave him a one-shot victory over Doug Ford and Fred Hawkins in the 1958 Masters.*

Now it was up to Palmer, who was playing the 13th hole; he needed one birdie to tie and two to win. His second shot to the par-5 hole went over the green and into a bunker, and he had to settle for par. At the par-5 15th, he missed the green right and let another birdie opportunity slip away. He also parred the 16th, missing a 35-footer. Now he needed a birdie-birdie finish to win, and he did it, sinking a 27-footer at 17 that hung tantalizingly on the lip before dropping in. At 18, he stroked one of the most memorable shots of his career, a six-iron that hit 2 feet right of the cup and stopped 6 feet away. He rolled it in, and his love affair with The Masters was heating up.

After losing the 1961 Masters to Gary Player with a double bogey from the sand on the last hole, Palmer came back the next year and survived a final-round 75—which included a chip-in birdie at 16, then a birdie-par finish—to tie Player and Dow Finsterwald. In the Monday playoff, Palmer again fell behind Player, trailed by three shots at the turn, then reeled off birdies at 10, 12, 13 and 14 to go from three strokes down to four up. He finished with a 68 to 71 for Player and 77 for Finsterwald, who by this time was sick and tired of losing The Masters.

Winning got a lot easier in 1964, when Palmer began with a 69 and followed with a 68 and 69 to open a five-shot gap over Bruce Devlin and six over Dave Marr. A final-round 70 gave Palmer a 276 and a six-stroke victory, which made him the first four-time winner at Augusta National. As he reached that hallowed 18th fairway, his playing partner, Marr, needed a birdie to tie Nicklaus for second. Palmer graciously asked if there was anything he could do. "Yeah," Marr said with a smile, "shoot 12."

Once again, the following spring it was the Big Three—Palmer, Player and Nicklaus—atop the leader board, but it was no dogfight: Nicklaus cruised around in 17-under-par 271 to break Ben Hogan's record by three shots and beat Palmer and Player by nine strokes.

WINNING FIRST MASTERS: *A seemingly subdued Palmer barely tips his cap to the roaring crowd after sinking the putt on the 18th green that gave him his first Masters victory in 1958.*

FAMILIAR FINISH: *Cocking his head to follow his shot in what would become his trademark, Palmer goes after a fifth Masters championship in 1965 at Augusta National, only to finish second to Jack Nicklaus.*

Afterward, Bobby Jones summed up Nicklaus' performance with words that would follow the Golden Bear throughout his brilliant career. "Palmer and Player played superbly," Jones said. "As for Nicklaus, he plays a game with which I am not familiar."

There would be no more green jackets for Palmer, who in 1966 missed a three-way playoff (which Nicklaus won by two shots) and in 1967 finished fourth after Nicklaus missed the cut. The run was over. Palmer would miss the cut the following year, and he would never finish in the top 10 for the next 24 years.

In fact, there would be no more major championships after the age of 34. Burned out? That's too simple. It was a combination of things, starting, of course, with the eroding confidence in his putting. He always had rammed his putts at the back of the hole, believing he could make the three- or four-footer coming back, if necessary. His boldness always had been his pride: hitch up your pants, take a deep drag of your cigarette, flip it away, grind your fingers around the club and let it fly. In his prime, he seemed to play better when he was behind, his best comeback being that final-round 65 to pass 14 players and win the 1960 U.S. Open.

In his prime, from 1960 to 1963, Palmer went into the final round of 38 tournaments on the PGA Tour with a reasonable chance of winning. He finished on top 27 times, a success ratio of a staggering 71 percent. In the next three years, however, he was in contention 22 times and only won 6.

His most infamous collapse came in the 1966 U.S. Open at Olympic Club in San Francisco. He led Billy Casper by seven strokes with nine holes to play, then fell into a playoff with some reckless gambles as he went for Hogan's record of 276, which was set at Riviera Country Club in Los Angeles in 1948. After a birdie on the 12th hole, Palmer still led by six; then he fired a four-iron at the pin on the 191-yard par-3 13th, pulled it and bounced it into the rough for another bogey, dropping his lead to five. Both contenders parred the

14th hole, and as Palmer described in his book *Go for Broke!*, he still was thinking more about Hogan's record than beating Casper.

"I knew what the record was. I had set the British Open record several years ago [276 at Royal Troon in 1962] and I thought it would be nice to have both." Then came the par-3 15th hole. "I was trying to play the perfect shot, going for the record, not just the title. With a lead like that why not be bold." After Casper hit safely in the middle of the green, Palmer fired at the pin, and the ball landed in a bunker. He blasted out and two-putted for a bogey, then Casper drained his 20-footer and Palmer's lead was cut to three.

"As I stood on the 16th tee, I knew I could play safe and cut Billy off completely," Palmer said. "Then I thought of how I'd look to myself: there goes Arnold Palmer playing safe with a 1-iron when he's got a three-shot lead with three holes to play. I couldn't do it. I have to play the hole as I feel it, so I decided to go for broke: to use my driver."

Palmer yanked his drive sharply into heavy rough no more than 150 yards from the tee. There he had another difficult decision. It was a par-5, and he could pitch out safely with a nine-iron or go toward the green with a three-iron. Naturally, he went for the green, only there was no way to get a ball airborne out of that heavy grass with a three-iron. The ball dribbled about 75 yards. Now Palmer went to the nine-iron, and his pitch still left him 270 yards to the green. He nailed a three-wood, but it fell into a greenside bunker. He exploded within 4 feet and sank the putt. "It was one of the greatest sixes the game has ever seen," says Casper, who hit driver, two-iron and five-iron, then sank a 13-footer for birdie to cut Palmer's lead to a single shot.

Palmer lost it on the 443-yard 17th. He missed the green to the left, then made a brilliant pitch out of the rough and over a bunker to within 8 feet below the hole. "The putt was slightly uphill and I hit it exactly as I wanted," Palmer said. "I thought I'd made it. The

NOT TO BE: *Once again, Palmer can't coax enough putts in and finishes within two shots of a three-way playoff among Jack Nicklaus, Tommy Jacobs and Gay Brewer in the 1966 Masters at Augusta National.*

ball was right on line and seemed to have the roll to carry to the cup. But it stopped an inch short. A lousy inch." Casper tapped in a 3-footer for par and Palmer's seven-shot lead was history.

After driving into the rough again, this time with a one-iron, Palmer made another magnificent recovery on the last hole. "My ball was caught deeply in the tangled rough and it would take a 9-iron to get it out of there," Palmer said. "The way the ball was sitting, it figured that I wouldn't hit more than halfway to the green. But I put everything I had into it, every muscle that could be brought to bear." The ball carried the lip of the bunker and rolled to the back of the green, some 25 feet above the hole. Palmer's first putt stopped 3 feet short and he recalls, "I remember looking at that putt and thinking everything is on the line. My pride. My business. My livelihood." He rammed it into the hole. Casper two-putted from 17 feet for his par, setting up a playoff the next day that was almost a carbon copy of the back nine and is often overlooked by historians. Palmer had a two-shot lead going into the 10th hole, but he fell apart again and lost 69-73.

For Casper, a recently converted Mormon who lost 50 pounds in the 18 months before, it would be his second U.S. Open (he won at Winged Foot in 1959 with a magnificent putting performance), and he would go on to win the 1970 Masters in a playoff with Gene Littler (69-74). In 1983, resplendent in plus fours and blinding colors, Casper became the second player after Palmer to win both the U.S. Open and the U.S. Senior Open when he outlasted Rod Funseth in a playoff after they tied at 288 at Hazeltine. Sixth on the all-time victory list with 51, Casper added 9 more on the Senior Tour before his 60th birthday.

For Palmer, it would be the start of a series of last-round disappointments. He went head-to-head with Nicklaus in the 1967 U.S. Open at Baltusrol after being tied a shot behind Marty Fleckman, but he was beaten by four shots when Nicklaus fired a 65. The next

T I P

"Sometimes it pays to go back to the basic fundamentals of the game when you're not playing your best golf. The major problem that I see with most of our amateurs in pro-ams is that they start away from the ball. If the amateur can think about taking the club back in a deliberate manner and in one piece, he should be able to deliver the club back to the ball smoothly. If the average player can keep his swing thoughts simple and fundamentally sound, he'll be able to improve his overall golf game faster."

Arnold Palmer

year, at the PGA Championship at Pecan Valley Country Club in San Antonio, Palmer made a miraculous second shot out of heavy rough with a three-wood to eight feet above the 18th hole Sunday. Then he missed the putt and watched as 48-year-old Julius Boros chipped within four feet and sank the putt to become the oldest winner of a major championship.

That was the second discouraging loss in the PGA Championship—the one major that he never won—in four years for Palmer. In 1964, he shot four rounds in the sixties (68-68-69-69) at Columbus Country Club in Ohio and tied Nicklaus for second, three shots behind wire-to-wire winner Bobby Nichols. Once again, in the 1970 PGA Championship, Palmer finished second, two shots behind Dave Stockton, despite a closing 70 for 281 at Southern Hills Country Club in Tulsa.

His next memorable PGA Championship came 19 years later, when he stirred nostalgia lovers everywhere and vaulted back to his prime for one glorious yet fleeting afternoon at Kemper Lakes, outside of Chicago. For a day, if only a day, the King lived and the crowd loved it. In the opening round, Palmer, at age 59, somehow toned up 20 years of aging muscles and decaying reflexes and made five consecutive birdies on the front nine.

Nicklaus and Tom Kite were on the 4th green when they heard the thunderous cheer from the 8th hole, where Palmer had rolled in a 25-footer for his fifth straight birdie. "Jack was over a bunker shot, and a tremendous roar went up at 8," Kite says. "Jack stepped back. The crowd was yelling, 'Go, Arnie,' and all of a sudden you could

ANOTHER DISAPPOINTMENT: *Palmer went head-to-head with archrival Jack Nicklaus in the final round of the 1967 U.S. Open at Baltusrol, but he shot 69 and lost by four strokes.*

see that look of determination in Jack's eyes. It was like we were back in the sixties."

After salvaging a par at No. 9 with a tricky 5-footer, Palmer made the turn in 31. The 7,197-yard municipal course seemed to tilt as everyone ran to the back side to watch golf's most popular player act out an emotional encore of his greatness. "It was great to watch him," says one of his playing partners, defending champion Jeff Sluman. "It was like Ponce de León out there." After scrambling for a couple of pars, Palmer made another birdie at 15 to go six-under-par and tie for the lead. After rifling a five-iron within 15 feet at the 469-yard 16th, he savored the moment, walking up the fairway with two-time PGA champion Larry Nelson.

"He had just hit a great five-iron shot, and I think he looked up and saw his name up there on the leader board," Nelson said afterward. "He came over to me and said, 'It's been a long time since I played like this.' I've played with a lot of great ones in my 16 years out here, but he played as well as anyone I've ever seen. He drove it really well. It was great to be in that situation, to have a front-row seat. You just have to watch and enjoy it. He's meant so much to the game."

Palmer missed his birdie attempt, then bogeyed the par-3 17th, pushing his tee shot to avoid the water on the left. At 18, a surge of adrenaline caused his nine-iron shot to fly over the green, and he made another bogey to finish with 68, two shots back of leader Mike Reid. "The adrenaline got going a little on the last two holes," he says. "I really thought I might shoot 65." He also let himself enjoy, for the moment, the fleeting thought that, maybe, just maybe, he

TRIES GLASSES: *Puzzled at first by his near-sightedness, Palmer experiments with glasses during a winless 1972 season.*

could finally win that PGA Championship that would mean so much to him and Deacon, the lifelong PGA club pro. "Can I win? If I play like I did today, yes. Whether that can happen is questionable. But I was thinking today, 'Why the hell can't you play the way you used to? What's so much different?' "

He couldn't, of course. He was back to 74 the next day; then an 81 with seven three-putt greens and a closing 70 left him where 59-year-old men usually finish, 17 strokes behind the winner. Why couldn't he continue to play the way he used to? What's so much different?

Let's count the ways. You could start with myopia, which struck back in 1972. While many of his peers were getting farsighted in their advancing years (Al Geiberger said he knew he was on the Senior Tour when he got to the registration desk and there was a pair of glasses for the players' use), Palmer was puzzled at first by his near-sightedness. He experienced a lot of problems judging distances before he started wearing soft contact lenses (at one point he switched briefly to regular glasses, then went back to the lenses). Then there were two long bouts with bursitis. In 1963, it hit in his left shoulder. Then in 1966, after he injured his back, he was bothered for several years by a pain in his right hip, which flared up so intensely in his last practice round before the 1969 PGA Championship in Dayton, Ohio, that he had to withdraw after shooting a career-high 82 in the first round. Ten weeks later, he was back on the Tour and finished strong, winning the Heritage Golf Classic at Hilton Head and the Danny Thomas–Diplomat Classic to finish ninth on the money list.

After Palmer won the Bob Hope Desert Classic for the fifth time in 1973, his putting turned from bad to worse, and the more he fiddled, fumed and fussed, the worse it got. He tried everything, but nothing sustained. In 1976 and 1977, he didn't have a top-10 finish. In 1979, he turned 50, made the cut in only 8 of 15 starts and earned just $9,276—about $1,300 more than he won as a rookie 24 years

SENIOR DEBUT: *Palmer stubbornly resisted the Senior Tour, playing only four times his first year in 1981 and seven the following year.*

before. The Senior Tour was beckoning, but Arnie's heels were dug in.

While most players, including great ones such as Player and Trevino, eagerly awaited their 50th birthday and an opportunity to win again, to compete, to earn prize money, Palmer and Nicklaus stood alone in their resistance. Although they both praised the concept, were impressed with the operation and were genuinely pleased that their pals were back in the spotlight again, well, it just wasn't for them. Playing against men in their fifties just wasn't much of a challenge. After all, they were still competing on the PGA Tour. Or were they?

"Quite frankly, when I turned 50, I thought my days in tournament golf were going to be limited to a few of the regular tour events and the major championships," Palmer says. "The rest would be centered around outings. I didn't plan on playing much on the Senior Tour."

It took a few years. Although he won the first Senior event he entered, beating Paul Harney on the first hole of a playoff at the 1980 PGA Seniors Championship in Palm Beach Gardens, Florida, Palmer only played four Senior events in 1981 and seven the following year. Despite his limited schedule, he won three times, including beating old nemesis Billy Casper and Bob Stone in an 18-hole playoff for the 1981 U.S. Senior Open at Oakland Hills, near Detroit. After a 15-month drought, Palmer avoided a shutout in 1983 by winning the season-ending Boca Grove Classic. At age 54, now settled into a 15-tournament schedule, he enjoyed his best year on the Senior Tour, winning the PGA Seniors Championship for the second time, winning the Senior Tournament Players Championship and repeating at Boca Grove to finish fourth on the money list with $184,582—the second highest yearly earnings of his entire career. He highlighted the next year with an 11-shot victory in successfully defending his Senior TPC title at Cleveland's Canterbury Golf Club, but there has been only one victory since, the 1988 Crestar Classic near Richmond.

"Nevertheless," says Chi Chi Rodriguez, "he'll always be the King. There will never be another like him. I'm just thankful to know him. If it wasn't for Arnold, I'd be back in Puerto Rico cleaning clubs."

Lee Trevino yields to no man in his love for the game, but what really makes him appreciate Palmer's contribution, he says, is that "Arnold is the only guy on the Senior Tour who loses money when he plays. He could make a lot more every week doing corporate outings or making appearances, but he loves to play."

A country club locker room can be a garden for cynicism. And because golf is an individual sport and the same players compete against each other every week, some subtle bitterness can fester. But despite all the attention he attracts, Palmer has remained above it all.

"He's the king of kings," says Doug Sanders. "There's a strength about the man that people want to be around. Anybody who resents Arnold Palmer getting more attention than the rest of us doesn't deserve to use his head for more than a hat rack."

"I made plans long ago to be in business at age 60," says Palmer, flashing the cover-boy smile that never seems to age. "Oh, I expected to be playing golf, and I suspected I would play occasionally in a tournament, but never to the extent that I do now. But I love to compete and I'm going to keep playing, maybe a little less and hopefully a little better. I'm not apologizing; I know I'm getting older. Don't you think it's time?"

JACK NICKLAUS

O h, there was more apprehension than he ever let us know about—his continuing back problems and, perhaps, more than his share of business failures—but Jack Nicklaus doesn't really belong here.

The greatest golfer of all time doesn't have a place in a book about growing up in poverty, about hardships, financial problems, divorces, victory droughts, overcoming adversity and rising again to success on the Senior Tour.

When you're discussing the future of the Senior Tour, however, the Golden Bear fits right in. We know who many of the headliners will be in the next few years. But will Nicklaus be among them? Certainly the potential is there. In the four tournaments he entered as a Senior rookie in 1990, he won two, finished second in the U.S. Senior Open to Trevino and wound up third in the PGA Seniors Championship to Gary Player. Despite a limited schedule that disappointed the fans, the media and his fellow players, Nicklaus still won $340,000. In 1991, he entered five tournaments, won three, including the U.S. Senior Open, and earned $343,734.

"I'm worried that he won't play very much," Trevino said in a rare serious moment in a locker room one day near the end of the season. "He came out and proved he could still win—he had a hell of a year—but I'm afraid the motivation just isn't there anymore. Jack's got too much pride to come out here if he's not prepared, or not playing well."

Arnold Palmer laughs when he hears that Nicklaus doesn't really have much desire to compete anymore, that his course-designing business is more challenging, that he's too busy flying all over the world opening golf courses to play on the Senior Tour.

"Jack's talking like I did 10 years ago," Palmer says. "But I know Jack. I know how much he likes to compete. He enjoys golf too much to walk away from all this. He'll be out here, not full-time, but he'll play a lot."

Some of the Senior players are upset that Nicklaus didn't play more in his first two seasons. Although they didn't relish the thought of competing against him, they all knew that he would attract more fans, more publicity, more media and more money from the sponsors with his appearances. Strong opinions abound.

"Personally, I don't think we ever have to worry about Nicklaus," says Rives McBee. "I would like to see people get off the Nicklaus situation because he's not going to play out here. His priorities now are building golf courses and the corporate world. His golf is secondary. It's funny because Arnold Palmer makes more money in the corporate world today than he does in golf, but he keeps playing. He loves to play. He loves the crowds; it keeps him going."

Some players are quick to point out that 4 tournaments Nicklaus entered—The Tradition, the PGA Seniors Championship, the U.S. Senior Open and the Senior Players Championship—were the 4 events all year that did not have pro-ams.

"A lot of the guys feel Jack snubbed his nose at us," Bob Goalby says. "There was all that publicity about him and Lee coming out, resuming their rivalry and all that, and then he doesn't show up. Nobody expected him to play in 30 tournaments like Lee, but everyone thought he'd play more than 4. Hell, you have to play 6 to be exempt for the following year." (By skipping the $1.5 million Vantage Championship and the $1 million New York Life Champions in Dorado Beach, Puerto Rico, in December, Nicklaus had to rely on sponsor invitations to enter tournaments in 1991 and 1992.)

Nicklaus got off to a bad start before he ever took a club back on the Senior Tour. In a long, far-ranging interview with insightful Jaime Diaz for the January 1990 issue of *Golf Digest*, Nicklaus discussed his future on the Senior Tour.

"Even though I love golf, I don't have any goals," he told Diaz. "I hate to admit that. I have been goal-oriented my entire career and I'm not goal-oriented now. That's my biggest problem. Senior golf doesn't give me any goals. I think the Senior Tour has been great for the game. It is terrific for the guys, giving them an opportunity to play. I should compete some because of that. But to be honest, playing pro-ams on short courses with no rough doesn't motivate me. If the course were more challenging, I might take a different attitude. Right now, I just see it as a way to have some fun."

Then he made the remark that was like a fingernail scraped across a blackboard to most of the Senior players, one they carried with them the entire year, or at least whenever Nicklaus was around.

"The problem for me," Nicklaus said, "is that the guys who are competing are the same guys that I have beaten for 30 years. Now, most of the guys who are playing well, with a few exceptions, are the guys who were marginal players when they played on tour. Because they were marginal players, they now have the desire to keep playing. The guys who are dominating, I suppose, are Bob Charles and Orville

Moody. They were good players, but marginal. They weren't exceptional."

Outspoken Dave Hill, who would take sides if two flies were crawling up a screen door, ripped into Nicklaus for labeling as "marginal" such players as Al Geiberger, winner of 11 PGA Tour events, including the 1966 PGA Championship; George Archer, a 12-time winner, including the 1969 Masters; Bruce Crampton, a 14-time winner and, damn right, his very own self, who won 13 times.

There was talk of hanging the article on Nicklaus' locker when he made his debut at The Tradition at Desert Mountain, a course he designed in the mountains of Carefree, just outside of Scottsdale, Arizona. But when the time came, the players all greeted him with open arms.

"Nah, nobody said anything at the dinner last night," Trevino said the next day. "Everybody likes Jack. The article bothered some guys, but everyone's glad to see him out here playing. It's great for our tour."

Trevino began a standing joke that turned out to be a little expensive. When he started off winning three of the first four tournaments without a challenge from the absent Nicklaus, he said he would send a dozen roses to Jack's wife, Barbara, every week that Nicklaus didn't show up.

"I'm still doing it," Trevino said before the Vantage Championship in October, "but I'm waiting until Thursday because he might show up. He's just liable to do that: get the flowers and then come to the tournament."

FIRST U.S. SENIOR OPEN: *Jack Nicklaus tees off in the opening round of the U.S. Senior Open at Ridgewood Country Club in Paramus, New Jersey, where he would suffer one of his most disappointing losses in a final-day showdown with Lee Trevino.*

Barbara could have started her own florist shop that summer, because Nicklaus' last Senior event was the U.S. Senior Open, June 28–July 1 in Paramus, New Jersey.

The stunning way he lost on that gloomy Sunday at historic Ridgewood Country Club might have had something to do with his lack of interest the rest of the year.

After starting slowly with a 71 to spot the front-running Trevino four shots, Nicklaus quietly moved up the leader board with a second-round 69. But he still was five behind Trevino—who had a one-shot lead on Jim Dent—and was tied with Gary Player at four-under-par 140.

Nicklaus began Saturday's round by rolling in a 23-foot birdie putt on the par-5 2nd hole and a 45-foot eagle from the fringe at the par-5 4th. He sank four more birdie putts on the back nine—including a 20-footer at the par-3 15th and an 18-footer at the par-5 17th—for a 67, and he snatched the lead at nine-under-par 207. The Bear was on the move and Trevino could feel the heat as he struggled to a 73 for 208.

"I've improved my score two shots every day, and I feel good about the way I'm playing," Nicklaus said late that Saturday. "This is the most major championship we have on the Senior Tour. But it's still a different feeling. I really don't feel I have anything to prove. When I started the regular tour, I had a lot to prove. When you start out, nobody knows who you are; you just go out and play. I can feel the difference between the two tours this year. The Senior Tour is not really blood and guts; there is a lot of nostalgia as well as competition."

There was plenty of competition left at Ridgewood from his two longtime adversaries, Trevino and Player. Nicklaus had beaten Player in the final round at The Tradition, and Player had won the PGA Seniors in a final-round duel with Nicklaus and Trevino.

This time, after Player and Trevino birdied the 2nd hole Sunday, the three were tied at nine-under-par with 16 holes to play when the heavens opened up, lightning flashed and there was a delay in the drama.

Player kept pace for nine holes, then crumbled, making bogeys on the 10th, 12th and 13th holes to fall out of contention. After Trevino, playing a group ahead, drove into the right rough and bogeyed the 545-yard 13th hole, and Nicklaus birdied it, they were tied at 11-under-par. Another pressure-packed stretch drive in this long-standing rivalry was about to unfold—with a bizarre ending that undoubtedly never will be duplicated.

There had been some exciting duels in the past. Trevino won four of his six major championships in down-the-stretch battles with Nicklaus: the 1968 U.S. Open—Trevino's first victory—at Oak Hill in Rochester, New York; the 1971 U.S. Open at Merion Golf Club in Ardmore, Pennsylvania, where he tossed a rubber snake at the Bear on the first playoff hole, then beat him 68-71; the 1972 British Open, where he holed out three chip shots and a bunker shot and won by a stroke, and the 1974 PGA Championship at Tanglewood Park, in Clemmons, North Carolina, where he matched Nicklaus' final-round 69 to protect a one-shot lead.

"He brought out the best in me every time," Trevino says. "If you match me with Nicklaus, I would beat him 8 out of 10 times. The reason is that I'd match him shot for shot: the better he'd hit it, the better I'd hit it. And nothing pleases me more. I didn't care who was leading the tournament as long as I beat Jack. That's the big difference. It's almost like boxing. A guy can beat the hell out of you, but you keep getting up. Finally the guy says, 'Man, when is this guy going to lie down?' I know there were times when Jack felt like that against me."

This might have been one of those times. Nicklaus pulled his three-wood off the 14th tee into the rough and bogeyed the hole to fall one back. Smelling victory, Trevino heightened his psych on his longtime rival after sinking birdie putts of 20 and 15 feet on the 15th and 16th holes. Both times he turned to the crowd and encouraged them to cheer louder.

"I was trying to send a message to Jack," he explained afterward. "I didn't think the cheers were loud enough, and I thought he might have figured [Jim] Dent had made the birdies. I wanted him to know I made them."

Nicklaus knew, and he answered like the champion he is, also making birdies on those two holes—hitting a seven-iron within 5 feet at the 151-yard 15th and draining a 12-footer at No. 16. Still needing another birdie to tie because of that bogey at 14, he hit a one-iron second shot to an ideal spot on the 554-yard 17th hole. Trevino, perhaps playing a little quicker than usual to magnify Nicklaus' methodical style, already had parred the last two holes for a 67 and 275, and he was headed to the ABC television tower. As Nicklaus prepared for his eight-iron approach shot, the sky darkened and the wind started blowing, like a scene from an Agatha Christie mystery.

With all eyes on him, Nicklaus chunked the shot—hit behind it—and the ball came up 10 yards short of the green. You could hear the gasps all the way to North Palm Beach.

"I knew I couldn't get to the green in two, so I hit a one-iron to leave myself a nine-iron or a pitching wedge for my third shot," Nicklaus patiently explained afterward. "I prefer to have a pitching wedge, but I hit the one-iron a little fat. I had 128 yards and was going to hit a nine-iron. When the storm came up, I decided to hit an easy eight. But when the light changes, when it gets dark like that, I have trouble with my contact lenses. I lose my depth perception to the ground. I caught the shot a little heavy."

Nicklaus chipped to 4 feet; then came another eerie moment. As he was hunched over his par putt, which still would leave him only a shot back going to the 18th hole, Trevino was telling his television audience, "Jack has a tendency to peek sometimes on these short putts. If he does, he'll miss it to the right." As if on cue, Nicklaus picked his head up ever so slightly as his putter approached the ball, and his putt lipped out on the right. A bogey. The championship was over and so was Nicklaus' rookie year on the Senior Tour. And for all intents and purposes, so was his year, period.

Oh, he went on to play at St. Andrews, where he had won two of his three British Opens—including his last in 1978, when he shot seven-under-par 281 in what he called the best he had ever played from tee to green. But even that may be coming to an end.

"I'm not going to keep playing the British Open on a regular basis," he said after he birdied the last hole in his final-round 71, which left him at one-over-par 289 and in a five-way tie for 63rd place. "I'll probably go back to Muirfield [site of his first British Open victory in 1966] in two years, and I could come back here [in 1996], but I'll decide depending on how I'm playing."

After St. Andrews, there was the awkward situation at the PGA Championship at Shoal Creek, a course he designed for a friend, Hall Thompson. It was Thompson who raised a racial furor weeks before the championship in Birmingham, Alabama. His remarks that his club would not be pressured into accepting black members, and that present members would feel uncomfortable if there were black guests because "that's just not done in Birmingham," sent repercussions rippling throughout the golf world.

Nicklaus, caught in the middle, said that Hall Thompson was a very generous man and had done a lot of wonderful things for the city of Birmingham. He said that private clubs should be able to select their own members but that there was an open policy at Muirfield Village, the club he founded near his birthplace in Columbus, Ohio. It wasn't any easier for Nicklaus on the course, which drew more complaints than any major championship in recent years because of its high, wiry, Bermuda-grass rough and brick-hard greens.

"I only hit three fairways, and that's no way to play this course," he said while walking to the locker room after an opening-round 76. He improved slightly to a 74 the next day, but he still missed the cut by a shot. He didn't play much better the next week at The International at Castle Pines, Colorado, another course he designed. And that was it for 1990, a year that started with so much promise at The Tradition and ended with more questions than answers.

Nicklaus, like every other player on the Senior Tour, went through a down period in his career during his late forties. Not even the skills of the world's best player were immune to the deterioration of aging muscles.

The magical back-nine, six-under-par 30 at the 1986 Masters brought him one of the most popular victories in golf history. It was his first win since his own Memorial in 1984, when Andy Bean missed a three-foot putt on the third playoff hole. Between that brisk May day at Muirfield Village and the Senior Tour, the 1986 Masters was his only victory in five and a half years.

But what a victory it was. When the week started, Nicklaus was classified among the also-rans. He hadn't won a major championship since the 1980 PGA Championship. In seven starts in 1986, he had missed the cut three times and withdrawn once. He arrived at Augusta ranked 160th on the money list. When veteran golf writer Tom McCollister of the *Atlanta Journal and Constitution* handicapped the field, he wrote that Nicklaus was over the hill and had no chance. In an effort to motivate Jack, someone staying with him that week at an Augusta home taped the article to the refrigerator door, and Nicklaus said it kept him focused all tournament.

EYE ON THE PRIZE: *In the second round of the 1986 Masters, Nicklaus shows his deep concentration as he blasts out of a bunker en route to a 71 that left him back in the pack.*

When Nicklaus opened with a 74, everyone nodded knowingly, rubbed their chins and proclaimed that, of course, at age 46 he had no chance. The consensus was that he couldn't putt anymore, and besides, his back had been bothering him. A second-round 71 merely assured Nicklaus of making the cut for the 18th straight year, discounting 1983 when he withdrew with back spasms. He certainly wasn't challenging front-running Seve Ballesteros, the dashing Spaniard who had become the youngest Masters champion at age 23 in 1980, and who won again in 1983. Even a third-round 69 merely put Nicklaus on the leader board at 214. There were eight players, including defending champion Bernhard Langer, Tom Watson, Tom Kite and Ballesteros, between Nicklaus and leader Greg Norman.

The most magnificent and best remembered charge of Nicklaus' unparalleled career began under unusual circumstances at the ninth green that unforgettable Sunday. Twice in the first eight holes he had missed putts of 4 feet; he was even-par for the day, two-under for the tournament and seemingly relegated to a sentimental journey through the famed back nine. But first, the birdie attempt at No. 9, with the usual cheering throng around the green.

As he addressed his 11-foot putt, a deafening roar erupted from over the hill at the par-5 eighth green. Kite had holed a sand wedge shot from 80 yards for an eagle to go five-under-par. Nicklaus smiled weakly and prepared to putt again. He was about to draw his putter back when, unbelievably, another roar boomed from the eighth green, even louder than before. Ballesteros, paired with Kite and trying to regain his second-round lead, had holed his 50-yard pitch shot for an eagle to go eight-under-par, one in front of Norman and six ahead of Nicklaus.

After backing off for a second time, Nicklaus smiled, looked at the gallery with a shrug and said, "Let's see if we can make a roar of our own." When his ball tumbled into the cup, they did, although it seemed more out of affection than the spontaneous explosions that came from the contenders' gallery.

So Nicklaus headed for the back nine, trailing by five and knowing that he needed to take no more than 30 strokes—and that several of the world's best players behind him all had to falter—for him to have a chance at his sixth Masters championship. He started quickly by rolling in 20-footers for birdies at the 10th and 11th holes, but he lapsed back with a bogey at the tricky little par-3 12th hole when he flew the shallow green.

"Oddly, I don't know why, but it was that hole that got me going," he said in the jammed press conference afterward. "Yesterday, I birdied the hole and got defensive. This time, after a bogey, I knew I was running out of time, that I had to be aggressive the rest of the way."

He birdied the par-5 13th hole with a daring tee shot, drawing a three-wood around the trees precariously close to Rae's Creek. A three-iron to the middle of the green set up a two-putt birdie that put him at five-under-par, two shots behind Ballesteros, who had bogeyed the 9th hole and started the back with three successive pars. A good chip gave Nicklaus a one-putt par at the 14th, and then he hit his best shot of the tournament at the par-5 15th. After a long drive, he had 202 yards to the flag, and he powered a four-iron within 12 feet, setting up an eagle putt. "I had the same putt before and didn't hit it hard enough, and it broke off," said the player with one of the most flawless memories in the game. "This time I hit it straight." The immense gallery, which had been growing with each hole of the Nicklaus charge, exploded with a roar maybe never exceeded at this famed course. "I couldn't hear anything," Nicklaus says. "I mean, nothing. All I knew was I was hitting greens and making birdies and I was going to keep doing it."

It was at the picturesque, water-guarded, par-3 16th hole, framed with tall pines and bright pink azaleas, that Nicklaus had made a 40-foot uphill birdie putt that broke a tie with Tom Weiskopf and Johnny Miller and sent him to his last Masters triumph in 1975. This time, Nicklaus hit a five-iron that landed just above the flag to the right,

drew back left and almost rolled into the cup, nestling 3 feet below the hole. After his playing partner, Sandy Lyle, holed out, Nicklaus sank his birdie putt, and again the roar was deafening.

Listening to it all, one ovation after the other, was Ballesteros, now standing back in the 15th fairway and contemplating the same gambling approach shot that Nicklaus had just fired at the flag to make eagle. After discussing it with his caddie, older brother Vicente, Seve selected a four-iron. But he was too quick with his swing and hooked it into a pond for a bogey. He was through. Although he was never over par in four rounds and finished seven-under, Ballesteros wound up fourth, two shots behind Nicklaus and one behind Kite and Norman.

Striding to his drive at the 17th hole, which he had hooked into trouble, Nicklaus was unaware of the misfortune that had befallen Ballesteros. All he knew was that he needed one more birdie. He made an excellent recovery, punching his ball within 11 feet of the flag. He realized he had made the putt when it was still rolling toward the cup, and as he stuck his tongue out and pointed his putter at the hole, dozens of cameras snapped one of golf's most famous photos.

A strong three-wood and a wind-battling five-iron left Nicklaus on the front edge of the 18th green, some 50 feet from the hole. He stroked his first putt within inches, tapped in his par and emotionally embraced his son, Jackie, who had caddied for him. Then they went to Bob Jones' cabin to watch on television as his challengers tried to spoil one of the most heartwarming stories in all of sports.

THE PUTT: *Perhaps the most famous—surely one of the best-remembered—birdie putts of Nicklaus' famed career came on the 17th green of the final round of the 1986 Masters. The birdie gave him a one-shot victory over Tom Kite and Greg Norman.*

Ballesteros three-putted the 17th green from far left of the hole—approximately the same area where Raymond Floyd three-putted in losing to Nick Faldo in the 1990 Masters. Now it was down to Kite and Norman. Kite, many times a contender at Augusta but still looking for his first major championship, needed a birdie at 18 to tie Nicklaus. His approach shot got to the back of the green, about 12 feet right of the hole. The putt looked good all the way before it trickled off below the hole. "I made that putt. It just didn't go in," Kite said after tying for second for the second time. "I read it dead straight. I could take 15 balls out there and there wouldn't be a one of them that would go left. I couldn't hit a better putt."

Now it was up to Norman, the flamboyant Great White Shark, he of seemingly unlimited potential who would come close so many times at Augusta in the 1980s. That day, after a double bogey at the 10th hole and missing a 4-foot birdie attempt at No. 13, he was threatening to eclipse Nicklaus's glowing performance with a record-smashing charge of his own. Starting at the 14th hole, he reeled off four consecutive birdies, hitting it 2 feet from the pin at the 16th and then, after an errant drive, knocking a wedge within 10 feet of the 17th hole and sinking that pressure putt to tie Nicklaus at nine-under-par.

At the 18th tee, Norman decided to use his three-wood to avoid the gaping fairway bunker on the left. That gave him a four-iron, and he took a gamble he still regrets.

"That was the first time all week I conceded to my ego," he says. "I tried to go for the flag instead of playing for a safe two-putt and a tie. Halfway through the shot, I knew I was in trouble." He came off the shot, pushing it 20 yards right into the gallery on the hill beside the green. Now he was faced with a difficult chip, and he did well to get it within 15 feet. But it was above the hole and he pulled the putt about 4 feet past.

Nicklaus was the champion again, but this time was different

A SIXTH GREEN JACKET: *Nicklaus is pre-sented his sixth green jacket, slipped on by 1985 champion Bernhard Langer, after shoot-ing a final-nine 30 to win again at Augusta National.*

from the other 19 major championships he had won over the past 27 years, starting with the 1959 U.S. Amateur title at the Broadmoor in Colorado Springs. This time, even Jack may have realized it might be his last.

"I had tears in my eyes several times today," he said after donning another green jacket. "When the crowd gets like that, I get pretty emotional. I sort of well up. And having your son share an experience like this is such a wonderful feeling. This might be the time for me to quit. Maybe I should say goodbye, but I still enjoy the competition, I love golf and I still think I can play a little, so I plan to keep competing."

It wasn't easy after that. There were no more victory speeches, no more emotional embraces with Jackie or hugs from Barbara at the 18th green. There was only the late-forties malaise that inflicts every professional golfer, even the best.

The following year, Nicklaus became, in his own words, a "ceremonial golfer." He reduced his schedule to 11 tournaments and had just one top-10 finish—a tie for 7th at The Masters, where he never broke 70. He finished four shots behind Larry Mize, Ballesteros and Norman, who played off to an incredible finish when Mize knocked in a 140-foot chip shot on the second extra hole to win. In 1988, Nicklaus played in just 9 events. His best effort was a tie for 21st at The Masters, and he finished the year 177th on the money list with only $28,845.

His back was bothering him all the time now. It first hit him in 1983 when he had to withdraw from The Masters, and it had gotten progressively worse. The problem was two herniated disks in his lower lumbar area, and as he grew older, he suffered from severe stiffness and numbness in his left leg. It affected his powerful lower-body swing action and forced him to compensate with an unnatural upper-body movement that made practicing difficult and unpleasant.

"You don't want to play when it hurts," he says. "I couldn't work on my game, and I got in some bad habits. Then you don't want to work on it and you get frustrated because you're not playing well. It's an endless circle."

This was as low as Nicklaus ever got. He was taking cortisone shots to relieve the pain, but now he couldn't even play tennis or go skiing, his two favorite pastimes. He consulted several specialists, and some recommended surgery.

One round of golf he'll never forget came on his 49th birthday, when he played nine holes at his home course at Loxahatchee Club in North Palm Beach, Florida, with Gardner Dickinson and his wife, Judy, who plays on the LPGA Tour.

"I actually shot my age, 49 for nine holes," Nicklaus eagerly reported at the AT&T Pebble Beach National Pro-Am two weeks later. "I was so weak I couldn't outhit Judy, but I feel so much better now."

The reason for his rapid improvement was that Nicklaus went to San Diego on his way to Pebble Beach and spent some time with Peter Eqoscue, a kinesiologist who recommended a rigorous stretching and exercise program. As is his nature, Nicklaus became a fanatic about the exercise program, and he would fall to the floor of a press room and put on a Jane Fonda imitation at the drop of a question.

Feeling better and trying to reduce his weight from 200 pounds, Nicklaus played a little better in 1989, making the cut in all four majors, finishing 9th at The International, coming in 10th at the Canadian Open and winning $96,595.

"I enjoyed myself more that year because, at times, I felt competitive again," he said. "I realize I don't have the strength I did when I was younger—nobody does—but I still hit it far enough. I think if I prepare, work on my game, I'm still capable of winning."

So after reaching his 50th birthday January 21, a slimmed-down, exercise-conscious Nicklaus set out with a new goal: he wanted to become the first player to win on the Senior Tour and the regular tour in the same year.

"It's been a long time since I've had a goal," he said. "The last time I remember was in 1980. I had a horrible year in '79 [dropping from 14th to a career-low 71st on the money list]. It revitalized me. I realized I had been neglecting my game, so I started working hard again, and to motivate myself I set a goal of winning a major championship." He won the U.S. Open at Baltusrol Golf Club in Springfield, New Jersey, that year, opening with a 63 and finally outlasting Japan's Isao Aoki with a birdie-birdie finish for a final-round 68 and a two-stroke victory. Then he tied Walter Hagen's record for most PGA Championships by winning his fifth in a six-shot runaway from Andy Bean at Oak Hill in Rochester, New York.

Now he had another goal—one more difficult, perhaps, because several players have won major championships after their 40th birthdays, but only Sam Snead, at 52 years and 10 months, ever won a PGA Tour event (the Greater Greensboro Open) on the sunny side of 50.

Nicklaus certainly gave no indication he could pull it off when he started the year finishing 61st at Pebble Beach, closing with a pair of 78s. Then it was on to Doral, one of his favorite tournaments, where he won in 1972 and 1975. With the death of his longtime guru, Jack Grout, the previous May, Nicklaus had been left without an advisor, so he went to see famed teacher Peter Kostis at Boca Raton, Florida, for the first time, and it strengthened his confidence.

"My son, Jackie, has been going to Pete, so I stopped by one day and he made three or four minor adjustments in my swing," Nicklaus said. "I've seen him four or five times in the last two weeks and I feel good about my game."

Then Nicklaus got a little sentimental. He talked of turning 50, of his father dying when he was 56, of what his business meant to him and his family, of how his days of being the best golfer in the world were over.

T I P

"One thing that never fails to excite galleries at pro tournaments is the approach shot that bites into the green and spins backward several feet. It's not only exciting to watch, but also highly functional to play, particularly when you're short of landing area in front of the flagstick.

"Maximum backspin is the product of high club-head speed combined with a sharply descending club-head path that leads directly into the back of the ball before chewing into the turf. You may not be able to equal the pros' club-head velocity, but there is no reason why you can't duplicate their path of club-head movement.

"Simply open the club face at address, then swing the club head up sooner and higher on a more upright plane than normal by cocking your wrists right from the start of the action. Return the club head to the ball at the same steep angle with a cutting type of action, keeping your left wrist firm and swinging the club head straight out toward the target. Delay the rolling of your right hand over your left to avoid closing the club face through impact, which would reduce backspin and drive the ball forward on too low a trajectory."

Jack Nicklaus

"I can't think too much about the Senior Tour because I'm having a hard time being 50," he admitted. "I still feel I can be competitive on the regular tour, so why am I supposed to run to another tour? I'm having a hard time getting excited about the Seniors. Sure, I said they were the same guys I've been beating for 30 years, but that was blown out of proportion. I certainly never meant to demean or downgrade the ability of the guys on the Senior Tour. I beat them for 30 years, but a lot of times they beat me, too.

"It's going to be difficult to play on both tours and maintain my business. I could be building golf courses from January to December. It's a darn good business and it continues to grow. It's a business for my five kids. I have 130 employees and I can't turn my back on them. So I've got to try to juggle all the things I want to do this year. Right now, I'm starting one of the busiest stretches I've had in many years. Between the two tours, I'm playing 7 of the next 11 weeks, so I'll just have to wait and see what happens."

What happened was that he still couldn't compete on the PGA Tour, tying for 68th at Doral and missing the cut at The Players Championship. Then he was off to Arizona to make his debut on the Senior Tour at The Tradition, and it would turn out to be one of the most enjoyable tournaments of his life.

"I can't say I looked forward to being 50 with enthusiasm, but after a while, I guess you get used to it," he said upon arriving in Arizona. "Actually, I am looking forward to this tournament although I'm not playing well. If you only play 10 tournaments a year, you're not going to be competitive, no matter what tour you're playing on. I'm not favoring my back anymore. Now I just have to convince myself to swing like I used to.

"But I'm the new kid on the block this week. I've put a lot of pressure on myself. The other players are waiting, saying, 'Come show us,' so I've got to prove myself again. Sure, there's pressure on me, but I've had that since I started playing tournaments when I was

SENIOR DEBUT: *In his first round on the Senior Tour, Nicklaus blasts out of a bunker and shoots 71 at The Tradition in Scottsdale, Arizona. He fired a final-round 68 to beat Gary Player by four shots and said, "I got the monkey off my back."*

13. Every tournament I've ever played, I was expected to do well, so really, this is no different."

Trevino, ever the con man, had made sure that Nicklaus understood his position by saying, "Jack has everything to lose and nothing to gain. It doesn't matter where he tees it up, what course, what tournament, he's always the man to beat. If he wins, it's expected. If he doesn't . . ."

By now, Nicklaus was admitting that his sessions with Kostis weren't very helpful. He said he didn't absorb much because he's not a mechanical player—he goes more by feel and tempo. When he first arrived at Desert Mountain for The Tradition, he started talking to Jim Flick, a member of the *Golf Digest* teaching school staff who had worked with Grout and watched Nicklaus swing thousands of times. Now Flick told him, "I don't see the Nicklaus swing."

So it was back to work. And Nicklaus worked, particularly on his short game, which had always been his nemesis. After a storm canceled the first round on Thursday, there was hail over the practice tee. It was about five o'clock—cocktail time for most of the players, who had spent the afternoon lounging by the fireplaces in the luxurious locker room spinning yarns. When the storm stopped, one player, bundled in a heavy sweater, headed for the practice range. It was Nicklaus.

In a quiet moment the next day, Nicklaus talked about his first day on the Senior Tour. Perhaps, he said, it was best that the round was rained out. It gave him a chance to do something he said he hadn't done in 20 years. He sat around the locker room and swapped lies with the other players.

"That's the big difference between this tour and the regular tour," he said. "On the regular tour, everybody seems so busy, so much in a hurry. Here, these guys are so much more relaxed. I sat around for four hours telling stories. It was a great afternoon. The guys couldn't have been nicer."

An opening-round 71 left Nicklaus two shots behind Phil Rodgers, Al Geiberger, Bruce Crampton and Mike Hill, but he passed them all by chipping from 30 feet with a sand wedge for an eagle on the 18th hole Saturday. That gave him a 67 and a two-shot lead over Rodgers, Crampton and Gary Player.

"The chip at 18 was the perfect situation for the shot that Jim Flick and I have been working on," Nicklaus said. "I had been chipping terribly and he just told me to choke down on the club and accelerate through the ball. One, you get better control going down on the club, and two, the ryegrass around the greens is very heavy, and you have to swing more firmly through it."

Nicklaus also was pleased with his iron play, which playing partner Gary Player said was as good as he'd seen Jack strike the ball in years.

"When you guys [reporters] asked me a few days ago if I thought Jack could still win on the regular tour, I said I thought it was unlikely," Player said. "Well, I take that back. From what I saw yesterday, Jack could win on any tour. He's striking the ball flush every time. His shots are going so long and so high, and they're coming down so softly, landing like a butterfly with sore feet."

Although he bogeyed two par-5s, Nicklaus was in command the final day, shooting 68 and beating Player by four shots. "I got the monkey off my back," he said. "But I had put it there. Now I don't have to worry about winning on the Senior Tour anymore. I didn't know how I'd react today. The most important thing is to keep your composure and I did that."

With The Masters looming on the immediate horizon the next week, Nicklaus' confidence was sky high. He said that the Cochise course he designed at Desert Mountain was similar to Augusta National in many ways, and that the way he played, the way he handled the pressure down the stretch, gave him a tremendous lift.

"This was terrific preparation because the grass is the same, the greens are the same—although not as slick—and I had to hit a lot of high shots," he said. "I think my chances are pretty good at Augusta.

NEVER BETTER? *In perhaps his best scoring performance ever, Nicklaus shot rounds of 65-68-64-64 for a record-breaking 27-under-par 261 to win the 1990 Senior Tournament Players Championship at Dearborn, Michigan.*

If I'm going to win on the regular tour, I think The Masters would be the easiest to win. Length won't be a factor and there's no rough. Also, I've won there six times; I know the course and how to play it."

He gave it his best shot. He trailed third-round leader Raymond Floyd by five strokes starting the final round, and everyone knows he made up that deficit in nine holes back in 1986. He drew one of the biggest ovations of the bright, sunny day when he holed a bunker shot for a birdie at the 7th hole, but it came after successive bogeys on the two previous holes. He also birdied the 12th and 13th holes, but he three-putted the 15th and hit his tee shot in the water at 16, drowning his last hopes.

Still, the sixth-place finish was his high point on the regular tour. He withdrew from the USF&G Classic with a sore hip after an opening 77, and he finished 26th at the Memorial. Then, as quickly as it had disappeared, his putting stroke returned on the Senior Tour, and he put on one of the most remarkable performances of his magnificent career in winning the Senior Tournament Players Championship at Dearborn, Michigan. En route to a record-breaking 27-under-par 261 with rounds of 65-68-64-64, he made 28 birdies and 2 eagles.

"I can't remember when I've made that many birdies," he said. "I holed a lot of 20-footers this week. I don't think I've ever putted this well for four days."

Just as The Tradition had given him confidence for The Masters, this winning performance had Nicklaus thinking about the U.S Open the following week at Medinah near Chicago, but he never got the feel for those greens and tied for 33d.

Then it was off to the U.S. Senior Open and another duel with Trevino—one that left him devastated and wondering about his future and the Senior Tour.

There was no reason to expect much more the next year, but once again the Golden Bear surprised his critics and solidified his place in history as the greatest golfer of all time.

It was at The Tradition again that he waved the red flag, signaling to the world that he never could be counted out of a tournament, that he still had the ability to overcome enormous odds and win. After an opening 71, Nicklaus trailed first-round leader and close friend Phil Rodgers by six shots. A second-round 73 left him an even dozen strokes behind Rodgers (65-67) and prompted a phone call to his old buddy.

"I called Phil that night and told him I thought I was too far back, but that I'd give it everything I had," Nicklaus recalls. "Realistically, the only chance I had was to shoot two very good rounds and have Phil back up. If he shoots 72-72 the last two rounds, I don't catch him."

Rodgers, who shared a room with Nicklaus many years ago in the Crows Nest—the cramped living quarters for amateur players on the top floor of the clubhouse at Augusta National—certainly was a candidate to fold. He hadn't won on the Senior Tour. In fact, the last of his five victories on the PGA Tour was the 1966 Buick Open. He did his part, shooting a pair of 73s, but Nicklaus still had plenty of work ahead. Never in his legendary career had he come from 12 shots back to win. Not many players have.

His third-round 66 had the leaders looking over their shoulders, but Nicklaus still was five behind Rodgers and Jim Colbert and four back of Jim Dent and Ben Smith, an auto mechanic who didn't turn pro until he was 48 and has never won in seven years on the Senior Tour.

The highlight for Nicklaus—a career highlight in a lifetime of them—came on the par-5 fourth hole, when he rolled in a 94-foot putt for eagle. "That was ridiculous," he said later. "I thought I'd be lucky to get down in two." It was later determined to be the second longest putt of his career, surpassed only by a 110-foot no-brainer at the Desert Inn in Las Vegas in the 1964 Tournament of Champions. With birdies at Nos. 7 and 8, Nicklaus made the turn in 32, and a

SUCCESSFUL DEFENSE: *Nicklaus returned to The Tradition in 1991 and staged one of the greatest comebacks of his career, overcoming a 12-shot deficit to successfully defend his title in Scottsdale, Arizona.*

steady 35 on the back enabled him to post a 67 that nobody could catch.

Of particular satisfaction was the fact that he got up and down from a bunker for par at 17, and chipped within 4 feet for a birdie at the last hole. Those were the shots that boosted his confidence going to The Masters, just as it had done a year ago.

Once again, he got into contention at Augusta with a first-round 68, and Friday he staged a show for the ages when he teamed with Tom Watson and shot one of the most spectacular 72s in Masters history. What's so difficult about an even-par 72? Well, it's not easy when you hit two balls into the water at the 155-yard 12th hole for a quadruple bogey (Nicklaus' first ever at Augusta). He was only two shots out of the lead before that hole, and six back when he scaled the 13th tee. He responded with four consecutive birdies, climaxed by a 35-footer at the par-3 16th. The 72 Saturday was more routine, and when he stumbled to a 76 Sunday, some wondered if a weary Nicklaus, after back-to-back emotionally draining tournaments at The Tradition and The Masters, could bounce back the next week at the PGA Seniors Championship.

Did he ever. In one of his most intimidating performances, he started with a pair of 66s and coasted to a six-shot victory at 17-under-par over the PGA National Course, rated one of the most difficult on the Senior circuit.

"I've never had more control over the ball," he said. "I'm hitting it long and straight, my putting has been exceptional and, believe it or not, my chipping has been consistently good."

Once again, the Golden Bear had wiped away all the doubts and proved that when he's on his game—when he focuses strictly on golf—he still can dominate and be the best player on the Senior Tour.

He proved it once more at the Senior tournament he wanted to win the most when he fired a five-under-par 65 to beat Chi Chi Rodriguez in a playoff for the U.S. Senior Open at famed Oakland Hills in Birmingham, Michigan.

First, the winner receives an exemption to the U.S. Open and Nicklaus needed it. His past exemptions had expired and he required a special invitation to play that June at Hazeltine.

"I want to play my way into the 1992 Open," he said before the U.S. Senior Open started, and then went out and played as well as he had all year.

Second, losing down the stretch to Lee Trevino in the 1991 U.S. Senior Open still gnawed at Nicklaus, particularly the way he lost, missing that four-footer after Trevino predicted he would on television.

"That was the best golf I've seen Jack play in 15 years," Rodriguez said following the playoff, ironically played out under the same type of threatening skies after a rain delay as the previous U.S. Senior Open.

Nicklaus opened with five birdies in the first eight holes, including a chip-in from 40 feet at No. 7 to lead by three at the turn and eliminate any pressure down the stretch. But there had been enough pressure Sunday to last a week.

Trevino, at even-par 210, started with a one-shot lead over Nicklaus, Rodriguez and J. C. Snead. Standing on the 17th tee, Trevino and Nicklaus were tied with Rodriguez and Al Geiberger after Snead had collapsed (79).

Trevino said he misclubbed after hitting a 5-iron short of the left bunker and making bogey. Nicklaus thought he had the lead after sinking a five-foot birdie putt, but the roar from the 18th green told him that Rodriguez had birdied and he needed a par on the difficult 447-yard dogleg 18th hole to force a playoff. He got it by hitting a 7-iron within 14 feet and two-putting. Geiberger, playing with Rodriguez, had driven into the rough and made bogey, so it was Nicklaus and Rodriguez on Monday and once again the Golden Bear rose to the occasion.

By winning, Nicklaus matched Arnold Palmer's record of winning the U.S. Amateur, the U.S. Open and the U.S. Senior Open, and now, one wonders, if there are any goals left. It was his last Senior event of the year and he gave no hint that he would alter his limited schedule in 1992.

His performance at Oakland Hills left no doubt that Nicklaus still will be the favorite in any Senior tournaments he enters this year, that when motivated and focused, he's still the best.

PHOTO CREDITS

THE SENIOR TOUR

p. 3 Jeff McBride
p. 4 Jeff McBride
p. 5 Jeff McBride
p. 5 Jeff McBride
p. 6 Sam Greenwood
p. 7 Sam Greenwood
p. 7 Jeff McBride
p. 8 Jeff McBride

STATISTICAL HIGHLIGHTS 1991

JIM DENT

EXEMPT STATUS: Top 31 on 1991 Senior Tour money list
HEIGHT: 6'3"   WEIGHT: 224
BIRTH DATE: May 9, 1939   BIRTHPLACE: Augusta, Georgia
RESIDENCE: Tampa, Florida
FAMILY: Wife, Willye; Children, Radiah Laceyette (4/1/73), James Antonio (6/2/76)
COLLEGE ATTENDED: Paine College (Augusta, Georgia)
TURNED PROFESSIONAL: 1966   JOINED PGA TOUR: 1970
PGA TOUR VICTORIES: None
PGA TOUR CAREER EARNINGS: $565,245   PLAYOFF RECORD: 0-0
PGA TOUR YEAR BY YEAR:

1971—$ 7,101—150	1980—$16,223—136
1972—$24,285— 93	1981—$26,523—116
1973—$26,393— 97	1982—$55,095— 82
1974—$48,486— 59	1983—$40,423—113
1975—$33,649— 69	1984—$49,941—109
1976—$20,102—102	1985—$30,102—144
1977—$46,411— 64	1986—$34,342—157
1978—$30,063— 86	1987—$ 1,322—276
1979—$30,709—109	1988—$44,365—156

JOINED SENIOR PGA TOUR: 1989
SENIOR PGA TOUR VICTORIES:
1989 MONY Syracuse Senior Classic, Newport Cup; 1990 Vantage at the Dominion, MONY Syracuse Senior Classic, Kroger Senior Classic, Crestar Classic (TOTAL: 6)
SENIOR TOUR CAREER EARNINGS: $1,560,221
ALL-TIME EARNINGS (Regular and Senior Tour combined): $2,125,466
SENIOR TOUR PLAYOFF RECORD: 0-0
SENIOR TOUR YEAR BY YEAR:
1989—$337,691—12
1990—$693,214— 6
1991—$529,315— 9
1991 SENIOR TOUR SUMMARY:
Tournaments entered—32; top 10 finishes—13; stroke average—70.79; best finishes—2 MONY Syracuse Classic, T2 The Tradition, T2 Newport Cup, T2 Vantage Championship
OTHER ACHIEVEMENTS:
Won three consecutive Florida PGA Championships starting in 1976 . . . winner of 1983 Michelob-Chattanooga Gold Cup Classic on Tournament Players Series . . . member of U.S. DuPont Cup team in 1990 and 1991.

					RANK	
					NO.	%
1. DRIVING DISTANCE	#DRIVES 200 TOT. DIST. 57,287		AVG.	286.4	1	100%
2. DRIVING ACCURACY	POSSIBLE FAIRWAYS 1,387 # HIT 847		PCT.	.611	61	15%
3. GREENS IN REGULATION (GIR)	HOLES PLAYED 1,800 GREENS HIT 1,289		PCT.	.716	9	88%
4. PUTTING	GREENS HIT 1,289 # PUTTS GIR 2,320		AVG.	1.800	24	67%
5. TOTAL DRIVING	TOTAL OF STATISTICS 1–2 RANKING			62	22	69%
6. EAGLES	TOTAL EAGLES			19	1	100%
7. BIRDIES	TOTAL BIRDIES			382	4	94%
8. SCORING AVERAGE				70.79	11	85%
9. SAND SAVES	BUNKERS HIT 152 SAVES 73		PCT.	.480	26	64%
10. ALL-AROUND	TOTAL OF STATISTICS 1–9 RANKING			159	7	90%
11. MONEY	TOTAL MONEY		$529,315.30		9	88%
12. PAR BREAKERS	HOLES PLAYED 1,800 BIRDIES/EAGLES 401		PCT.	.223	4	94%

OTHER STATISTICS

PUTTS PER ROUND	ROUNDS PLAYED 100 TOTAL PUTTS 3,018	AVG.	30.18	49	32%
PAR 3 BIRDIES	PAR 3 HOLES PLAYED 413 BIRDIES MADE 41	PCT.	.099	58	19%
PAR 4 BIRDIES	PAR 4 HOLES PLAYED 1,006 BIRDIES MADE 163	PCT.	.162	12	83%
PAR 5 BIRDIES	PAR 5 HOLES PLAYED 381 BIRDIES MADE 178	PCT.	.467	1	100%
BIRDIE CONVERSION PERCENTAGE	BIRDIES 382 DIVIDED BY GIR 1,289	PCT.	.296	8	89%

AL GEIBERGER

EXEMPT STATUS: Top 31 on 1991 Senior Tour money list
HEIGHT: 6'2"   WEIGHT: 185
BIRTH DATE: September 1, 1937   BIRTHPLACE: Red Bluff, California
RESIDENCE: Solvang, California
FAMILY: Wife, Carolyn; Children, Lee Ann (9/14/63), John (5/20/68), Brent (5/22/68), Bryan (9/28/76), Al, Jr. (1/2/88), Kathleen Marie (1/11/91)
COLLEGE ATTENDED: University of Southern California
TURNED PROFESSIONAL: 1959   JOINED PGA TOUR: 1960
PGA TOUR VICTORIES:
1962 Ontario Open; 1963 Almaden Open; 1965 American Golf Classic; 1966 PGA Championship; 1974 Sahara Invitational; 1975 Tournament of Champions, Tournament Players Championship; 1976 Greater Greensboro Open, Western Open; 1977 Danny Thomas Memphis Classic; 1979 Colonial National Invitation (TOTAL: 11)
PGA TOUR CAREER EARNINGS: $1,256,548   PLAYOFF RECORD: 1-1

PGA TOUR YEAR BY YEAR:

1960—$ 10,511— 37	1973—$ 63,467— 45
1961—$ 18,656— 30	1974—$ 91,628— 23
1962—$ 26,045— 20	1975—$175,693— 6
1963—$ 34,126— 8	1976—$194,821— 5
1964—$ 36,323— 13	1977—$ 88,645— 30
1965—$ 59,699— 8	1978—$ 20,477—107
1966—$ 63,220— 10	1979—$ 70,625— 58
1967—$ 63,315— 14	1980—$ 15,379—139
1968—$ 64,931— 22	1981—$ 8,508—176
1969—$ 26,868— 65	1982—$ 21,089—148
1970—$ 21,233— 91	1983—$ 13,477—172
1971—$ 20,848— 99	1984—$ 9,807—181
1972—$ 29,710— 80	1985—$ 11,001—176
	1986—$ 8,212—212

JOINED SENIOR PGA TOUR: 1987
SENIOR PGA TOUR VICTORIES:
1987 Vantage Championship, Hilton Head Seniors International, Las Vegas Senior Classic; 1988 Pointe/Del E. Webb Arizona Classic; 1989 GTE Northwest Classic; 1991 Kroger Senior Classic (TOTAL: 6)

SENIOR TOUR CAREER EARNINGS: $2,034,115

ALL-TIME EARNINGS (Regular and Senior Tour combined): $3,299,303

SENIOR TOUR PLAYOFF RECORD: 1-0

SENIOR TOUR YEAR BY YEAR:
1987—$264,798— 9
1988—$348,735— 6
1989—$527,033— 3
1990—$373,624—13
1991—$519,926—10

OTHER SENIOR VICTORIES:
1989 Liberty Mutual Legends of Golf (with Harold Henning)

1991 SENIOR TOUR SUMMARY:
Tournaments entered—25; top 10 finishes—12; stroke average—70.39; best finishes—1 Kroger Senior Classic, T2 Southwestern Bell Classic, 3 U.S. Senior Open, 3 Ameritech Senior Open

OTHER ACHIEVEMENTS:
1954 National Jaycee Champion . . . 1967 and 1975 Ryder Cup teams . . . winner of 1962 Caracas Open, 1982 Frontier Airlines Open and 1985 Colorado Open

					RANK	
					NO.	%
1. DRIVING DISTANCE	#DRIVES 152	TOT. DIST. 40,461		AVG.	266.2	8	89%
2. DRIVING ACCURACY	POSSIBLE FAIRWAYS 1,052	# HIT 697		PCT.	.663	41	43%
3. GREENS IN REGULATION (GIR)	HOLES PLAYED 1,368	GREENS HIT 971		PCT.	.710	11	85%
4. PUTTING	GREENS HIT 971	# PUTTS GIR 1,728		AVG.	1.780	10	86%
5. TOTAL DRIVING	TOTAL OF STATISTICS 1–2	RANKING			49	9	88%
6. EAGLES	TOTAL EAGLES				9	12	83%
7. BIRDIES	TOTAL BIRDIES				277	34	53%
8. SCORING AVERAGE					70.39	7	90%
9. SAND SAVES	BUNKERS HIT 87	SAVES 37		PCT.	.425	44	39%
10. ALL-AROUND	TOTAL OF STATISTICS 1–9 RANKING				176	12	83%
11. MONEY	TOTAL MONEY				$519,925.60	10	86%
12. PAR BREAKERS	HOLES PLAYED 1,368	BIRDIES/EAGLES 286		PCT.	.209	9	88%

OTHER STATISTICS

					NO.	%
PUTTS PER ROUND	ROUNDS PLAYED 76	TOTAL PUTTS 2,259		AVG.	29.72	27	63%
PAR 3 BIRDIES	PAR 3 HOLES PLAYED 316	BIRDIES MADE 43		PCT.	.136	16	78%
PAR 4 BIRDIES	PAR 4 HOLES PLAYED 769	BIRDIES MADE 131		PCT.	.170	7	90%
PAR 5 BIRDIES	PAR 5 HOLES PLAYED 283	BIRDIES MADE 103		PCT.	.364	19	74%
BIRDIE CONVERSION PERCENTAGE	BIRDIES 277 DIVIDED BY GIR 971			PCT.	.285	12	83%

DAVE HILL

EXEMPT STATUS: Top 31 on 1991 Senior Tour money list

HEIGHT: 5'11"   WEIGHT: 152

BIRTH DATE: May 20, 1937   BIRTHPLACE: Jackson, Michigan

RESIDENCE: Jackson, Michigan

FAMILY: Wife, Joyce

TURNED PROFESSIONAL: 1958   JOINED PGA TOUR: 1959

PGA TOUR VICTORIES:
1961 Home of the Sun Open, Denver Open; 1963 Hot Springs Open; 1967 Memphis Open; 1969 Memphis Open, Buick Open, IVB-Philadelphia Classic; 1970 Danny Thomas Memphis Open; 1972 Monsanto Open; 1973 Danny Thomas Memphis Classic; 1974 Houston Open; 1975 Sahara Invitational; 1976 Greater Milwaukee Open (TOTAL: 13)

PGA TOUR CAREER EARNINGS: $1,130,430   PLAYOFF RECORD: 4-2

PGA TOUR YEAR BY YEAR:
1959—$ 1,655— 84
1960—$ 7,424— 46
1961—$ 21,560— 22
1962—$ 22,731— 25
1963—$ 18,906— 25
1964—$ 13,333— 56
1965—$ 14,674— 58
1966—$ 26,857— 35
1967—$ 49,774— 23
1968—$ 34,036— 48
1969—$156,423— 2
1970—$118,415— 10
1971—$ 61,410— 36
1972—$ 98,464— 18
1973—$ 95,574— 17
1974—$133,674— 11
1975—$ 80,533— 24
1976—$116,606— 19
1977—$ 17,059—116
1978—$ 3,781—177
1979—$ 5,779—175
1980—$ 43,187— 79
1981—$ 8,838—175
1982—$ 8,758—175
1983—$ 2,276—226
1984—$ 0
1985—$ 1,813—230

JOINED SENIOR PGA TOUR: 1987

SENIOR PGA TOUR VICTORIES:
1987 Fairfield Barnett Senior Golf Classic; 1988 MONY Senior Tournament of Champions, MONY Syracuse Senior Classic, PaineWebber Invitational; 1989 Bell Atlantic Classic, Rancho Murieta Senior Gold Rush (TOTAL: 6)

SENIOR TOUR CAREER EARNINGS: $1,741,837

ALL-TIME EARNINGS (Regular and Senior Tour combined): $2,872,266

SENIOR TOUR PLAYOFF RECORD: 1-1

SENIOR TOUR YEAR BY YEAR:
1987—$232,189—11
1988—$415,594— 3
1989—$488,541— 5
1990—$354,046—14
1991—$251,467—30

OTHER SENIOR VICTORIES:
1988 Mazda Champions (with Colleen Walker)

1991 SENIOR TOUR SUMMARY:
Tournaments entered—25; top 10 finishes—2; stroke average—71.55; best finishes—T2 Senior Players Championship, 7 Security Pacific Classic

OTHER ACHIEVEMENTS:
Won 1969 Vardon Trophy (70.34) . . . member 1969, 1973, 1977 Ryder Cup teams

				RANK	
				NO.	%
1. DRIVING DISTANCE	# DRIVES 150 TOT. DIST. 37,386	AVG.	249.2	56	22%
2. DRIVING ACCURACY	POSSIBLE FAIRWAYS 1,040 # HIT 702	PCT.	.675	35	51%
3. GREENS IN REGULATION (GIR)	HOLES PLAYED 1,350 GREENS HIT 908	PCT.	.673	31	57%
4. PUTTING	GREENS HIT 908 # PUTTS GIR 1,625	AVG.	1.790	18	75%
5. TOTAL DRIVING	TOTAL OF STATISTICS 1–2 RANKING		91	58	19%
6. EAGLES	TOTAL EAGLES		6	27	63%
7. BIRDIES	TOTAL BIRDIES		246	47	35%
8. SCORING AVERAGE			71.55	24	67%
9. SAND SAVES	BUNKERS HIT 111 SAVES 54	PCT.	.486	25	65%
10. ALL-AROUND	TOTAL OF STATISTICS 1–9 RANKING		321	35	51%
11. MONEY	TOTAL MONEY		$251,467.01	30	58%
12. PAR BREAKERS	HOLES PLAYED 1,350 BIRDIES/EAGLES 252	PCT.	.187	23	68%

OTHER STATISTICS

PUTTS PER ROUND	ROUNDS PLAYED 75 TOTAL PUTTS 2,209	AVG.	29.45	12	83%
PAR 3 BIRDIES	PAR 3 HOLES PLAYED 310 BIRDIES MADE 38	PCT.	.123	29	60%
PAR 4 BIRDIES	PAR 4 HOLES PLAYED 747 BIRDIES MADE 112	PCT.	.150	15	79%
PAR 5 BIRDIES	PAR 5 HOLES PLAYED 293 BIRDIES MADE 96	PCT.	.328	35	51%
BIRDIE CONVERSION PERCENTAGE	BIRDIES 246 DIVIDED BY GIR 908	PCT.	.271	21	71%

MIKE HILL

EXEMPT STATUS: Top 31 on 1991 Senior Tour money list

HEIGHT: 5'10"   WEIGHT: 170

BIRTH DATE: January 27, 1939   BIRTHPLACE: Jackson, Michigan

RESIDENCE: Brooklyn, Michigan

FAMILY: Wife, Sandra; Children, Kimberly (5/16/63), Kristen (12/11/69), Michael, Jr. (4/15/72)

COLLEGE ATTENDED: Arizona State University

TURNED PROFESSIONAL: 1967   JOINED PGA TOUR: 1968

PGA TOUR VICTORIES:
1970 Doral-Eastern Open; 1972 San Antonio-Texas Open; 1977 Ohio Kings Island Open (TOTAL: 3)

PGA TOUR CAREER EARNINGS: $573,724   PLAYOFF RECORD: 0-0

PGA TOUR YEAR BY YEAR:

1968—$30,892— 55	1978—$17,648—110
1969—$16,239— 97	1979—$38,087—102
1970—$56,693— 32	1980—$28,341—108
1971—$48,188— 53	1981—$ 627—243
1972—$67,067— 33	1982—$ 4,753—205
1973—$44,635— 70	1983—$ 384—274
1974—$76,802— 28	1984—$ 0
1975—$41,696— 63	1985—$ 2,898—218
1976—$58,478— 45	1986—$ 4,800—229
1977—$50,323— 63	

JOINED SENIOR PGA TOUR: 1989

SENIOR PGA TOUR VICTORIES:
1990 GTE Suncoast Classic, GTE North Classic, Fairfield Barnett Space Coast Classic, Security Pacific Senior Classic, New York Life Champions; 1991 Doug Sanders Kingwood Classic, Ameritech Senior Open, GTE Northwest Classic, Nationwide Championship, New York Life Champions (TOTAL: 10)

SENIOR TOUR CAREER EARNINGS: $2,373,439

ALL-TIME EARNINGS (Regular and Senior Tour combined): $2,947,163

SENIOR TOUR PLAYOFF RECORD: 3-0

SENIOR TOUR YEAR BY YEAR:
1989—$ 412,104—9
1990—$ 895,678—2
1991—$1,065,657—1

OTHER SENIOR VICTORIES:
1989 Mazda Champions (with Patti Rizzo), 1991 Liberty Mutual Legends of Golf (with Lee Trevino)

1991 SENIOR TOUR SUMMARY:
Tournaments entered—32; top 10 finishes—21; stroke average—69.98; best finishes—five wins, two seconds, six thirds

OTHER ACHIEVEMENTS:
Winner of the 1990 Merrill Lynch Senior Shoot-Out Championship . . . member of the 1990 and 1991 U.S. DuPont Cup teams . . . 1991 Senior Tour co–Player of the Year

				RANK	
				NO.	%
1. DRIVING DISTANCE	# DRIVES 199 TOT. DIST. 51,855	AVG.	260.6	25	65%
2. DRIVING ACCURACY	POSSIBLE FAIRWAYS 1,387 # HIT 956	PCT.	.689	27	63%
3. GREENS IN REGULATION (GIR)	HOLES PLAYED 1,800 GREENS HIT 1,324	PCT.	.736	3	96%
4. PUTTING	GREENS HIT 1,324 # PUTTS GIR 2,335	AVG.	1.764	5	93%
5. TOTAL DRIVING	TOTAL OF STATISTICS 1–2 RANKING		52	14	81%
6. EAGLES	TOTAL EAGLES		6	27	63%
7. BIRDIES	TOTAL BIRDIES		400	1	100%
8. SCORING AVERAGE			69.98	5	93%
9. SAND SAVES	BUNKERS HIT 125 SAVES 53	PCT.	.424	47	35%
10. ALL-AROUND	TOTAL OF STATISTICS 1–9 RANKING		154	6	92%
11. MONEY	TOTAL MONEY		$1,065,656.83	1	100%
12. PAR BREAKERS	HOLES PLAYED 1,800 BIRDIES/EAGLES 406	PCT.	.226	2	97%

OTHER STATISTICS

PUTTS PER ROUND	ROUNDS PLAYED 100	TOTAL PUTTS 2,964		AVG.	29.64	21	71%
PAR 3 BIRDIES	PAR 3 HOLES PLAYED 413	BIRDIES MADE 65	PCT.	.157	4	94%
PAR 4 BIRDIES	PAR 4 HOLES PLAYED 1,006	BIRDIES MADE 174	PCT.	.173	3	96%
PAR 5 BIRDIES	PAR 5 HOLES PLAYED 381	BIRDIES MADE 161	PCT.	.423	3	96%
BIRDIE CONVERSION PERCENTAGE	BIRDIES 400 DIVIDED BY GIR 1,324		PCT.	.302	3	96%

ORVILLE MOODY

EXEMPT STATUS: Top 31 on 1991 Senior Tour money list (net 31st)

HEIGHT: 5'10"   WEIGHT: 210

BIRTH DATE: December 9, 1933   BIRTHPLACE: Chickasha, Oklahoma

RESIDENCE: Sulphur Springs, Texas

FAMILY: Wife, Beverly; Children, Michelle (11/24/69), Sabreena (2/17/70), Kelley Rhea (9/14/73), Jason (4/16/75)

COLLEGE ATTENDED: University of Oklahoma

TURNED PROFESSIONAL: 1967   JOINED PGA TOUR: 1967

PGA TOUR VICTORIES: 1969 U.S. Open (TOTAL: 1)

PGA TOUR CAREER EARNINGS: $389,915   PLAYOFF RECORD: 0-2

PGA TOUR YEAR BY YEAR:
1968—$12,950—103	1977—$15,521—121
1969—$79,176— 21	1978—$44,204— 73
1970—$50,086— 44	1979—$48,483— 81
1971—$25,256— 83	1980—$13,619—145
1972—$13,672—126	1981—$ 1,534—218
1973—$74,286— 36	1982—$ 0
1974—$13,283—130	1983—$ 5,928—198
1975—$ 2,813—185	1984—$ 0
1976—$ 2,866—195	1985—$ 980—253

JOINED SENIOR PGA TOUR: 1984

SENIOR PGA TOUR VICTORIES:
1984 Daytona Beach Seniors Classic, MONY Tournament of Champions; 1987 Rancho Murieta Senior Gold Rush, GTE Kaanapali Classic; 1988 Vintage Chrysler Invitational, Senior Players Reunion, Greater Grand Rapids Open; 1989 Mazda Senior TPC, U.S. Senior Open; 1991 PaineWebber Invitational (TOTAL: 10)

SENIOR TOUR CAREER EARNINGS: $2,364,006

ALL-TIME EARNINGS (Regular and Senior Tour combined): $2,753,922

SENIOR TOUR PLAYOFF RECORD: 2-4

SENIOR TOUR YEAR BY YEAR:
1984—$183,920— 5
1985—$134,643—12
1986—$128,755—16
1987—$355,793— 4
1988—$411,859— 4
1989—$647,985— 2
1990—$273,224—22
1991—$227,826—32

OTHER SENIOR VICTORIES:
1984 Viceroy Panama Open; 1987 and 1988 Liberty Mutual Legends of Golf (with Bruce Crampton)

1991 SENIOR TOUR SUMMARY:
Tournaments entered—28; top 10 finishes—5; stroke average—71.98; best finishes—1 PaineWebber Invitational, T5 Murata Reunion Pro-Am, T8 PGA Seniors Championship, T8 GTE Suncoast Classic

OTHER VICTORIES:
1969 World Cup team title (with Lee Trevino); 1969 World Series of Golf (then unofficial); 1971 Hong Kong Open; 1971 Morocco Grand Prix; 1977 International Caribbean Open; 1986 and 1987 Australian PGA champion; 1958 All-Army Championship and 1962 All-Service Championship

					RANK	
					NO.	%
1. DRIVING DISTANCE	# DRIVES 172 TOT. DIST. 44,212		AVG.	257.0	34	53%
2. DRIVING ACCURACY	POSSIBLE FAIRWAYS 1,192 # HIT 819		PCT.	.687	28	61%
3. GREENS IN REGULATION (GIR)	HOLES PLAYED 1,548 GREENS HIT 1,014		PCT.	.655	41	43%
4. PUTTING	GREENS HIT 1,014 # PUTTS GIR 1,841		AVG.	1.816	37	49%
5. TOTAL DRIVING	TOTAL OF STATISTICS 1–2 RANKING			62	22	69%
6. EAGLES	TOTAL EAGLES			4	41	43%
7. BIRDIES	TOTAL BIRDIES			274	36	50%
8. SCORING AVERAGE				71.98	33	54%
9. SAND SAVES	BUNKERS HIT 150 SAVES 70		PCT.	.467	28	61%
10. ALL-AROUND	TOTAL OF STATISTICS 1–9 RANKING			300	31	57%
11. MONEY	TOTAL MONEY		$227,826.06		32	56%
12. PAR BREAKERS	HOLES PLAYED 1,548 BIRDIES/EAGLES 278		PCT.	.180	31	57%

OTHER STATISTICS

PUTTS PER ROUND	ROUNDS PLAYED 86	TOTAL PUTTS 2,572		AVG.	29.91	34	53%
PAR 3 BIRDIES	PAR 3 HOLES PLAYED 356	BIRDIES MADE 44	PCT.	.124	28	61%
PAR 4 BIRDIES	PAR 4 HOLES PLAYED 869	BIRDIES MADE 120	PCT.	.138	31	57%
PAR 5 BIRDIES	PAR 5 HOLES PLAYED 323	BIRDIES MADE 110	PCT.	.341	30	58%
BIRDIE CONVERSION PERCENTAGE	BIRDIES 274 DIVIDED BY GIR 1,014		PCT.	.270	22	69%

JACK NICKLAUS*

*Note: A Senior Tour statistical composite is not available for Jack Nicklaus, who played fewer than the required minimum 59 rounds in 1991.

HEIGHT: 5'11"   WEIGHT: 185

BIRTH DATE: January 21, 1940   BIRTHPLACE: Columbus, Ohio

RESIDENCE: North Palm Beach, Florida, and Muirfield Village, Ohio

FAMILY: Wife, Barbara; Children, Jack II (9/23/61), Steven (4/11/63), Nancy Jean (5/5/65), Gary (1/15/69), Michael (7/24/73); two grandchildren

COLLEGE ATTENDED: Ohio State University

TURNED PROFESSIONAL: 1961   JOINED PGA TOUR: 1962

PGA TOUR VICTORIES:
1962 U.S. Open, Seattle World's Fair Open, Portland Open; 1963 Palm Springs Golf Classic, Masters, Tournament of Champions, PGA Championship, Sahara Invitational; 1964 Portland Open, Tournament of Champions, Phoenix Open, Whitemarsh Open; 1965 Portland Open, Masters, Memphis Open, Thunderbird Classic, Philadelphia Golf Classic; 1966 Masters, Sahara Invitational; 1967 U.S. Open, Sahara Invitational, Bing Crosby National Pro-Am, Western Open, Westchester Classic; 1968 Western Open, American Golf Classic; 1969 Sahara Invitational, Kaiser International, Andy Williams-San Diego Open; 1970 Byron Nelson Golf Classic, PGA National Four-Ball Championship (with Arnold Palmer); 1971 PGA Championship, Tournament of Champions, Byron Nelson Golf Classic, PGA National Team Championship (with Arnold Palmer), Walt Disney World Open; 1972 Bing Crosby National Pro-Am, Doral-Eastern Open, Masters, U.S. Open, Westchester Classic, U.S. Professional Match Play Championship, Walt Disney World Open; 1973 Bing Crosby National Pro-Am, Greater New Orleans Open, Tournament of Champions, Atlanta Classic, PGA Championship, Ohio Kings Island Open, Walt Disney World Classic; 1974 Hawaiian Open, Tournament Players Championship; 1975 Doral-Eastern Open, Sea Pines Heritage Classic, Masters, PGA Championship, World Open; 1976 Tournament Players Championship, World Series of Golf; 1977 Jackie Gleason Inverrary Classic, MONY Tournament of Champions, Memorial Tournament; 1978 Jackie Gleason Inverrary Classic, Tournament Players Championship, IVB-Philadelphia Classic; 1980 U.S. Open, PGA Championship; 1982 Colonial National Invitation; 1984 Memorial Tournament; 1986 Masters (TOTAL: 70)

PGA TOUR CAREER EARNINGS: $5,294,262 PLAYOFF RECORD: 13-10

PGA TOUR YEAR BY YEAR:

1962—$ 61,869—	3		1965—$140,752—	1		
1963—$100,040—	2		1966—$111,419—	2		
1964—$113,285—	1		1967—$188,998—	1		
1968—$155,286—	2		1980—$172,386—	13		
1969—$140,167—	3		1981—$178,213—	16		
1970—$142,149—	4		1982—$232,645—	12		
1971—$244,490—	1		1983—$256,158—	10		
1972—$320,542—	1		1984—$272,595—	15		
1973—$308,362—	1		1985—$165,456—	43		
1974—$238,178—	2		1986—$226,014—	34		
1975—$298,149—	1		1987—$ 64,685—127			
1976—$266,438—	1		1988—$ 28,845—177			
1977—$284,509—	2		1989—$ 96,595—129			
1978—$256,672—	4		1990—$ 68,054—160			
1979—$ 59,434—	71		1991—$123,797—122			

JOINED SENIOR PGA TOUR: 1990

SENIOR PGA TOUR VICTORIES:
1990 The Tradition at Desert Mountain, Mazda Senior TPC; 1991 The Tradition at Desert Mountain, PGA Seniors Championship, U.S. Senior Open (TOTAL: 5)

SENIOR TOUR CAREER EARNINGS: $683,734

ALL-TIME EARNINGS (Regular and Senior Tour combined): $5,977,996

SENIOR TOUR PLAYOFF RECORD: 1-0

SENIOR TOUR YEAR BY YEAR:
1990—$340,000—15
1991—$343,734—17

1991 SENIOR TOUR SUMMARY:
Tournaments entered—5; top 10 finishes—4; stroke average—69.79; best finishes—1 The Tradition, 1 PGA Seniors Championship, 1 U.S. Senior Open

OTHER VICTORIES:
1966, 1970 and 1978 British Open; 1964, 1968, 1971, 1975, 1976 and 1978 Australian Open; 1962, 1963, 1967 and 1970 World Series of Golf (then unofficial); 1970 World Match Play; three-time World Cup medalist; 1966 PGA Team Championship (with Arnold Palmer); 1983 Chrysler Team Championship (with Johnny Miller); 1959 and 1961 U.S. Amateur; 1961 NCAA Championship

OTHER ACHIEVEMENTS:
1967, 1972, 1973, 1975 and 1976 PGA Player of the Year . . . named Athlete of the Decade, 1970–79 . . . received 1982 Card Walker Award for outstanding contributions to junior golf . . . member of World Golf Hall of Fame . . . named Golfer of the Century in 1988 . . . Walker Cup team member in 1959 and 1961 . . . World Cup team member in 1963, 1964, 1966, 1967, 1971 and 1973 . . . Ryder Cup team member in 1969, 1971, 1973, 1975, 1977 and 1981 . . . Ryder Cup captain in 1983 and 1987

ARNOLD PALMER*

*Note: A Senior Tour statistical composite is not available for Arnold Palmer, who player fewer than the required minimum 59 rounds in 1991.

EXEMPT STATUS: Top 31 on all-time money list

HEIGHT: 5'10"   WEIGHT: 178

BIRTH DATE: September 10, 1929   BIRTHPLACE: Latrobe, Pennsylvania

RESIDENCE: Bay Hill, Florida

FAMILY: Wife, Winifred Walzer; Children, Margaret (2/26/56), Amy (8/4/58); three grandchildren

COLLEGE ATTENDED: Wake Forest University

TURNED PROFESSIONAL: 1954   JOINED PGA TOUR: 1955

PGA TOUR VICTORIES:
1955 Canadian Open; 1956 Insurance City Open, Eastern Open; 1957 Houston Open, Azalea Open, Rubber City Open, San Diego Open; 1958 St. Petersburg Open, Masters, Pepsi Championship; 1959 Thunderbird Invitational, Oklahoma City Open, West Palm Beach Open; 1960 Palm Springs Golf Classic, Texas Open, Baton Rouge Open, Pensacola Open, Masters, U.S. Open, Insurance City Open, Mobile Sertoma Open; 1961 San Diego Open, Phoenix Open, Baton Rouge Open, Texas Open, Western Open; 1962 Palm Springs Golf Classic, Phoenix Open, Masters, Texas Open, Tournament of Champions, Colonial National Invitation, American Golf Classic; 1963 Los Angeles Open, Phoenix Open, Pensacola Open, Thunderbird Classic, Cleveland Open,

Western Open, Whitemarsh Open; 1964 Masters, Oklahoma City Open; 1965 Tournament of Champions; 1966 Los Angeles Open, Tournament of Champions, Houston Champions International; 1967 Los Angeles Open, Tucson Open, American Golf Classic, Thunderbird Classic; 1968 Bob Hope Desert Classic, Kemper Open; 1969 Heritage Golf Classic, Danny Thomas-Diplomat Classic; 1970 PGA National Four-Ball Championship (with Jack Nicklaus); 1971 Bob Hope Desert Classic, Florida Citrus Invitational, Westchester Classic, PGA National Team Championship (with Jack Nicklaus); 1973 Bob Hope Desert Classic (TOTAL: 60)

PGA TOUR CAREER EARNINGS: $1,902,698 PLAYOFF RECORD: 14-10

PGA TOUR YEAR BY YEAR:

Year	Earnings	Rank		Year	Earnings	Rank
1955	$ 7,958	32		1974	$ 36,293	72
1956	$ 16,145	19		1975	$ 59,017	36
1957	$ 27,803	5		1976	$ 17,017	115
1958	$ 42,608	1		1977	$ 21,950	101
1959	$ 32,462	5		1978	$ 27,073	94
1960	$ 75,263	1		1979	$ 9,276	159
1961	$ 61,091	2		1980	$ 16,589	133
1962	$ 81,448	1		1981	$ 4,164	197
1963	$128,230	1		1982	$ 6,621	198
1964	$113,203	2		1983	$ 16,904	159
1965	$ 57,770	10		1984	$ 2,452	217
1966	$110,467	3		1985	$ 3,327	214
1967	$184,065	2		1986	$ 0	
1968	$114,602	7		1987	$ 1,650	269
1969	$105,128	9		1988	$ 0	
1970	$128,853	5		1989	$ 2,290	253
1971	$209,603	3		1990	$ 0	
1972	$ 84,181	25		1991	$ 7,738	237
1973	$ 89,457	27				

JOINED SENIOR PGA TOUR: 1980

SENIOR PGA TOUR VICTORIES:
1980 PGA Seniors Championship; 1981 USGA Senior Open; 1982 Marlboro Classic, Denver Post Champions; 1983 Boca Grove Senior Classic; 1984 PGA Seniors Championship, Senior TPC, Quadel Seniors Classic; 1985 Senior TPC; 1988 Crestar Classic (TOTAL: 10)

SENIOR TOUR CAREER EARNINGS: $1,323,729

ALL-TIME EARNINGS (Regular and Senior Tour combined): $3,226,427

SENIOR TOUR PLAYOFF RECORD: 1-1

SENIOR TOUR YEAR BY YEAR:

Year	Earnings	Rank
1980	$ 0	
1981	$ 55,100	4
1982	$ 73,848	4
1983	$106,590	6
1984	$184,582	4
1985	$137,024	11
1986	$ 99,056	21
1987	$128,910	19
1988	$185,373	17
1989	$119,907	38
1990	$ 66,519	65
1991	$143,967	46

1991 SENIOR TOUR SUMMARY:
Tournaments entered—17; top 10 finishes—4; stroke average—71.96; best finishes—T4 Transamerica Senior Golf Championship, T7 Nationwide Championship, 8 Vantage Championship

OTHER VICTORIES:
1954 U.S. Amateur; 1961 and 1962 British Open; 1966 PGA Team Championship (with Jack Nicklaus); 17 other foreign titles through 1980 Canadian PGA

OTHER ACHIEVEMENTS:
Member of Ryder Cup team in 1961, 1963, 1965, 1967, 1971 and 1973; nonplaying captain in 1975 . . . member of World Cup team in 1960, 1962, 1963, 1964, 1965, 1966 and 1967

GARY PLAYER

EXEMPT STATUS: Top 31 on 1991 Senior Tour money list
HEIGHT: 5'7"   WEIGHT: 147
BIRTH DATE: November 1, 1935   BIRTHPLACE: Johannesburg, South Africa

RESIDENCE: Alaqua, Florida

FAMILY: Wife, Vivienne; Children, Jennifer (4/12/59), Marc (2/17/61), Wayne (4/22/62), Michele (12/19/63), Theresa (6/7/65), Amanda (3/11/73); two grandchildren

TURNED PROFESSIONAL: 1953   JOINED PGA TOUR: 1957

PGA TOUR VICTORIES:
1958 Kentucky Derby Open; 1961 Lucky International Open, Sunshine Open, Masters; 1962 PGA Championship; 1963 San Diego Open; 1964 "500" Festival Open, Pensacola Open; 1965 U.S. Open; 1969 Tournament of Champions; 1970 Greater Greensboro Open; 1971 Greater Jacksonville Open, National Airlines Open; 1972 Greater New Orleans Open, PGA Championship; 1973 Southern Open; 1974 Masters, Danny Thomas Memphis Classic; 1978 Masters, MONY Tournament of Champions, Houston Open (TOTAL: 21)

PGA TOUR CAREER EARNINGS: $1,811,251   PLAYOFF RECORD: 3-11

PGA TOUR YEAR BY YEAR:

Year	Earnings	Rank		Year	Earnings	Rank		Year	Earnings	Rank
1957	$ 3,286			1963	$ 55,455	5		1980	$ 45,471	76
1958	$ 18,592			1964	$ 61,449	7		1981	$ 22,483	122
1959	$ 5,694	58		1965	$ 69,964	5		1982	$ 22,059	145
1960	$ 13,879	28		1966	$ 26,391	38		1983	$ 20,567	147
1961	$ 64,540	1		1967	$ 55,820	18		1984	$ 93,258	70
1962	$ 45,838	6		1968	$ 51,950	33		1985	$ 11,032	175
				1969	$123,897	5		1986	$ 0	
				1970	$101,212	15		1987	$ 4,257	231
				1971	$120,916	5		1988	$ 0	
				1972	$120,719	7		1989	$ 11,000	225
				1973	$ 48,878	63				
				1974	$108,372	19				
				1975	$ 73,943	27				
				1976	$ 53,668	53				
				1977	$112,485	21				
				1978	$117,336	9				
				1979	$ 74,482	53				

JOINED SENIOR PGA TOUR: 1985

SENIOR PGA TOUR VICTORIES:
1985 Quadel Seniors Classic; 1986 General Foods PGA Seniors Championship, United Hospital Classic, Denver Post Champions; 1987 Mazda Senior TPC, USGA Senior Open, PaineWebber World Seniors Invitational; 1988 General Foods PGA Seniors Championship, Aetna Challenge, Southwestern Bell Classic, USGA Senior Open, GTE North Classic; 1989 GTE North Classic, RJR Championship; 1990 PGA Seniors Championship; 1991 Royal Caribbean Classic (TOTAL: 16)

SENIOR TOUR CAREER EARNINGS: $2,449,180

ALL-TIME EARNINGS (Regular and Senior Tour combined): $4,260,431

SENIOR TOUR PLAYOFF RECORD: 4-1

SENIOR TOUR YEAR BY YEAR:
1985—$ 30,000—44
1986—$291,190— 5
1987—$333,439— 6
1988—$435,914— 2
1989—$514,116— 4
1990—$507,268— 9
1991—$337,253—18

OTHER SENIOR VICTORIES:
1988 Volvo Seniors British Open, 1990 Volvo Seniors British Open

1991 SENIOR TOUR SUMMARY:
Tournaments entered—20; top 10 finishes—9; stroke average—70.57; best finishes—1 Royal Caribbean Classic, T2 GTE West Classic, T3 Aetna Challenge, 3 Las Vegas Senior Classic

OTHER VICTORIES:
1959, 1968 and 1974 British Open; winner of the South African Open 13 times since 1956; 7-time winner of the Australian Open and 5-time Suntory World Match Play champion; individual titleist in 1965 and 1977 World Cup; winner of 1965, 1968 and 1972 World Series of Golf (then unofficial), 1957 Australian PGA; 1972 and 1974 Brazilian Open; 1976 South African Dunlop Masters; 1980 Chile Open; 1984 Johnnie Walker tournament (Spain)

OTHER ACHIEVEMENTS:
Leading money winner on the PGA Tour in 1961 . . . inducted into the World Golf Hall of Fame in 1974

				RANK	
				NO.	%
1. DRIVING DISTANCE	# DRIVES 126 TOT. DIST. 32,110	AVG.	254.8	39	46%
2. DRIVING ACCURACY	POSSIBLE FAIRWAYS 870 # HIT 626	PCT.	.720	11	85%
3. GREENS IN REGULATION (GIR)	HOLES PLAYED 1,134 GREENS HIT 803	PCT.	.708	12	83%
4. PUTTING	GREENS HIT 803 # PUTTS GIR 1,441	AVG.	1.795	22	69%
5. TOTAL DRIVING	TOTAL OF STATISTICS 1–2 RANKING		50	10	86%
6. EAGLES	TOTAL EAGLES		8	16	78%
7. BIRDIES	TOTAL BIRDIES		214	56	22%
8. SCORING AVERAGE			70.57	9	88%
9. SAND SAVES	BUNKERS HIT 81 SAVES 48	PCT.	.593	1	100%
10. ALL-AROUND	TOTAL OF STATISTICS 1–9 RANKING		176	12	83%
11. MONEY	TOTAL MONEY		$337,252.60	18	75%
12. PAR BREAKERS		PCT.	.196	18	75%

OTHER STATISTICS

PUTTS PER ROUND	ROUNDS PLAYED 63 TOTAL PUTTS 1,876	AVG.	29.78	29	60%
PAR 3 BIRDIES	PAR 3 HOLES PLAYED 264 BIRDIES MADE 30	PCT.	.114	36	50%
PAR 4 BIRDIES	PAR 4 HOLES PLAYED 636 BIRDIES MADE 90	PCT.	.142	24	67%
PAR 5 BIRDIES	PAR 5 HOLES PLAYED 234 BIRDIES MADE 94	PCT.	.402	8	89%
BIRDIE CONVERSION PERCENTAGE.	BIRDIES 214 DIVIDED BY GIR 803	PCT.	.267	24	67%

CHI CHI RODRIGUEZ

EXEMPT STATUS: Top 31 on 1991 Senior Tour money list
HEIGHT: 5'7"   WEIGHT: 132
BIRTH DATE: October 23, 1935   BIRTHPLACE: Bayamón, Puerto Rico
RESIDENCE: Naples, Florida
FAMILY: Wife, Iwalani; Children, Donnette (4/6/62)
TURNED PROFESSIONAL: 1960   JOINED PGA TOUR: 1960

PGA TOUR VICTORIES:
1963 Denver Open; 1964 Lucky International, Western Open; 1967 Texas Open; 1968 Sahara Invitational; 1972 Byron Nelson Classic; 1973 Greater Greensboro Open; 1979 Tallahassee Open (TOTAL: 8)

PGA TOUR CAREER EARNINGS: $1,037,105   PLAYOFF RECORD: 3-1

PGA TOUR YEAR BY YEAR:
1960—$ 2,137— 94
1961—$ 2,269— 99
1962—$ 6,389— 68
1963—$ 17,674— 48
1964—$ 48,339— 9
1965—$ 26,568— 37
1966—$ 35,616— 28
1967—$ 48,608— 24
1968—$ 58,323— 30
1969—$ 56,312— 33
1970—$ 53,102— 38
1971—$ 30,390— 74
1972—$113,503— 12
1973—$ 91,307— 23
1974—$ 58,940— 44
1975—$ 13,955—115
1976—$ 29,870— 75
1977—$ 56,018— 55
1978—$ 39,565— 77
1979—$ 58,225— 72
1980—$ 35,906— 92
1981—$ 65,152— 68
1982—$ 7,119—182
1983—$ 8,190—187
1984—$ 30,989—137
1985—$ 38,956—134
1986—$ 16,145—185

JOINED SENIOR PGA TOUR: 1985

SENIOR PGA TOUR VICTORIES:
1986 Senior TPC, Digital Seniors Classic, United Virginia Bank Seniors; 1987 General Foods PGA Seniors Championship, Vantage at the Dominion, United Hospitals Classic, Silver Pages Classic, Senior Players Reunion, Digital Seniors Classic, GTE Northwest Classic; 1988 Doug Sanders Kingwood Classic, Digital Seniors Classic; 1989 Crestar Classic; 1990 Las Vegas Senior Classic, Ameritech Senior Open, Sunwest Bank/Charley Pride Senior Golf Classic; 1991 GTE West Classic, Vintage ARCO Invitational, Las Vegas Senior Classic, Murata Reunion Pro-Am (TOTAL: 20)

SENIOR TOUR CAREER EARNINGS: $3,029,172

ALL-TIME EARNINGS (Regular and Senior Tour combined): $4,066,277

SENIOR TOUR PLAYOFF RECORD: 1-6

SENIOR TOUR YEAR BY YEAR:
1985—$ 7,700—71
1986—$399,172— 2
1987—$509,145— 1
1988—$313,940—10
1989—$275,414—17
1990—$729,788— 5
1991—$794,013— 4

1991 SENIOR TOUR SUMMARY:
Tournaments entered—32; top 10 finishes—17; stroke average—70.29; best finishes—four wins, five seconds, one third

OTHER VICTORIES:
1976 Pepsi Mixed Team Championship (with JoAnn Washam)

OTHER ACHIEVEMENTS:
Member 1973 Ryder Cup team . . . represented Puerto Rico on 12 World Cup teams . . . winner of Ambassador of Golf Award

in 1981 . . . received the Card Walker Award from the PGA Tour in 1986 for outstanding contributions to junior golf . . . 1987 National Puerto Rico Coalition Life Achievement Award . . . 1988 Fred Raphael Award winner . . . received 1988 Old Tom Morris Award . . . recipient of the 1989 Bob Jones Award, the U.S. Golf Association's highest honor

					AVG./PCT.	RANK NO.	%
1.	DRIVING DISTANCE	# DRIVES 198	TOT. DIST. 52,539		AVG. 265.3	10	86%
2.	DRIVING ACCURACY	POSSIBLE FAIRWAYS 1,374	# HIT 982		PCT. .715	15	79%
3.	GREENS IN REGULATION (GIR)	HOLES PLAYED 1,782	GREENS HIT 1,293		PCT. .726	5	93%
4.	PUTTING	GREENS HIT 1,293	# PUTTS GIR 2,311		AVG. 1.787	14	81%
5.	TOTAL DRIVING	TOTAL OF STATISTICS 1–2	RANKING		25	2	97%
6.	EAGLES	TOTAL EAGLES			10	5	93%
7.	BIRDIES	TOTAL BIRDIES			362	5	93%
8.	SCORING AVERAGE				70.29	6	92%
9.	SAND SAVES	BUNKERS HIT 175	SAVES 93		PCT. .531	10	86%
10.	ALL-AROUND	TOTAL OF STATISTICS 1–9	RANKING		72	2	97%
11.	MONEY	TOTAL MONEY			$794,013.48	4	94%
12.	PAR BREAKERS	HOLES PLAYED 1,782	BIRDIES/EAGLES 372		PCT. .209	9	88%

OTHER STATISTICS

			AVG./PCT.	NO.	%
PUTTS PER ROUND	ROUNDS PLAYED 99	TOTAL PUTTS 2,953	AVG. 29.83	31	57%
PAR 3 BIRDIES	PAR 3 HOLES PLAYED 408	BIRDIES MADE 52	PCT. .127	25	65%
PAR 4 BIRDIES	PAR 4 HOLES PLAYED 1,005	BIRDIES MADE 165	PCT. .164	11	85%
PAR 5 BIRDIES	PAR 5 HOLED PLAYED 369	BIRDIES MADE 145	PCT. .393	10	86%
BIRDIE CONVERSION PERCENTAGE	BIRDIES 362	DIVIDED BY GIR 1,293	PCT. .280	17	76%

LEE TREVINO

EXEMPT STATUS: Top 31 on 1991 Senior Tour money list

HEIGHT: 5'7" WEIGHT: 180

BIRTH DATE: December 1, 1939 BIRTHPLACE: Dallas, Texas

RESIDENCE: Jupiter Island, Florida

FAMILY: Wife, Claudia; Children, Richard (11/21/62), Lesley Ann (6/30/65), Tony Lee (4/13/69), Troy (9/13/73), Olivia Leigh (2/3/89)

TURNED PROFESSIONAL: 1960 JOINED PGA TOUR: 1967

PGA TOUR VICTORIES:
1968 U.S. Open, Hawaiian Open; 1969 Tucson Open; 1970 Tucson Open, National Airlines Open; 1971 Tallahassee Open, Danny Thomas Memphis Classic, U.S. Open, Canadian Open, Sahara Invitational; 1972 Danny Thomas Memphis Classic, Greater Hartford Open, Greater St. Louis Classic; 1973 Jackie Gleason Inverrary Classic, Doral-Eastern Open; 1974 New Orleans Open, PGA Championship; 1975 Florida Citrus Open; 1976 Colonial National Invitation; 1977 Canadian Open; 1978 Colonial National Invitation; 1979 Canadian Open; 1980 Tournament Players Championship, Danny Thomas Memphis Classic, San Antonio-Texas Open; 1981 MONY Tournament of Champions; 1984 PGA Championship (TOTAL: 27)

PGA TOUR CAREER EARNINGS: $3,478,450 PLAYOFF RECORD: 5-5

PGA TOUR YEAR BY YEAR:
1967—$ 26,472—	45	1977—$ 85,108—	33
1968—$132,127—	6	1978—$228,723—	6
1969—$112,418—	7	1979—$238,732—	4
1970—$157,037—	1	1980—$385,814—	2
1971—$231,202—	2	1981—$134,801—	23
1972—$214,805—	2	1982—$ 34,293—	113
1973—$210,017—	4	1983—$111,100—	52
1974—$203,422—	4	1984—$282,907—	12
1975—$134,206—	9	1985—$140,883—	56
1976—$136,963—	13	1986—$ 86,315—	98
		1987—$ 51,212—	152
		1988—$ 26,286—	184
		1989—$118,628—	114
		1990—$ 14,500—	219
		1991—$ 3,533—	261

JOINED SENIOR PGA TOUR: 1989

SENIOR PGA TOUR VICTORIES:
1990 Royal Caribbean Classic, Aetna Challenge, Vintage Chrysler Invitational, Doug Sanders Kingwood Celebrity Classic, NYNEX Commemorative, U.S. Senior Open, Transamerica Senior Golf Championship; 1991 Aetna Challenge, Vantage at the Dominion, Sunwest Bank/Charley Pride Classic (TOTAL: 10)

SENIOR TOUR CAREER EARNINGS: $1,922,940

ALL-TIME EARNINGS (Regular and Senior Tour combined): $5,401,390

SENIOR TOUR PLAYOFF RECORD: 1-1

SENIOR TOUR YEAR BY YEAR:
1989—$ 9,258—93
1990—$1,190,518— 1
1991—$ 723,163— 5

OTHER SENIOR VICTORIES:
1991 Liberty Mutual Legends of Golf (with Mike Hill)

1991 SENIOR TOUR SUMMARY:
Tournaments entered—28; top 10 finishes—20; stroke average—69.50; best finishes—three wins, four seconds, four thirds

OTHER VICTORIES:
1971 and 1972 British Open; 1974 World Series of Golf (then unofficial); 1975 Mexican Open; 1977 Morocco Grand Prix; 1978 Benson & Hedges; 1978 Lancome Trophy; 1979 and 1983 Canadian PGA; 1987 Skins Game (aced 17th hole to win $175,000)

OTHER ACHIEVEMENTS:
1971 PGA Player of the Year . . . 1968, 1969, 1970, 1971 and
1974 World Cup teams . . . 1969, 1971, 1973, 1975, 1979 and

1981 Ryder Cup teams . . . captain of 1985 Ryder Cup
team . . . 1970, 1971, 1972, 1974, 1980 Vardon Trophy winner . . . inducted into the World Golf Hall of Fame in 1981

				RANK	
				NO.	%
1. DRIVING DISTANCE	# DRIVES 168 TOT. DIST. 44,381	AVG.	264.2	15	79%
2. DRIVING ACCURACY	POSSIBLE FAIRWAYS 1,164 # HIT 871	PCT.	.748	3	96%
3. GREENS IN REGULATION (GIR)	HOLES PLAYED 1,512 GREENS HIT 1,125	PCT.	.744	2	97%
4. PUTTING	GREENS HIT 1,125 # PUTTS GIR 1,991	AVG.	1.770	6	92%
5. TOTAL DRIVING	TOTAL OF STATISTICS 1–2 RANKING		18	1	100%
6. EAGLES	TOTAL EAGLES		10	5	93%
7. BIRDIES	TOTAL BIRDIES		316	21	71%
8. SCORING AVERAGE			69.50	1	100%
9. SAND SAVES	BUNKERS HIT 103 SAVES 55	PCT.	.534	8	89%
10. ALL-AROUND	TOTAL OF STATISTICS 1–9 RANKING		62	1	100%
11. MONEY	TOTAL MONEY		$723,163.24	5	93%
12. PAR BREAKERS	HOLES PLAYED 1,512 BIRDIES/EAGLES 326	PCT.	.216	5	93%

Other Statistics

PUTTS PER ROUND	ROUNDS PLAYED 84 TOTAL PUTTS 2,474	AVG.	29.45	12	83%
PAR 3 BIRDIES	PAR 3 HOLES PLAYED 348 BIRDIES MADE 55	PCT.	.158	3	96%
PAR 4 BIRDIES	PAR 4 HOLES PLAYED 858 BIRDIES MADE 145	PCT.	.169	9	88%
PAR 5 BIRDIES	PAR 5 HOLES PLAYED 306 BIRDIES MADE 116	PCT.	.379	14	81%
BIRDIE CONVERSION PERCENTAGE	BIRDIES 316 DIVIDED BY GIR 1,125	PCT.	.281	14	81%

WALT ZEMBRISKI

EXEMPT STATUS: Top 31 on 1991 Senior Tour money list
HEIGHT: 5'8" WEIGHT: 160
BIRTH DATE: May 24, 1935 BIRTHPLACE: Mahwah, New Jersey
RESIDENCE: Orlando, Florida
TURNED PROFESSIONAL: 1965 JOINED PGA TOUR: 1967
PGA TOUR VICTORIES: None
PGA TOUR CAREER EARNINGS: None
JOINED SENIOR PGA TOUR: 1985
SENIOR PGA TOUR VICTORIES: 1988 Newport Cup, Vantage Cham-
pionship; 1989 GTE West Classic (TOTAL: 3)
SENIOR TOUR CAREER EARNINGS: $1,522,611
ALL-TIME EARNINGS (Regular and Senior Tour combined):
$1,522,611
SENIOR TOUR PLAYOFF RECORD: 0-1

SENIOR TOUR YEAR BY YEAR:
1985—$ 47,023—35
1986—$103,551—19
1987—$189,403—15
1988—$348,531— 7
1989—$291,861—15
1990—$276,292—20
1991—$265,951—26

1991 SENIOR TOUR SUMMARY:
Tournaments entered—30; top 10 finishes—5; stroke average—
71.60; best finishes—2 Las Vegas Senior Classic, T4 GTE West
Classic, T5 Bank One Classic, T7 Southwestern Bell Classic

OTHER VICTORIES: 1966 New Jersey Amateur champion

OTHER ACHIEVEMENTS: Was the only public-course player to win
the "Ike" Championship, a prestigious amateur tournament, cap-
turing the event in 1964 at Winged Foot . . . won 10 tournaments
on the 1982 Space Coast mini-tour in Florida

				RANK	
				NO.	%
1. DRIVING DISTANCE	# DRIVES 184 TOT. DIST. 45,629	AVG.	248.0	57	21%
2. DRIVING ACCURACY	POSSIBLE FAIRWAYS 1,273 # HIT 941	PCT.	.739	4	94%
3. GREENS IN REGULATION (GIR)	HOLES PLAYED 1,656 GREENS HIT 1,126	PCT.	.680	29	60%
4. PUTTING	GREENS HIT 1,126 # PUTTS GIR 2,035	AVG.	1.807	28	61%
5. TOTAL DRIVING	TOTAL OF STATISTICS 1–2 RANKING		61	20	72%
6. EAGLES	TOTAL EAGLES		4	41	43%
7. BIRDIES	TOTAL BIRDIES		298	27	63%
8. SCORING AVERAGE			71.60	26	64%
9. SAND SAVES	BUNKERS HIT 120 SAVES 51	PCT.	.425	44	39%
10. ALL-AROUND	TOTAL OF STATISTICS 1–9 RANKING		276	26	64%
11. MONEY	TOTAL MONEY		$265,951.48	26	64%
12. PAR BREAKERS	HOLES PLAYED 1,656 BIRDIES/EAGLES 302	PCT.	.182	28	61%

Other Statistics

PUTTS PER ROUND	ROUNDS PLAYED 92 TOTAL PUTTS 2,764	AVG.	30.04	42	42%
PAR 3 BIRDIES	PAR 3 HOLES PLAYED 383 BIRDIES MADE 42	PCT.	.110	44	39%
PAR 4 BIRDIES	PAR 4 HOLES PLAYED 926 BIRDIES MADE 136	PCT.	.147	18	75%
PAR 5 BIRDIES	PAR 5 HOLES PLAYED 347 BIRDIES MADE 120	PCT.	.346	26	64%
BIRDIE CONVERSION PERCENTAGE	BIRDIES 298 DIVIDED BY GIR 1,126	PCT.	.265	27	63%

ALL-TIME MONEY LEADERS (Through 1991 Season)
(Regular and Senior Tour combined)

NAME

1	Jack Nicklaus	$ 5,977,996	51	Bert Yancey	$ 871,900
2	Lee Trevino	5,401,390	52	Phil Rodgers	860,320
3	Miller Barber	4,379,949	53	Terry Dill	857,944
4	Gary Player	4,260,431	54	Joe Jimenez	843,023
5	Chi Chi Rodriguez	4,066,277	55	Jimmy Powell	823,266
6	Bruce Crampton	4,038,232	56	Gardner Dickinson	818,414
7	Bob Charles	3,707,760	57	Howie Johnson	770,090
8	George Archer	3,689,750	58	Billy Maxwell	764,700
9	Gene Littler	3,305,973	59	Bob Brue	735,086
10	Al Geiberger	3,299,303	60	Doug Ford	727,685
11	Arnold Palmer	3,226,427	61	Sam Snead	726,700
12	Don January	3,216,907	62	Kermit Zarley	722,579
13	Charles Coody	3,172,647	63	Richard Rhyan	695,491
14	Billy Casper	3,129,606	64	Dick Hendrickson	693,799
15	Dale Douglass	2,953,020	65	Charles Owens	671,385
16	Mike Hill	2,947,163	66	DeWitt Weaver	659,758
17	Dave Hill	2,872,266	67	Mike Fetchick	647,590
18	Orville Moody	2,753,922	68	Paul Harney	631,035
19	J. C. Snead	2,568,952	69	Bob Erickson	624,474
20	Jim Colbert	2,433,884	70	Jerry Barber	599,780
21	Harold Henning	2,370,265	71	Mason Rudolph	595,079
22	Lee Elder	2,288,716	72	Dow Finsterwald	591,675
23	Jim Dent	2,125,466	73	Al Kelley	590,086
24	Bobby Nichols	2,094,320	74	Bill Collins	585,873
25	Lou Graham	2,001,116	75	Roberto De Vicenzo	584,174
26	Gay Brewer	1,993,269	76	Jack Fleck	573,758
27	Don Bies	1,709,978	77	Lionel Hebert	556,019
28	Frank Beard	1,680,425	78	John Brodie	549,599
29	Walter Zembriski	1,522,611	79	Bob Rosburg	540,563
30	Jim Ferree	1,494,935	80	Larry Laoretti	539,461
31	Gibby Gilbert	1,447,824	81	Fred Hawkins	527,455
32	Bruce Devlin	1,401,452	82	John Paul Cain	504,524
33	Tommy Aaron	1,394,724	83	John Schlee	497,729
34	Butch Baird	1,364,808	84	Babe Hiskey	453,946
35	Dave Stockton	1,288,418	85	Gordon Jones	451,736
36	Larry Mowry	1,271,237	86	J. C. Goosie	451,562
37	Doug Sanders	1,264,361	87	Bob Wynn	447,114
38	Homero Blancas	1,228,098	88	Mike Souchak	428,275
39	Bob Goalby	1,227,325	89	George Bayer	427,601
40	Tom Shaw	1,214,472	90	Al Balding	407,618
41	Julius Boros	1,155,995	91	Fred Marti	404,643
42	Larry Ziegler	1,138,454	92	Doug Dalziel	389,814
43	Peter Thomson	1,126,059	93	Dave Marr	377,706
44	Charles Sifford	1,118,910	94	Johnny Pott	373,022
45	Ken Still	1,115,225	95	Ted Kroll	371,511
46	Don Massengale	1,103,217	96	Bill Johnston	370,666
47	Art Wall	1,026,536	97	Jim King	367,355
48	Ben Smith	952,631	98	Simon Hobday	353,654
49	Rives McBee	948,806	99	Tommy Bolt	351,966
50	Rocky Thompson	906,438	100	R. H. Sikes	350,680

Senior Tour Career Money Leaders (Through 1991 Season)

	NAME				
1	Bob Charles	$ 3,168,642	51	Homero Blancas	$ 557,106
2	Chi Chi Rodriguez	3,029,172	52	John Brodie	549,599
3	Miller Barber	2,777,540	53	Larry Laoretti	539,461
4	Bruce Crampton	2,662,039	54	John Paul Cain	504,524
5	Gary Player	2,449,180	55	Bruce Devlin	494,383
6	Dale Douglass	2,375,069	56	Tommy Aaron	491,964
7	Mike Hill	2,373,439	57	Doug Sanders	491,367
8	Orville Moody	2,364,006	58	Howie Johnson	489,194
9	Harold Henning	2,153,218	59	Jack Fleck	443,861
10	Don January	2,075,981	60	Jerry Barber	421,932
11	Al Geiberger	2,034,115	61	Larry Ziegler	405,177
12	Charles Coody	1,964,457	62	Gordon Jones	401,372
13	Lee Trevino	1,922,940	63	Bill Collins	396,542
14	George Archer	1,811,208	64	Roberto De Vicenzo	395,882
15	Dave Hill	1,741,837	65	J. C. Goosie	394,093
16	Gene Littler	1,727,347	66	Gibby Gilbert	392,351
17	Jim Dent	1,560,221	67	Doug Dalziel	389,814
18	Walter Zembriski	1,522,611	68	Billy Maxwell	389,102
19	Billy Casper	1,438,022	69	Art Wall	387,720
20	Jim Ferree	1,387,217	70	DeWitt Weaver	387,257
21	Arnold Palmer	1,323,729	71	Phil Rodgers	377,549
22	Lee Elder	1,267,267	72	Simon Hobday	353,654
23	Gay Brewer	1,192,306	73	J. C. Snead	349,781
24	Larry Mowry	1,183,522	74	Jim O'Hern	345,359
25	Don Bies	1,171,769	75	Jim King	345,341
26	Bobby Nichols	1,101,315	76	Fred Hawkins	331,084
27	Peter Thomson	1,061,118	77	Bill Johnston	318,008
28	Butch Baird	1,035,019	78	Jim Albus	315,839
29	Ben Smith	952,631	79	Doug Ford	313,022
30	Don Massengale	896,554	80	Chick Evans	291,798
31	Jim Colbert	880,749	81	Gardner Dickinson	284,066
32	Rives McBee	s880,561	82	Quinton Gray	280,291
33	Joe Jimenez	839,691	83	Paul Harney	269,152
34	Jimmy Powell	795,470	84	Babe Hiskey	251,597
35	Tom Shaw	795,179	85	Bob Toski	247,869
36	Charles Sifford	777,566	86	Robert Rawlins	242,429
37	Rocky Thompson	762,009	87	Jim Cochran	242,178
38	Bob Brue	692,377	88	Al Balding	240,642
39	Jack Nicklaus	683,734	89	Dan Morgan	240,475
40	Dick Hendrickson	679,194	90	George Baver	238,733
41	Frank Beard	661,983	91	Al Chandler	235,513
42	Charles Owens	655,923	92	Art Silvestrone	219,610
43	Lou Graham	625,008	93	Robert Boldt	213,681
44	Ken Still	610,675	94	Paul Moran	205,029
45	Terry Dill	602,895	95	Bob Stone	198,876
46	Richard Rhyan	595,010	96	Dow Finsterwald	189,573
47	Al Kelley	582,638	97	Bob Wynn	185,054
48	Bob Goalby	582,313	98	Bob Betley	183,765
49	Bob Erickson	581,100	99	Bert Yancey	181,563
50	Mike Fetchick	569,606	100	Fred Haas	178,949

Year-by-Year Growth of
the Senior Tour
1980–92

YEAR	NUMBER OF EVENTS	OFFICIAL PRIZE MONEY
1980	2	$ 250,000
1981	5	$ 750,000
1982	11	$ 1,372,000
1983	18	$ 3,364,768
1984	24	$ 5,156,000
1985	27	$ 6,076,000
1986	32	$ 6,300,000
1987	38	$ 8,700,000
1988	37	$10,275,352
1989	41	$14,195,000
1990	42	$18,323,968
1991	42	$19,788,218
1992	42	$21,500,000

WEEK	1980 (2)	1981 (5)	1982 (11)	1983 (18)
1				
2				
3				
4				
5				
6				
7				
8				(Indian Wells, CA)
9				
10		(Indian Wells, CA)	(Indian Wells, CA)	
11				Daytona Beach, FL
12				
13			Tampa, FL	
14		Tampa, FL		
15				
16	(Austin, TX)	(Austin, TX)	(Austin, TX)	(Houston, TX)
17				Austin, TX
18				
19				
20				Pinehurst, NC
21	(Winged Foot, NY)			
22				Reno, NV
23		San Francisco, CA	Marlborough, MA	Cleveland, OH
24		Vancouver, British Columbia		
25	Atlantic City, NJ		Winnipeg, Manitoba	Calgary, Alberta
26		Marlborough, MA		Marlborough, MA
27			Portland, OR	Syracuse, NY
28		(Birmingham, MI)		Newport, RI
29				Chaska, MN
30				
31				
32			Denver, CO	
33			Syracuse, NY	Denver, CO
34			Park City, UT	Park City, UT
35				Lexington, KY
36				
37			Newport, RI	
38		(Charlotte, NC)	(Charlotte, NC)	Charlotte, NC
39				Richmond, VA
40				
41		Melbourne, FL	(Houston, TX)	Melbourne, FL
42			Melbourne, FL	Hilton Head, SC
43			Hilton Head, SC	
44				
45		(Scottsdale, AZ)		
46	Melbourne, FL			
47				
48	(Palm Beach Gardens, FL)	(Palm Beach Gardens, FL)	Palm Beach Gardens, FL	Boca Raton, FL
49		(North Miami, FL)		
50				
51				
52				

( ) = non-cosponsored or unofficial event

WEEK	1984 (24)	WEEK	1985 (27)	WEEK	1986 (32)	WEEK	1987 (35)
1	Tucson, AZ	1		1		1	
2		2		2	Carlsbad, CA	2	Carlsbad, CA
3	Palm Beach Gardens, FL	3		3		3	
4	(Panama)	4		4		4	
5		5		5		5	
6		6	Fort Pierce, FL	6	Fort Pierce, FL	6	Palm Beach Gardens, FL
7		7		7	Palm Beach Gardens, FL	7	
8		8		8		8	
9		9		9		9	Sun City West, AZ
10		10		10		10	Indian Wells, CA
11		11	Indian Wells, CA	11	Sun City West, AZ	11	Los Angeles, CA
12	Indian Wells, CA	12	Sun City West, AZ	12	Indian Wells, CA	12	
13		13	Los Angeles, CA	13	Los Angeles, CA	13	Sarasota, FL
14	Daytona Beach, FL	14		14		14	
15		15		15		15	(Houston, TX)
16	Sun City West, AZ	16		16	(Houston, TX)	16	Austin, TX
17	Austin, TX	17	Austin, TX	17	Austin, TX	17	Albuquerque, NM
18	Carlsbad, CA	18	Carlsbad, CA	18	Albuquerque, NM	18	San Antonio, TX
19		19	San Antonio, TX	19	San Antonio, TX	19	Philadelphia, PA
20		20	Philadelphia, PA	20	Philadelphia, PA	20	Oklahoma City, OK
21		21		21		21	Denver, CO
22	Reno, NV	22	Denver, CO	22	Denver, CO	22	Dallas, TX
23		23	Reno, NV	23	Dallas, TX	23	Ponte Vedra, FL
24	Tulsa, OK	24	Dallas, TX	24		24	(Long Island, NY)
25	Cleveland, OH	25	Cleveland, OH	25	Cleveland, OH	25	Grand Rapids, MI
26	Rochester, NY	26	Lake Tahoe, NV	26	Columbus, OH	26	Greenbrier, WV
27	Syracuse, NY	27	Greenbrier, WV	27		27	Fairfield, CT
28	Newport, RI	28		28	Greenbrier, WV	28	Syracuse, NY
29		29	Syracuse, NY	29	Grand Rapids, MI	29	
30	Denver, CO	30	Newport, RI	30	Syracuse, NY	30	Scarborough, NY
31		31	Concord, MA	31	Newport, RI	31	Concord, MA
32	Aylmer, Quebec	32		32	Concord, MA	32	Sacramento, CA
33		33	Vancouver, British Columbia	33	Seattle, WA	33	Seattle, WA
34	Park City, UT	34	Park City, UT	34	Park City, UT	34	Park City, UT
35	Lexington, KY	35	Lexington, KY	35	Lexington, KY	35	Lexington, KY
36	Richmond, VA	36		36	Potomac, MD	36	Charlotte, NC
37	Charlotte, NC	37	Richmond, VA	37	Richmond, VA	37	Richmond, VA
38	Concord, MA	38	Charlotte, NC	38	Charlotte, NC	38	Newport, RI
39		39		39		39	Winston-Salem, NC
40		40		40		40	Atlanta, GA
41	Melbourne, FL	41	Hilton Head, SC	41	Melbourne, FL	41	Hilton Head, SC
42	Hilton Head, SC	42	Melbourne, FL	42	Hilton Head, SC	42	Las Vegas, NV
43		43	Tucson, AZ	43	Atlanta, GA	43	
44		44		44	Tucson, AZ	44	
45		45		45	Las Vegas, NV	45	Melbourne, FL
46		46		46		46	Key Biscayne, FL
47		47	Boca Raton, FL	47	Delray Beach, FL	47	
48	Boca Raton, FL	48		48		48	
49	Palm Beach Gardens, FL	49		49		49	Maui, HI
50		50	Jamaica	50		50	Jamaica
51		51		51	Jamaica	51	
52		52		52		52	

( ) = non-cosponsored or unofficial event

WEEK	1988 (38)	WEEK	1989 (41)	WEEK	1990 (42)	WEEK	1991 (42)
1		1	Carlsbad, CA	1	Carlsbad, CA	1	Carlsbad, CA
2	Carlsbad, CA	2		2		2	
3		3	La Quinta, CA	3		3	
4	Oahu, HI	4		4	Kohala Coast, HI	4	Kohala Coast, HI
5		5		5	Key Biscayne, FL	5	Key Biscayne, FL
6	Palm Beach Gardens, FL	6	Palm Beach Gardens, FL	6	Tampa, FL	6	Tampa, FL
7	Tampa, FL	7	Tampa, FL	7	Naples, FL	7	Naples, FL
8	Naples, FL	8	Naples, FL	8	Sarasota, FL	8	Sarasota, FL
9	Indian Wells, CA	9	Indian Wells, CA	9	Indian Wells, CA	9	Ojai, CA
10	Los Angeles, CA	10	Phoenix, AZ	10		10	
11	Sun City West, AZ	11		11	San Antonio, TX	11	San Antonio, TX
12	(Narita, Japan)	12	(Narita, Japan)	12	(Narita, Japan)	12	Indian Wells, CA
13		13	Dallas, TX	13	Scottsdale, AZ	13	(Narita, Japan)
14		14		14		14	Scottsdale, AZ
15	Houston, Texas	15	Scottsdale, AZ	15	Palm Beach Gardens, FL	15	
16	Sarasota, FL	16	Sarasota, FL	16	Austin, TX	16	Palm Beach Gardens, FL
17	Austin, TX	17	Austin, TX	17	Dallas, TX	17	Houston, TX
18	San Antonio, TX	18	San Antonio, TX	18	Las Vegas, NV	18	Las Vegas, NV
19	Philadelphia, PA	19	Philadelphia, PA	19	Oklahoma City, OK	19	Dallas, TX
20	Scarborough, NY	20	Scarborough, NY	20	Houston, TX	20	Austin, TX
21	Albuquerque, NM	21	Oklahoma City, OK	21	Philadelphia, PA	21	Philadelphia, PA
22	Dallas, TX	22	Houston, TX	22	Scarborough, NY	22	Scarborough, NY
23	Ponte Vedra, FL	23	Ponte Vedra, FL	23	Dearborn, MI	23	Dearborn, MI
24	Long Island, NY	24	Long Island, NY	24	Syracuse, NY	24	Syracuse, NY
25	Oklahoma City, OK	25	Syracuse, NY	25	Concord, MA	25	Charlotte, NC
26	Sacramento, CA	26	Ligonier, PA	26	Ridgewood, NJ	26	Kansas City, MO
27	Seattle, WA	27	Concord, MA	27	Long Island, NY	27	Cincinnati, OH
28	Park City, UT	28	Grand Rapids, MI	28	Kings Island, OH	28	Newport, RI
29	Newport, RI	29	Cleveland, OH	29	Traverse City, MI	29	Chicago, IL
30	Concord, MA	30	Newport, RI	30	Newport, RI	30	Detroit, MI
31	Chicago, IL	31		31	Charlotte, NC	31	Long Island, NY
32	Syracuse, NY	32	Sacramento, CA	32	Albuquerque, NM	32	Park City, UT
33	Grand Rapids, MI	33	Seattle, WA	33	Park City, UT	33	Seattle, WA
34	Lexington, KY	34	Albuquerque, NM	34	Seattle, WA	34	Albuquerque, NM
35		35	Lexington, KY	35	Indianapolis, IN	35	Indianapolis, IN
36	Indianapolis, IN	36	Indianapolis, IN	36	Lexington, KY	36	Grand Rapids, MI
37	Richmond, VA	37	Richmond, VA	37	Grand Rapids, MI	37	Concord, MA
38	Charlotte, NC	38	Charlotte, NC	38	Richmond, VA	38	Atlanta, GA
39	Atlanta, GA	39	Melbourne, FL	39	Melbourne, FL	39	Lexington, KY
40	Winston-Salem, NC	40	Winston-Salem, NC	40	Winston-Salem, NC	40	Winston-Salem, NC
41		41	Abilene, TX	41	Abilene, TX	41	Sacramento, CA
42		42	Napa, CA	42	Napa, CA	42	Napa, CA
43	Las Vegas, NV	43		43	Sacramento, CA	43	Los Angeles, CA
44	(Narita, Japan)	44		44	Los Angeles, CA	44	
45	Melbourne, FL	45	Las Vegas, NV	45	Batoh, Japan	45	
46	Key Biscayne, FL	46	Batoh, Japan	46		46	Sawara City, Japan
47		47		47		47	
48	Maui, HI	48	Ojai, CA	48		48	
49		49	Maui, HI	49	Maui, HI	49	Maui, HI
50	Dorado, Puerto Rico	50	Dorado, Puerto Rico	50	Dorado, Puerto Rico	50	Dorado, Puerto Rico
51		51		51		51	
52		52		52		52	

(   ) = non-cosponsored or unofficial event

324

WEEK   1992 (42)

1		27	Cincinnati, OH
2	Carlsbad, CA	28	Bethlehem, PA
3		29	Chicago, IL
4	Kohala Coast, HI	30	Newport, RI
5	Key Biscayne, FL	31	Long Island, NY
6	Naples, FL	32	Concord, MA
7	Tampa, FL	33	Birmingham, AL
8		34	Seattle, WA
9	Sarasota, FL	35	Park City, UT
10	Ojai, CA	36	Grand Rapids, MI
11	San Antonio, TX	37	Lexington, KY
12	Indian Wells, CA	38	Indianapolis, IN
13	(Narita, Japan)	39	Atlanta, GA
14	Scottsdale, AZ	40	Winston-Salem, NC
15		41	Sacramento, CA
16	Palm Beach Gardens, FL	42	Napa, CA
17	Austin, TX	43	Los Angeles, CA
18	Las Vegas, NV	44	Maui, HI
19	Dallas, TX	45	
20	Houston, TX	46	Sawara City, Japan
21	Philadelphia, PA	47	
22	Scarborough, NY	48	
23	Charlotte, NC	49	
24	Dearborn, MI	50	Dorado, Puerto Rico
25	Syracuse, NY	51	
26	Kansas City, MO	52	

( ) = non-cosponsored or unofficial event

325

INDEX

INDEX

INDEX

INDEX